The Society for French Historical Studies holds an annual conference on the history of France and the Francophone world and sponsors this journal. In recognition of outstanding scholarship, it bestows the David H. Pinkney Prize, the William Koren Jr. Prize, the Natalie Zemon Davis Award, and the Marjorie M. and Lancelot L. Farrar Memorial Awards, and in collaboration with the Western Society for French History, the Research Travel Award. Finally, supported by the Institut Français d'Amérique fund, it awards the Gilbert Chinard Book Prize and the IFA Research Fellowships. For a list of membership benefits, see dukeupress.edu/sfhs.

To submit an article, please visit editorialmanager.com/fhs. Articles may be submitted in English or French and should be typed double-spaced, including notes, block quotes, and tables. To ensure anonymity, the author's name should not appear on the title page or in the body of the manuscript. Please follow *The Chicago Manual of Style*, seventeenth edition, and the journal's style guide. Manuscripts should not exceed 10,000 words in length (excluding notes). All other editorial correspondence should be sent to the editors, Kathryn A. Edwards and Carol E. Harrison, at fhs@sc.edu.

Visit the SFHS at societyforfrenchhistoricalstudies.net and Duke University Press Journals at dukeupress.edu/journals.

Direct inquiries about advertising to Journals Advertising Coordinator, journals_advertising@dukeupress.edu.

French Historical Studies

Volume 45 · Number 2 · April 2022

Music and French History
JONATHYNE BRIGGS and WILLIAM WEBER, Special Issue Editors

Introduction

Articles

News and Publications

La Langue Universelle?
French Music and Its Rhythms of Cultural Engagement

JONATHYNE BRIGGS and WILLIAM WEBER

Henry Longfellow's remark that music is the universal language of mankind does not apply well to French musical culture. There musical culture has often had a particular accent, whether in the spectacular performances at the eighteenth-century Opéra and the nineteenth-century Philharmonie de Paris, in the mundane, quotidian voices of twentieth-century buskers and radio broadcasts, or in twenty-first-century streaming platforms such as Deezer. Even though opera is certainly one of the more significant examples of French music, the dynamics that played out within it during the eighteenth and nineteenth centuries were evident in French encounters with other musical forms in the twentieth century, whether jazz, beguine, chanson, rock, folk, electronica, or rap. The five articles contained in this special issue of *French Historical Studies* on music in French history reveal the importance of music as a method of studying the history of France. Music and sound have long occupied a privileged place in French history, often directly tied to France's cultural power and its efforts to incorporate external cultural influences. The dynamics at work in the history of French music operate at the highest levels of recognition and support in its institutions as well as at the margins of cultural acceptance. The articles that follow trace these dynamics to reveal how French musicians, composers, librettists, critics, and audiences participated in and reacted to them. The examples here point to how music and sound were critical in understanding efforts of political outreach, both foreign and domestic; how musical classification and the creation of repertoires have often obscured the reality of how French musicians and audiences experienced their works; and how French cultural norms have remained consistent in the production of French music in the modern period no matter the genre or players. Taken together, these articles

French Historical Studies • Vol. 45, No. 2 (April 2022) • DOI 10.1215/00161071-9531940
Copyright 2022 by Society for French Historical Studies

underscore the important role that French music has played along multiple registers in its political, social, and cultural history.

The study of French music encompasses investigation of authorities that were embodied in the form of institutions, aesthetics in the form of artists, reception in the form of critics, or technology in the form of recording and broadcasting, just as a sampler to the vast amount of scholarship. This issue focuses on genres such as opera, vaudevilles, and so-called world music, as well the performance of music as part of political ceremony in the diplomacy of early modern France. The scholars included draw on a variety of historiographic approaches, as well as elements of musicology, literary analysis, cultural studies, and sound studies, to show how the study of music calls for a rich combination of analytic tools to provide a nuanced understanding. In this introduction, we wish to highlight three specific themes that emerge across the spectrum of the articles: the role of repertory in defining institutional power in musical production, the emphasis on distinct French variations of genres and styles, and the importance of engagement with foreign musical styles and forms in defining specific genres. Thus did specific musical ideas and forms persist in France, often as part of the interaction between performers and audiences. Furthermore, French musical culture developed in a complex tandem of engagement with and isolation from foreign musical styles. Opera offers a rich example of how these phenomena operated in French music, as do the other genres covered in this issue.

In the history of opera, we can see how authority was embedded in repertoires, performing institutions, and the tastes of audiences. Even though opera is certainly one of the more significant examples of how repertory shaped musical style and meaning during the nineteenth century, the dynamics that played out there during the eighteenth and nineteenth centuries were evident in French encounters with other musical forms throughout the modern period. The tensions between internal canons and the acceptance of perceived foreign influence defined much of the development of these musics in France, especially with the advent of recording technology and broadcasting. French audiences embraced these new genres and styles, and French musicians developed their own variations of each, with critics serving as an important conduit for shaping their meaning. In these musical styles, the fusion of genres developed through interactions with new ideas of rhythm, timbre, and arrangement, often intersecting with French encounters with new populations. That intersection included African American soldiers after the First World War, migrant workers during the various phases of economic development in the French mainland, young artists capitalizing of the expansion of radio and television in the postwar period, and indeed, missionary artists such as Afrika Bambaataa performing in France during the 1980s.[1] Each of these moments led to new innovations in musical style and expanded audiences but also helped confirm specific French iterations of those styles, especially at moments of great cultural change in French society.

The role of music became more pronounced beyond institutions thanks to music's increased ubiquity and potential for shared experience as it became a larger part of mass culture beginning in the late nineteenth century. New canons developed that shaped the perception and reception of musical ideas, creating new fusions of musical thought and reconfiguring a type of aural Frenchness in these various genres. For that matter, major canons emerged in French musical life, rising and falling with the evolution of new tastes since the eighteenth century.[2] By the end of the twentieth century, the internet brought new possibilities of musical exchange and encounters, just as the French government increasingly found value in supporting music as a distinct expression of French culture. This support included the passage of the Pelchat amendment in 1996 to protect French-language popular music in France.[3] With the continued dominance of the English language in the global music marketplace, the Pelchat amendment established institutional methods of supporting localized forms of global pop music, again showing the power of institutions in shaping the course of music.[4] And French music continues to develop, as French rap remains a robust form of French-language music and recent pop acts such as Daft Punk, David Guetta, and Christine and the Queens have found international success. Associations such as La Souterraine suggest the fecundity of French popular music and remain connected to a model of Frenchness rooted in the French language.[5]

The five articles included in this issue bring into focus this dynamic of engagement and distancing, exploring the sounds of Siam in the late seventeenth century as experienced through the aural norms of French diplomats; the influence of Italian-style music in the eighteenth century and the durability of French popular musical forms in response; the connection between the grand opera and French political identity in the nineteenth century; and the influence of the imperial project on the perception of genre in contemporary music. For example, France's imperial expansion echoes in the late twentieth-century music

---

1. See, e.g., Jackson, *Making Jazz French*; Gillett, *At Home in Our Sounds*; Moore, *Soundscapes of Liberation*; McGregor, *Jazz and Postwar French Identity*; Aidi, *Rebel Music*; Briggs, *Sounds French*; and Durant, *Hip-Hop en Français*.

2. Weber, *Canonic Repertories and the French Press*; Weber, *Rise of Musical Classics*.

3. Petterson, "No More Song and Dance."

4. Northrup, *How English Became the Global Language*, 130.

5. Mansuy, "Unearthing the Future of French Pop." French scholars have responded to this situation by turning their attention to the study of popular music in France. See, e.g., Guibert and Rudent, *Made in France*; and Dauncey and Le Guern, *Stereo*. See also *Volume! The French Journal of Popular Music Studies*, founded in 2002 by Gérôme Guibert, Marie-Pierre Bonniol, and Samuel Etienne.

of Kassav, with the categorization of the musical culture of DOM-TOM operating outside the established canon of French music despite the group's long presence with France. The continuity of sound, or at least its principal meaning, suggests the resilience of the model of French music as a distinct category from other European examples. The articles in this issue illustrate that French music was vibrant yet periodically quite static during the modern period. This nature of French music in the modern period charted the cultural boundaries that dictated French engagement with the musical other and the construction of an aural Frenchness.

In "The Sounds of Siam: Sonic Environments of Seventeenth-Century Franco-Siamese Diplomacy," Downing A. Thomas reveals that the diplomatic encounters between the agents of the Sun King and the King of Siam involved not merely exchange of ideas and goods. The diplomats who arrived in Siam in the seventeenth century noted the sonic environment they encountered and how it shaped their perception of the kingdom. Much of their response, which was recorded in their personal recollections of their journeys, reinforced attitudes that they developed from court culture and the meaning of sound in the absolutist politics of Louis XIV. These fading echoes that Thomas gleans reveal how the new and novel sounds were an important part of the efforts to bring these two kingdoms into greater diplomatic harmony. As French perspectives entrenched notions of French cultural superiority in the realm of music, the recognition of the sounds of Siam shows how diplomats were attuned to the role of sound and music in pomp and circumstance that greeted them on their arrival. This reaction from the diplomats reveals how French engagement with foreign sounds reinforced a particular French understanding of sound and music. Drawing from the discipline of sound studies, Thomas's article underscores the role sound had in the diplomats' interpretation of Siamese culture and its position vis-à-vis French music and politics.

In eighteenth-century France a *vaudeville* was a contrafact, a musical composition based on a well-known melody whose chord progressions were adapted to a new text, often with comedic or satirical implications. Jenna Harmon demonstrates how such pieces drew from sources as various as folk melodies, popular songs, and opera airs. However, she also shows that in the middle of the eighteenth century a new style of composition, the *ariette*, became more dominant within the musical world, reflecting the growing influence of the Italian *bouffon*. Nevertheless, under the Old Regime *vaudevilles* continued to appear in newspapers and literature, recalling the singers on the famous Pont Neuf who would write and sell songs that capitalized on the week's gossip. Her article, "'It Is No Longer in Fashion—More's the Pity': Reconsidering the Obsolescence of the

Eighteenth-Century Vaudeville," explains how the melodies selected by authors of *vaudeville* were not an idle choice, because they carried important interpretive implications for the public. As Harmon notes, "Virtually any preexisting melody could serve as the basis for a *vaudeville*, from old folk melodies to opera airs." Until the mid-eighteenth century, an *ariette* referred to a piece with virtuosic singing, such as found in French opera, "especially when it came to long melismas on particular vowel sounds." However, after the arrival of the Italian Bouffon players in 1752, the term *ariette* referred to newly composed songs used in the French comic opera genre, *opéra-comique*. Harmon shows how the policing of genre by critics in this period obfuscated the reality of practice for composers and performers and again offers another case of foreign engagement reinforcing French concepts of music. Additionally, she reveals the influence of repertory and canonization in the defining of French music.

Historical factors pervaded many aspects of French opera. Annelies Andries, in "Mobilizing Historicity and Local Color in *Fernand Cortez* (1809): Narratives of Empire at the Opéra," notes that a great deal of historical research went into producing Gaspare Spontini's newest opera, *Fernand Cortez ou la conquête du Mexique* (*Hernan Cortés or the Conquest of Mexico*) for its premiere at the Paris Opéra on November 28, 1809. The opera depicts an important episode in the Spanish colonization of the Americas: the siege and fall of the Aztec capital, México-Tenochtitlan, in 1521 at the hands of the Spanish conquistador Hernán Cortés. The libretto, written by Etienne de Jouy and Joseph-Alphonse Esménard, focused on well-known historical events. Historical sources were consulted not only for the set and costume designs but also for musical instruments and possibly even the choreography. Since the artists producing *Fernand Cortez* thought that fidelity to history was central to their work, Andries explores the ideological significance of a source-based methodology in the construction of historical knowledge and meaning around 1800 and the reception of those ideas. Even though the ascendancy of this historiographical methodology tends to be associated with a new generation of historians that arose in France in the 1820s, Andries suggests the influence of grand opera in this knowledge production as part of its elevation within French cultural worlds. Her article points to how the perception of foreign music had an aesthetic influence through opera's embrace of historical fidelity, although in a manner that reinforced French notions of music.

Diana R. Hallman, in "Napoleonic Commemoration on the Operatic Stage: The *Retour des Cendres* and Halévy's *La Reine de Chypre*," chronicles the pivotal intersection between grand opera and political culture in the July Monarchy. The *retour de cendres*, the return of Napoléon's remains from Sainte-Hélène to

France in 1840, represented an important gesture of Napoleonic restoration in the July Monarchy, along with the creation of monuments, paintings, histories, plays, and encomiums to the defeated emperor. In 1841 Napoleonic commemoration expanded to the stage of the Paris Opéra (the Académie Royale de Musique) with the appearance of *La reine de Chypre*, the five-act grand opera by French composer Fromental Halévy and librettist Henri de Saint Georges. The opera offers a poignant portrayal of the exiled French warriors within a theatrical reframing of Catarina Cornaro's early fifteenth-century rise to power in Cyprus and defiance of Venetian tyranny. Hallman analyzes how *La reine de Chypre* was tied to the political moment of the early 1840s. It expands the study of French grand opera's role in confronting and transforming national memory with a particular focus on the evocation of Napoleonic memory within the July Monarchy. It shows how French operas during this and earlier periods were affected by both preventive and external censorship, mediation of the past and the present, and complexes of visual, musical, and intertextual references. The intersection of opera and politics of repertory becomes apparent in Hallman's study of grand opera as well.

As we move into the late twentieth century, Paul Cohen's "'Zouk Is the Only Medicine We Need': Kassav and the Cultural Politics of Music in the French Caribbean" asserts the significance of a form of French music far from the Parisian capital and how musical groups there have contributed greatly to French popular culture with little recognition of their Frenchness. While less known in the Anglophone world outside the Caribbean diaspora, the musical group Kassav boasts a formidable legacy for musical innovation based in the Creole culture of Martinique and Guadeloupe, as well as a profound commercial impact in France. Kassav's significance lies in the group's engagement with the market while also critiquing it. Their success at creating a new form of commodified pop culture on their own musical, linguistic, and productive terms appeared during a multicultural moment in metropole France. Despite its massive success in France, the music of Kassav is often placed outside the narrative of French pop music and is instead contained within the amorphous genre of "world music." Over their forty-year existence Kassav produced a seamless synthesis of diverse influences: a little hard rock, a touch of metal, a measure of funk, a taste of disco, lots of R&B and 1980s synthesizer pop, and healthy doses of a range of Caribbean styles from salsa and merengue to reggae and ska. By insisting on performing in Creole, the ensemble helped rewrite the terms of *antillais* identity and reminded an unmindful metropole of important imperial histories and legacies. Cohen argues for the need to center the work of Kassav fully in the realm of French pop music to understand the contours and limits of the era of multiculturalism. Again, Cohen shows the continuation of the French tendency to engage with "foreign" culture—although in this case it is part of French culture—as a method of distinguishing a notion of Frenchness deep into the twentieth century. With the death of Kassav founder Jacob Desvarieux from COVID-19, a reassessment of the group's place will be sure to follow, but Cohen's article articulates the challenges that will confront such efforts.

Taken as a whole, these articles suggest the rich polyphony of French musical history and the various realms with which it connects, whether in prestigious or popular permutations. They show musicians and audiences attendant to sounds beyond France but often with an ear toward domestic tastes and styles. As these articles reveal, French music offers an ideal means of understanding the dilemma of a Frenchness paradoxically rooted in a cosmopolitan engagement and a simultaneous sense of distance—one buttressed by institutions that often did not embrace all styles and sounds within French culture and perhaps found that distinctions so tightly drawn were beginning to fade in importance in contemporary art worlds. These tendencies that play out in the articles in this issue have perhaps reached their coda, suggesting that a new era in French music will have new dynamics.

JONATHYNE BRIGGS is professor of history and associate dean of humanities and the arts at Indiana University Northwest. He is author of *Sounds French: Globalization, Cultural Communities, and Pop Music, 1958–1980* (2015) and is at work on a history of autism in France since 1950.

WILLIAM WEBER is professor emeritus of history at California State University, Long Beach. He is author of *Canonic Repertories and the French Press, Lully to Wagner* (2021) and editor, with Cormac Newark, of *The Oxford Handbook of the Operatic Canon* (2020).

Acknowledgments

The authors thank all of those who submitted to the issue, Kathryn A. Edwards for her editorial assistance, and Jamie Holeman for her aid in finding images for the issue's cover.

References

Aidi, Hisham. *Rebel Music: Race, Empire, and the New Muslim Youth Culture*. New York, 2014.

Briggs, Jonathyne. *Sounds French: Globalization, Cultural Communities, and Pop Music, 1958–1980*. New York, 2015.

Dauncey, Hugh, and Philippe Le Guern, eds. *Stereo: Comparative Perspectives on the Sociological Study of Popular Music in France and Britain*. Farnham, 2011.

Durant, Alain-Philippe, ed. *Hip-Hop en Français: An Exploration of Hip-Hop Culture in the Francophone World*. Lanham, MD, 2020.

Gillett, Rachel. *At Home in Our Sounds: Music, Race, and Cultural Politics in Interwar Paris*. New York, 2021.

Guibert, Gérôme, and Catherine Rudent, eds. *Made in France: Studies in Popular Music*. New York, 2018.

Jackson, Jeffrey H. *Making Jazz French: Music and Modern Life in Interwar Paris*. Durham, NC, 2003.

Mansuy, Anthony. "Unearthing the Future of French Pop." *Pitchfork*, Sept. 9, 2015. pitchfork.com /features/article/9717-unearthing-the-future-of-french-pop.

McGregor, Elizabeth Vihlen. *Jazz and Postwar French Identity: Improvising the Nation*. Lanham, MD, 2016.

Moore, Celeste Day. *Soundscapes of Liberation: African American Music in Postwar France*. Durham, NC, 2021.

Northrup, David. *How English Became the Global Language*. New York, 2013.

Petterson, James. "No More Song and Dance: French Radio Broadcast Quotas, Chansons, and Cultural Exceptions." In *Transactions, Transgressions, Transformations: American Culture in Western Europe and Japan*, edited by Uta G. Poiger and Heide Fehrenbach, 109–23. New York, 2000.

Weber, William. *Canonic Repertories and the French Press, Lully to Wagner*, with Beverly Wilcox. Rochester, NY, 2021.

Weber, William. *The Rise of Musical Classics in Eighteenth-Century England*. Oxford, 1992.

The Sounds of Siam

Sonic Environments of Seventeenth-Century Franco-Siamese Diplomacy

DOWNING A. THOMAS

ABSTRACT   A series of diplomatic contacts between France and Siam was initiated in the 1660s primarily through missionary efforts and the expansion of France's global trade network. These diplomatic drives and their historical significance have been described by previous commentators in relation to Louis XIV's global ambitions and his efforts at royal image building. An aspect of these exchanges that has attracted relatively little commentary is the attention given by the participants and chroniclers to the sounds the French travelers experienced in Siam: how the sounds, musical or otherwise, that engaged their attention might have impeded or furthered diplomatic efforts. Within the context of the Louis XIV's attempts to expand France's influence in the world, the sounds and silences described by the French travelers provide additional insight about the diplomatic initiatives and how they understood, or misunderstood, Siam and its culture.

KEYWORDS   Siam, Louis XIV, diplomatic history, sound studies

I n his *Mémoire* on the diplomatic relationship between France and Siam that developed under Louis XIV, the priest Bénigne Vachet announced that Somdet Phra Narai Maharat, the king of Siam, had conveyed an important message to him before he returned to France. The king had told him "in the clearest terms that on [Vachet's] return he wanted to carry out a plan about which he had informed no one, and that would bring great joy to many."[1] Vachet understood these veiled words as an opening to the king's, and thereby to the entire kingdom's, conversion to Christianity, an opportunity the priest may have fantasized as his epoch's equivalent to the conversion of the Roman emperor Constantine. He also apparently did not hesitate to broadcast his interpretation of the king's words to others.

---

1. Quoted in Launay, *Histoire de la mission de Siam*, 1:155. All translations are my own unless otherwise noted.

French Historical Studies • Vol. 45, No. 2 (April 2022) • DOI 10.1215/00161071-9531954

The message conveyed to Vachet is at the epicenter of a series of remarkable Franco-Siamese contacts that began in the 1660s and lasted through the 1680s, launched primarily through missionary efforts and the expansion of France's global trade network. Had Phra Narai decided to embrace Christianity, it would have been the coup of the century for the priest-voyagers of the Missions Etrangères de Paris. Not only was the king's message quite opaque, however, but archival sources in the Missions Etrangères de Paris indicate that King Phra Narai did not convey it directly to Vachet. Rather, the oracle-like message came through the intermediary of the king's powerful minister, Constantine Phaulkon, who had his own reasons to bait Vachet and the French delegation, namely, to develop the relationships necessary for an exit strategy for himself in the event of regime change in Siam. Though the king never converted to Christianity, the diplomatic efforts surrounding this initiative had a significant impact, judging from the spike in references to Siam in French texts during this period (fig. 1).[2] Looking back on the complex series of missionary efforts, commercial enterprises, and military ventures from this first period of French contact with Siam from the perspective of the mid-eighteenth century, the chevalier de Jaucourt remarked that "the famous Siamese embassy in France during the previous century has given us the accounts of that kingdom written by Fr. Tachard, the abbé de Choisy, Messrs. de Lisle, Gervaise, de Chaumont, & de la Loubere." But he closes the *Encyclopédie* entry on "Siam" by noting that "all these accounts contradict each other," pointing to the cultural misunderstandings, miscommunication, self-deluding missionary zeal, and conflicting goals of the Missions Etrangères de Paris and of the Jesuits—all of which, together with regime change on the Siamese side, fed into the collapse of diplomatic initiatives in the late 1680s.[3]

Previous commentators have described these diplomatic drives and their historical significance, in particular how they fit into Louis XIV's global ambitions and his efforts at royal image building.[4] Scholars have studied engravings, precious objects, and other material evidence to document various aspects of the embassies, bringing to light the expansive mercantile and scientific dimensions of the voyages.[5] The Siamese diplomats also experienced French musical culture firsthand: they were taken to operatic performances, met Jean-Baptiste

2. The ARTFL-FRANTEXT time series, which displays lexical usage over time drawing on the ARTFL database, reveals a similar pattern, with almost no references before 1675, a spike of mentions between 1675 and 1699, and slow decline in the eighteenth century: artflsrv03-uchicago-edu.proxy.lib.uiowa.edu/philologic4/frantext0917/query?report=time_series&method=proxy&q=siam&start=0&end=0&year_interval=50.
3. Jaucourt, "Siam," in Diderot and d'Alembert, *Encyclopédie*, 15:152.
4. See, e.g., Love, "Rituals of Majesty."
5. See, e.g., Kerssenbrock-Krosigk, "Glass for the King of Siam."

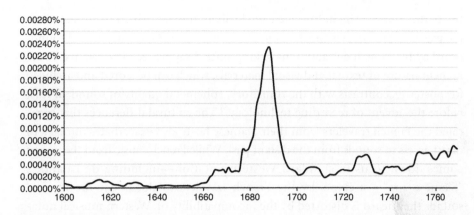

FIGURE 1 Graphic drawn from Google's Ngram database of French-language sources showing occurrences of the word *Siam* through the seventeenth and eighteenth centuries. See Michel et al., "Quantitative Analysis of Culture."

Lully, heard organs in churches, and encountered other performances along their route. Two "Siamese airs" written by the French composer Michel-Richard de Lalande testify to the cultural effects of the diplomatic encounter, and recent work by musicologists has analyzed these dimensions of the embassies.[6] More broadly, Ellen R. Welch has explored the important role of the arts in diplomatic visits from Moscow, the Ottoman Empire, Morocco, and Siam during the reign of Louis XIV, remarking that "music, dance, and theater helped to mediate these global relationships just as much as intra-European relations."[7] Other scholars have examined how opera served as a vehicle for advancing the Sun King's political ambitions and representing the culture of absolutism.[8]

One of the more intriguing but less examined aspects of Franco-Siam exchanges is the attention participants and chroniclers gave to what could be called the sonic environment of these encounters and how this sonic environment intersected with and affected the diplomatic efforts. While virtually all trace of Siamese perspectives on these exchanges was lost when the royal city of Ayuttaya was sacked by the Burmese in the eighteenth century, the French left numerous memoirs and other written documents testifying that they were intrigued, confused, amused, and astonished by the sounds, musical or otherwise, that they encountered during their travels. Compounding the constraints imposed by the one-sided historical record, our access to the sounds they encountered can only be indirect. Unlike the written record and other material

6. For recent musicological perspectives, see Yamprai, "Richard-Michel de Lalande"; and Irving, "Lully in Siam."

7. Welch, *Theater of Diplomacy*, 159. Chapter 7 explores the Franco-Siamese diplomatic exchanges.

8. A recent example is Bloechl, *Opera and the Political Imaginary in Old Regime France.*

traces that remain (including the Rue de Siam in Brest, which commemorates the place the Siamese visitors first entered France in 1686), the music and sounds heard by the French delegation have long since disappeared. The relatively permanent nature of textual and visual materials, which can be stored and archived for posterity, contrasts with the transitory, ephemeral quality of sound, at least before the advent of recording technology.[9] The cultural differences that separated the French travelers from their Siamese hosts also exacerbates our lack of direct access to sounds from the distant past. While French music from the period comes down to us in standard Western notation—including de Lalande's "Siamese airs"—attempts by the French travelers to document the musical sounds they heard is distorted by the incompatibility of Western musical notation and seventeenth-century Siamese music and by the cultural gap that separated European musical practices from those of contemporary Siam.[10]

In what follows, I explore the fleeting traces of what the French delegations heard during their travels by adopting the methodologies of sound studies. The developing field of sound studies offers insights into histories and cultures that may otherwise be lost in the priority we tend to give to the visual over the auditory. Lending an ear to the sounds of the past can add higher fidelity—greater richness and texture—to our representations of the past, which most often focus solely on the visual record. I do not delve into such questions as how closely seventeenth-century Western attempts to notate Siamese music approached the original, or what vestiges of Siamese music might be found in a French composer's airs inspired by the Siamese visitors to France. Instead, I examine the soundscapes the French missionaries, diplomats, and officers recorded in words to understand better how sound may have facilitated or impeded cross-cultural understanding and thereby contributed to the diplomatic successes and failures of these encounters. As Philippe Le Guern notes about sound studies generally, "It is not only a question of discovering how historical actors develop specific perceptual and sensorial schemas but also of indicating why the perceptual field, far from being given as a cognitive mechanism *sub specie aeternitatis*, is socially constructed and even hierarchized in function of cultural, social, and political interests."[11] The social construction of sound (and silence) has been a focus of the work of Alain Corbin within a broader project he has referred to as

---

9. For a discussion of this point, see Hammond, *Powers of Sound and Song*, 9.

10. Both Nicolas Gervaise and Simon de la Loubère attempted to notate Siamese airs. On the problematic nature of this enterprise, see Miller and Chonpairot, "History of Siamese Music," 137–49.

11. Le Guern, "Sound studies," 25. For a broad overview of scholarly opportunities opened by the field of sound studies, see Bull, *Routledge Companion to Sound Studies*. For recent sound studies scholarship on early modern France, see Hamilton and Hammond, "Soundscapes." See also the resources available through the international research network Early Modern Soundscapes: emsoundscapes.co.uk.

"a historical anthropology of the senses."[12] Corbin has drawn attention to the historically grounded differences in modes of attention, sense perceptions, and the meanings attributed to them. He has also remarked on the social divisions that influence our use of the senses and understanding of the impact and meaning of sights, sounds, smells, and touch.[13] Social distinctions of the kind that Corbin describes, dividing manual laborers in the countryside from those who lived more comfortably in towns, are not in direct play in diplomatic soundscapes, because these interactions took place within relatively homogeneous social strata. However, cross-cultural differences manifestly had an enormous influence on the perception of, and meanings attributed to, sound by Louis XIV's envoys, and sound was deliberately appropriated to serve political purposes. Normative understandings of sound during this period were both challenged and reinforced by the auditory experiences of the travelers.

Sound studies provides an interdisciplinary framework that allows us to interrogate cross-cultural differences and invites questions that may vary from those the historian or the musicologist might commonly ask. While much of the scholarship within sound studies has tended to focus on the modern period following the advent of recording technology, it may be the case, as Nicholas Hammond has argued, that the lack of recording technology before the twentieth century meant that sounds "carried even greater urgency," so the need to listen to them and capture them was felt intensely.[14] When the French travelers encountered sounds and heard musical performances, what was it that they noticed and chose to record about these experiences, and why? Which cultural frameworks enabled, or impeded, the travelers' understanding of the sounds they heard? How did the French actively engage with the sounds they encountered to further their aims? More generally, what can we learn from the echoes of sounds from the distant past, with respect to both those sounds themselves— their function in the Siamese context—and the cultural frameworks that informed and constrained the understanding of the travelers documenting them?

Following earlier Portuguese and Dutch ventures in Southeast Asia, the French push into Siam began in 1662, with the arrival of Monseigneur Pierre Lambert de la Motte, and was marked by the striking interdependence of global commercial expansion and missionary fervor, though this interdependence was not always without its conflicts. Letters from Pope Clement IX and Louis XIV brought to Phra Narai by François Pallu, bishop of Heliopolis, a decade later

---

12. Corbin, *Time, Desire, and Horror*, 181. For a contribution to the history of sensory culture during this period, see Vila, *Cultural History of the Senses*.

13. See Corbin's discussion of church bells in a small town in Normandy in *Time, Desire, and Horror*, 183–84.

14. Hammond, *Powers of Sound and Song*, 11.

helped kindle the intense diplomatic relationship with France that lasted for most of the 1680s. The first Siamese delegation that attempted to reach France in 1680–81 was lost at sea. In 1684–85 Phra Narai sent a second delegation, and France reciprocated, naming the chevalier de Chaumont and the abbé de Choisy to lead an embassy to the Siamese kingdom. In 1686–87 came a new volley of reciprocal embassies, with the seasoned Siamese diplomat Kosa Pan arriving in France to great fanfare and returning home with another French delegation under the leadership of Simon de la Loubère.[15] The *Mercure galant* published special editions offering voluminous descriptions of the 1686 Siamese delegation and its activities, even describing for the curious public small observations such as the ingenious way the Siamese peeled their fruit (which was deemed superior to the French way).[16] In January 1688 a fourth Siamese delegation left for France. Only after the fact would they learn of the death of Phra Narai that July and of the political upheaval that followed, bringing to a close active diplomatic exchange between the two countries. As Meredith Martin has argued, through these diplomatic connections Phra Narai and Louis XIV "facilitated a reciprocal understanding or 'mirroring' between the two powers based on shared notions of commerce and kingship."[17]

On the commercial side, the French sought to counter the Dutch trade networks established in the early to mid-seventeenth century and to connect with French operations in Pondicherry and Madagascar. As for the Siamese, Phra Narai had instructed his delegations to France to return with luxury goods in enormous quantities. These included more than four thousand Saint Gobain and other manufacturers' mirrors, "signalling the potential for Louis XIV's gifts not only to express France's cultural and technological prowess, but also to create a market for French luxury goods in Asia."[18] Commerce also fed missionary efforts to convert the indigenous population, perhaps most notably by providing the ships on which priests could travel to Asia and by opening supply routes to sustain them in their missions.

The economic and missionary expansion into southeast Asia set the stage for the reciprocal embassies of the 1680s and provided French travelers the

---

15. The record this Siamese diplomat left of his experiences, only a fragment of which remains, is one of the very few Siamese accounts of the diplomatic encounters of the 1680s: Pan, *Diary of Kosa Pan*.

16. "Rien n'égale l'adresse, & la propreté avec laquelle ils pelent du fruit. Leur manière est à rebours de la nostre. Nous le pelons en dedans, & eux en dehors; ils font de mesme de tout ce qu'ils coupent. Ils dissent *qu'en coupant ainsi on n'est point au hazard de se blesser*, & ils ont raison" (Nothing equals the skill and the neatness with which they peel their fruit. Their way is the reverse of ours. We peel our fruit with an inward motion, and they do so with an outward motion. They do likewise with everything they cut. They say *in cutting this way, one does not risk getting injured*, and they are right) (Donneau de Vizé, *Voyage*, 98–99).

17. Martin, "Mirror Reflections," 654.

18. Martin, "Mirror Reflections," 662.

opportunity to remark on the novel sights and sounds they heard in the kingdom of Siam. At the same time, some of the first accounts of the sonic environments focus on familiar songs and religious practices, which could be a comfort
in often dangerous circumstances so far from home. At sea, the efforts of those
on board regularly broke the sonic and visual tedium of the ocean and raised
passengers' and sailors' spirits. The embassy of the chevalier de Chaumont left
Batavia (present-day Jakarta) for Siam in 1685 and encountered winds that made
them fear losing a mast. Joachim Bouvet wrote that the crew divided into two
choirs to sing litanies to the Virgin Mary, and this act "safeguarded us from any
accident."[19] The sound of a double choir at sea, battling the wind, was memorable enough to be singled out by Bouvet in his narrative. Sound also marked
death at sea, at least for those of noble birth. Bouvet noted that on the death of a
Normand gentleman five cannon shots sounded, and before the body was put
to rest in the ocean, a *Libera Me*, the responsory in the Office for the Dead, was
sung.[20] Rituals surrounding daily devotion and important events such as death
were elements of a sonic environment that would have been similar on any
European expedition at sea, with some sectarian variation. Such practices created continuity with devotional practices at home and thereby reassured those
on board, with song and other sounds marking the significance of events and
linking them to a common purpose and a familiar and shared set of religious
experiences and beliefs.

Once in Siam, the commentators remarked on the cultural and natural
environment they encountered, including the familiar and novel sounds they
heard. One sound that emanated both from the ships and from shore in Siam
was cannon fire. Cannons were most obviously an instrument and symbol of
military might. Figuring at the top of the list of gifts the Siamese king sent to
Louis XIV in 1686, significantly, were two six-foot-long Siamese cannons decorated with silver.[21] Louis XIV in turn sent cannons and other arms to Phra
Narai on the return embassy in 1687, led by Loubère.[22] Such gifts from one monarch to another functioned, on the one hand, as a raw display of might and, on
the other hand, as a demonstration of the value both sides placed on the alliance. Beyond this symbolic exchange, and outside of combat, cannon fire was
understood as a sign or signal. As church bells marked time and punctuated the

19. Bouvet, *Voiage de Siam*, 90.
20. Bouvet, *Voiage de Siam*, 91.
21. Michel Jacq-Hergoualc'h claims that these cannons are conserved in the Musée de l'Armée in the
Hôtel des Invalides, Paris ("Les ambassadeurs siamois à Versailles," 34). More recently, Antoine Leduc has
reevaluated the evidence, tracing one cannon to the collections of the Royal Artillery Museum in London
and indicating that the other, likely sent to Berlin after France's defeat in 1815, has not been located ("Le
canon offert à Louis XIV," 162).
22. Van der Cruysse, *Siam and the West*, 382.

sonic space for significant purposes in an urban or town setting, cannon fire could function as a mode of communication at a distance, namely, as an aural salute.[23] In the case of death at sea mentioned above, it served to acknowledge the individual's passage from the living to the dead. The cannon fire the French delegations heard in Siam similarly marked the transition from a long and difficult journey at sea to safe arrival at their destination.

Just as the exchange of cannon between Louis XIV and Phra Narai provided a cross-cultural platform to express might and shared purpose, cannon fire as salute served as a form of mutual recognition that was understood across cultural divides. The governor of Bangkok, for example, welcomed Chaumont to Siam, sending to his ship two high-ranking nobles, referred to in the French texts as *mandarins*.[24] As they left, Chaumont noted, "I saluted them with nine rounds of cannon fire."[25] As the French delegation was escorted up the river to the capital, Chaumont was extremely meticulous in recording the number of cannon shots the French ships received to welcome them because it allowed him to document the perceived significance of their arrival and the specific and official gestures of recognition on the part of the Siamese and the European powers present in Siam. While an English ship "saluted me with twenty-one rounds of cannon fire," the fortresses on both sides of the river "saluted me, one with twenty-nine rounds, and the other with thirty-one."[26] Further along, an English ship and a Dutch ship pulled out all the stops in his honor and "saluted me with all their artillery."[27] The Jesuit missionary Guy Tachard, who was part of Chaumont's delegation, also recorded the welcoming Dutch cannon fire and further indicated that their arrival in Siam was acknowledged by the sound of a church bell rung by an elderly Portuguese cleric on their passage.[28] On his second trip to Siam, Tachard noted with exacting detail the number of cannon on each of the vessels, and on their departure from France cannon fire alerted the group of ships that it was time to raise anchor and begin their voyage.[29] Upon arriving in Siam, the Siamese ambassadors who were traveling with the French delegation went ashore to meet Constantine Phaulkon, the Greek man Phra Narai had appointed as a trusted minister. The returning Siamese embassy disembarked "to the sound of cannon fire which came from every ship."[30] As was

---

23. In the seventeenth century towns such as Beauvais in northern France and Lodi in northern Italy had well over a hundred bells of different sizes and purposes (Garrioch, "Sounds of the City," 9).

24. Dhiravat na Pombejra notes that the *mandarins* mentioned in the French texts are referred to as *khunnang* (ขุนนาง), or nobility, in the Thai language (*Siamese Court Life*, 120).

25. Chaumont, *Relation de l'ambassade*, 23.

26. Chaumont, *Relation de l'ambassade*, 26.

27. Chaumont, *Relation de l'ambassade*, 27.

28. Tachard, *Voyage de Siam*, 193.

29. Tachard, *Second voyage*, 12–14.

30. Tachard, *Second voyage*, 186.

the case for the burial at sea recounted by Bouvet, cannon fire functioned as a salute, emphasizing the significance of arrivals and departures, and had the advantage of being able to communicate meaning at great distance through a shared code. As such, cannon fire constituted a form of aural diplomacy, one that would have been understood by the Siamese, the French, and the other Europeans present in Siam.

Many of the other sounds the travelers described consisted of vocal or instrumental music at official events. Seventeenth-century French travelers would have expected to encounter differences in cultural practices, including musical ones, and would have understood them to arise at least in part from variations in *moeurs* and climate. As Claude-François Ménestrier wrote regarding music and musical theater, "Although nature is the same everywhere, it varies so significantly under different climates that customs [*moeurs*] are not the same in every country."[31] Travelers thus approached the different sounds they encountered through their understanding of a range of cultural and natural differences that separated the Siamese from Europeans. In terms of the language, on the one hand, the French considered Siamese speech to be "a kind of song" and likened it to Chinese because of its use of tones.[32] On the other hand, the language was deemed harsh and unpleasant, at least by François Henri Turpin: "The Siamese language cannot be very harmonious, being composed only of monosyllables and harsh diphthongs. Their historic and moral poetry always relies on the support of music, which erases its imperfections."[33] For Turpin, the pleasant sounds of music corrected or beautified the language whose sounds on their own were condemned as rough and ugly.

French observers remarked that there was little or no theoretical knowledge of music in Siam, which was indeed based on traditional oral and improvisatory practices.[34] Loubère, for example, wrote that the Siamese had no knowledge of notation: "They compose airs through inspiration [*génie*] and do not know how to notate them."[35] He went on to assert that they did not know multipart composition but only practiced monody: "They understand no better than

31. Ménestrier, *Des représentations en musique anciennes et modernes*, 138–39.
32. Diderot and d'Alembert, *Encyclopédie*, vol. 19, sec. 20, p. 10, plate 21, "Caractères et alphabets de langues mortes et vivantes," artflsrv03.uchicago.edu/philologic4/encyclopedie1117/navigate/19/25/23/?byte= 541496.
33. Turpin, *Histoire civile et naturelle*, 134. Unlike the other works cited here, Turpin's volume is a compilation of observations by missionaries and others and therefore not a firsthand account. The phrasing of his judgment on the Siamese language, moreover, does not imply that he has any working knowledge of it. An *Arrest du conseil d'Etat du roi* of 1772 claims that the publication was based on manuscripts left by the bishop of Tabraca and other missionaries and forbade its reimpression and distribution, accusing Turpin of unacceptable imaginative flights of fancy.
34. See Myers-Moro, "Musical Notation in Thailand," 101.
35. Loubère, *Du royaume de Siam*, 1:261.

the Chinese the variety of songs for the various parts of a piece of music. They do not even understand the diversity of voices [*la diversité des Parties*]: they all sing in unison."[36] Nicolas Gervaise, in a similar vein, considered Siamese trumpets inferior to the more sophisticated European variety, likening those he heard in Siam to those that "our peasants use to call their cows."[37] After witnessing a number of theatrical and musical performances, Bouvet remarked that they were a thousand times more "insolent" than the performances offered for public entertainment on the Pont Neuf in Paris, denigrating what he saw and heard in Siam by placing them below even the lowest of Parisian street performers.[38] The comparisons offered by Gervaise and Bouvet reflected the cultural chasm that separated their experiences of music and theater in France from the performances they encountered in Siam, and they also resulted from a tendency to compare peoples encountered outside Europe to peasants or other unsophisticated Europeans.[39]

In other words, the new experiences were rejected as lowly, unsophisticated, or simply unpleasant and at the same time perceived and understood with reference to a French hierarchy of musical sound coming from the courtly experience of the French diplomats. Cultural cleavages within French society therefore served as models for understanding cross-cultural differences encountered abroad. It is also intriguing to consider that the sound profile of some Siamese instruments might indeed have resembled in certain respects the sound of a Pont-Neuf performer playing, for example, a hurdy-gurdy or perhaps a wind instrument. More specifically, Terry E. Miller and Jarernchai Chonpairot remarked that two aspects of Siamese music repelled foreigners: the "lack of a single clear melody supported by harmony" and the timbre of certain instruments, "especially the double-reed aerophones," which have a nasal sonority.[40] These Thai instruments thus may have reminded the French travelers of instruments from Europe that they disdained either because the instruments were associated with street performers or peasant music or because they resembled older European instruments such as the crumhorn or cornamuse that the envoys of Louis XIV would have rejected as entirely antiquated.

Aside from the royal audiences, which held primary documentary importance for those representing the French crown, without question the ceremonial activities that most frequently captured the interest of the French travelers were

36. Loubère, *Du royaume de Siam*, 1:262.
37. Gervaise, *Histoire naturelle et politique*, 130.
38. Bouvet, *Voiage de Siam*, 132–33.
39. Jean-Jacques Rousseau later argued that distant cultures, such as those of America, were comparable to that of the ancient patriarchs. See Thomas, *Music and the Origins of Language*, 109–10.
40. Miller and Chonpairot, "History of Siamese Music," 26.

those that took place on the river. Indeed, a river procession of long, elegant *balons* (or *ballons*), as the Thai river boats are referred to in the French sources, must have been a breathtaking sight (fig. 2). However, the sounds of these processions were equally important: the sounds made by human interaction with water, the coordinated voices of the oarsmen, and the musical instruments that were played from the boats. These descriptions stand out because they contrast with the overwhelming censure of musical performances elsewhere in the French sources. Turpin noted that the Thai people "prefer to travel only by water in boats called *ballons* which, though made from a single tree, sometimes measure from sixteen to twenty *toises* [a *toise* measures about 6.5 feet]: one can accommodate up to 120 oarsmen all arranged in pairs."[41] The river processions featuring the king impressed the French visitors with their enormous scale. Commenting on a visit by Phra Narai and the chevalier de Chaumont to the most important religious leaders of the country, Tachard counted 149 boats, "of which the largest were nearly 120 feet in length and barely six feet at their widest," with more than fourteen thousand men aboard in total.[42] Traveling upriver with the French embassy on its way to Ayuttaya, Louis XIV's letter to Phra Narai was treated with as much respect as if it were the king's person and was conveyed in its own golden boat, as Bouvet describes it: "A large *ballon*, gilded all the way to the waterline, carried the king's letter which rested on a kind of throne, open in the middle on all sides and covered by a high, fully gilded pyramid. Four other *ballons* of the [king's] guard, of the same form and magnificence as the one carrying the letter, served as escort."[43]

Tachard noted that music accompanied the Siamese ships carrying the chevalier de Chaumont, his delegation, the gifts from Louis XIV, the king's letter in its own vessel, and various mandarins: "Mr. Ambassador came next in a magnificent *Balon* which gleamed on all sides from the gold covering it. On his right and left were six galleys of the guard containing the trumpets, drums, and other instruments that preceded the king in his public appearances."[44] In addition to the music played on the river, which is mentioned but not described in detail, Tachard remarked in particular the coordinated sound of the rowers' voices: "The often redoubled cries of joy that the oarsmen voiced, following Siamese custom, as if they were making a military charge," inviting crowds to the banks to watch and listen to the procession.[45] Gervaise, too, made a point of noting the joyful sounds of processions on the river: "Though they seem a bit melancholic

41. Turpin, *Histoire civile et naturelle*, 34.
42. Tachard, *Voyage de Siam*, 223–24.
43. Bouvet, *Voiage de Siam*, 117.
44. Tachard, *Voyage de Siam*, 191.
45. Tachard, *Voyage de Siam*, 192.

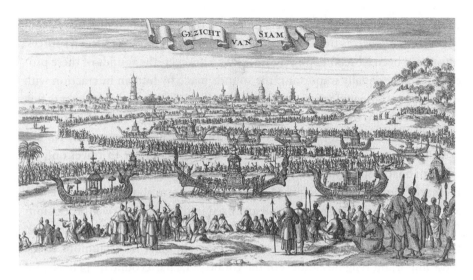

FIGURE 2 Guy Tachard, *Reis na Siam, gedaan door den ridder de Chaumont* (Amsterdam, 1687), 148. Image courtesy of Rijksmuseum, Amsterdam.

to us, the Siamese are nevertheless joyful. Often they have *balon* races on the river that they enliven with concerts of voices, musical instruments, and rhythmic hand clapping."[46] Turpin also noted that the "oarsmen sing in time" to accompany and match their rhythmic rowing efforts.[47] The abbé de Choisy, too, made a point of celebrating the impressive sounds of official delegations on the river, with the lead oarsman and the crew entering into a dialogue that harmonized with the strokes of the oars: "Their lead oarsman is a good musician: he sings, and does nothing but that. The others row and sing, repeating everything that the lead oarsman says on the same tone. The chords are perfect, and all at once one witnesses a hundred voices perfectly harmonized with a hundred oars."[48] Here, the sounds of the river, the oars, and the oarsmen created a rhythmic and sonorous "performance" that impressed the French ambassador, forming a moving concert as the procession flowed on the water. Referring to more ordinary, daily travel by boat, Turpin noted that "every time they take out their *ballons* the men and women blend their voices to create a concert that inspires an innocent joy."[49] Turpin described a sonorous daily dialogue between passing boats or between the boats and those on shore: "Those who go out in their *ballons* attack with couplets all passersby who never fail to reply on the same

46. Gervaise, *Histoire naturelle et politique*, 129.
47. Turpin, *Histoire civile et naturelle*, 34.
48. Choisy, *Journal du voyage de Siam*, 232.
49. Turpin, *Histoire civile et naturelle*, 123.

tone."[50] All of these accounts highlight the effect an interactive, sonorous, and mobile tableau on the river created, with additional sonorous interaction between river and shore, both on official occasions and as part of the sonic environment of everyday life. While the accounts of Choisy and others who visited Siam testify to the strong impression these river processions had on them and the novel sight and sounds they experienced, that of Turpin—which, as noted earlier, was an armchair exercise, written decades after the events—layers on an additional moral tone and implicit judgment that betrays a post-Rousseauesque attitude to the supposed "innocent joy" of the Siamese people.

How can we understand the significant attention given to these river processions and the universal praise French chroniclers lavished on them, when in equal measure they denigrated so many other aspects of Siamese religion and culture? Certainly, the sight and sound of so many vessels moving together on the water, with the choreographed efforts of thousands of oarsmen, must have been magnificent in and of itself. We can postulate further that some degree of cultural familiarity may have also contributed to the French delegation's admiration, namely, the preeminence of water in Louis XIV's gardens at Versailles and its uses in state events. Water was one of the most dominant elements of the gardens as they were developed from the 1660s and figured prominently in the activities of the king and court there, creating both visual and aural effects for visitors to the gardens. An engineering feat of the day, the construction of several reservoirs made possible magnificent water jets that animated the basins and played on sculptural forms drawn from the mythological tales in Ovid's *Metamorphoses*, creating memorable sights and sounds. Madeleine de Scudéry introduced the reservoirs on the very first pages of her *La promenade de Versailles* as keys to the wonders within.[51] André Félibien singled out water as "one of the most beautiful ornaments of this house," and the water features of the gardens figure prominently in each of the six days he chronicled for Louis XIV's 1674 *Divertissements de Versailles*, which included theatrical performances, cannon fire, fireworks, and notably promenades in gondolas for the royal family and members of the court accompanied by musicians in their own gondolas.[52] At

---

50. Turpin, *Histoire civile et naturelle*, 123–24.

51. "Je vous prie de regarder avec quelque attention cet étang paisible que vous voiez, & qui n'estant pas fort grand ne meriteroit peut-estre pas d'être fort considéré, si je n'avois à vous dire qu'il est la source de mille belles choses que vous verrez tantost" (I encourage you to consider attentively this peaceful pool that you see, which, not being so large, would not warrant being considered further if I did not tell you that it is the source of a thousand beautiful things that you will soon see) (Scudéry, *La promenade de Versailles*, 2–3). Indeed, water was such an essential element of Versailles's mise-en-scène that for official visitors, "if a section of the gardens lacked one or more displays of water, it was not visited" (Berger and Hedin, *Diplomatic Tours*, 17).

52. Félibien, *Les fêtes de Versailles*, 32.

several points in his account, Félibien remarks on the importance for the experience of the gardens of the pleasurable sounds made by the fountains and by groups enjoying promenades on the water.

Promenades on the Grand Canal accompanied by music were also a regular feature of diplomatic visits.[53] The Siamese delegation of 1686 was taken through the gardens over the course of four days during which time they boarded a galley on the Grand Canal with gondolas accompanying them to the sound of trumpets, drums, and other instruments.[54] The water features were clearly a signal part of their visit, with the *Mercure galant* emphasizing that the delegation counted the water jets they could view from the Trianon and that Kosa Pan himself was invited to turn several of the spigots that controlled water flow at the labyrinth.[55] Familiarity with the gardens of Versailles, including the water features and their visual and aural integration in formal state events, most notably diplomatic ones, may have favorably colored the judgment of the travelers as they witnessed the Siamese river processions and recorded the sounds they heard, creating a common measure of understanding that helped advance the diplomatic effort. The sounds of the rowers, noted by the travelers in Siam, may have been an additional element of commonality to the experience of water by visitors to Versailles. Meredith Martin and Gillian Weiss have documented the expansion of Louis XIV's fleet of galleys during precisely this time period, galleys that were powered by convicts and slaves, including the model vessels commissioned by the crown for the gardens of Versailles.[56] The "joyful" sounds made by the Siamese rowers may have created a form of sympathetic resonance for the French travelers who heard in them the sound of the galleys that Jean-Baptiste Colbert amassed for Louis XIV and a comparable expression of sovereign power. The sounds made by men in vessels on water created both a pleasurable sonorous rhythm and a reminder that mastery of the water was at least in part generated by forced labor.

The royal audiences were understandably a primary focus of many of the travel writings because they documented the culmination of months of travel and years of diplomatic effort. The French visitors remarked on the particular sounds and silences connected with the appearance of King Phra Narai. Indeed, perhaps the most remarkable distinction for the French voyagers between the

---

53. During his 1670 visit concerning the secret Treaty of Dover, for example, the Duke of Buckingham was treated to a full visit of the grounds, including a musical promenade on the Grand Canal (Berger and Hedin, *Diplomatic Tours*, 78).

54. Donneau de Vizé, *Suite du voyage*, 94.

55. Donneau de Vizé, *Suite du voyage*, 103–4, 136. For a full account of the visit of the Siamese delegation to the gardens, see Berger and Hedin, *Diplomatic Tours*, 31–42.

56. Martin and Weiss, "'Turks' on Display," 101–2. See also the introduction to their forthcoming work *Sun King at Sea*.

sounds of royal appearances at Versailles and in Ayuttaya was the extreme silence that reigned whenever Phra Narai was present. Quiet is most certainly not a word that would have come to mind in the context of Louis XIV's Versailles, where courtiers continued their conversations and gossip even in the presence of Louis XIV and jostled each other to vie for the best places to see and be seen, and for the king's attention. At Siamese royal audiences, sounds and silences functioned as signals, alerting all those in attendance to the king's arrival and departure and other significant events during the audiences.

Claude de Forbin, a naval officer who participated in the embassy of Chaumont, mentioned that as the French delegation left by boat on their way to the audience with the king, "we departed to the sound of trumpets and drums," signaling in this case not the presence of the king but that the purpose of their expedition was an audience with the king.[57] Forbin described arriving at the king's palace, after passing through several courtyards, and entering the room designated for royal audiences: "Once all was ready, a large drum was struck. At this signal, the Mandarins . . . prostrated themselves and remained on the ground on their hands and knees. The position of these Mandarins with their pointed hats in each other's asses made all the French laugh."[58] It is impossible to know if the mirth of the French, provoked by the posture of the bowing Siamese nobles in tight rows each wearing a conical hat tapering to a point, called *lomphok* (ลอมพอก), was or was not expressed loudly enough for the Siamese to hear it. If the French had laughed out loud, a serious diplomatic incident surely would have ensued, but there is no mention in the sources of any kind of repercussion from the gaffe, which is one of the more remarkable examples of cross-cultural dissonance in these accounts. The drum was struck several times again slowly—Forbin insisted on the deliberateness and measured quality of the beat—and "at the sixth drumbeat, the king opened up and appeared at the window."[59] After the presentation of Louis XIV's letter and some polite exchange, "next the large drum was struck, the king closed his window, and the Mandarins stood up," with this final drumbeat signaling the end of the audience and the opportunity for the Siamese to resume their affairs.[60]

In the account of his second voyage to Siam, Tachard remarked that the musical flourishes both signaled the arrival of the king and directed the courtiers to prostrate themselves and perform a deep *wai* (ไหว้): "Immediately we heard the drums and other instruments that accompanied the Siamese king on his outings, alerting everyone to assume an appropriate position."[61] Tachard also

57. Forbin, *Mémoires*, 1:105.
58. Forbin, *Mémoires*, 1:107–8.
59. Forbin, *Mémoires*, 1:108.
60. Forbin, *Mémoires*, 1:109.
61. Tachard, *Second voyage*, 268.

noted that "the trumpets and drums always remain outside, indicating from time to time with their fanfares of what was transpiring in the royal reception chambers."[62] Though he did not indicate exactly how the sounds of the instruments informed those outside of the activities taking place within, it is nonetheless clear that the musical signals could demarcate key moments of the audience. In his *Journal*, Choisy described instruments both inside and outside the audience chamber, the latter echoing the sounds of the former to allow those who did not have direct access to the audience to bear aural witness to it: "As soon as the gentlemen were in place we heard the trumpets and drums sound from inside; those outside responded, which is the signal that the king will appear on his throne."[63]

The French accounts are consistent in noting that trumpets and percussion composed the soundscape of royal appearances and audiences, but these sounds were only some of those experienced by the voyagers. Loubère, who was more meticulous than most in his descriptions of Siamese culture and practices, mentioned other instruments for royal audiences. After giving an overview of Siamese musical instruments in some detail (stringed instruments [*rebecs ou violons*], oboes, a variety of percussive instruments), he indicated that "the march that was played at the entrance of the king's envoys was a racket of all those instruments together. The same is played for the processions of the king of Siam; and this noise, as strange as it is, does not sound unpleasant particularly on the river."[64] Here again, the experience of formal river processions, and possibly the cultural echo of those experiences in the gardens of Versailles, favorably disposed Loubère to the music when it was integrated into the river excursions. Aside from Loubère, and outside of official royal audiences, mentions of vocal song are rare in the accounts. Some described a few other instruments used in different contexts, such as theatrical performances. For example, Loubère and a few others referred to an instrument the Europeans found pleasing, the *khawng wong* (ฆ้องวง), which came in a variety of sizes: "The bells are aligned one after the other, each on a short stick and arranged on a half circle of wood similar to a small carriage wheel. He who plays this instrument is seated, legs crossed, in the center or hub; and he strikes the bells with two sticks, one held in the right hand and the other in the left hand."[65] Aside from these instances, where there is some degree of analogy to European musical sounds or contextual framing, as

---

62. Tachard, *Second voyage*, 268.
63. Choisy, *Journal du voyage de Siam*, 250–51.
64. Loubère, *Du royaume de Siam*, 1:264–65.
65. Loubère, *Du royaume de Siam*, 1:264. Bouvet mentions this instrument as well (*Voiage de Siam*, 127). See also Miller and Chonpairot, "History of Siamese Music," 53–55. On the *khawng wong*, see Morton, *Traditional Music of Thailand*, 51.

may have been the case with river soundscapes in Siam, cultural gaps created obstacles for French travelers to appreciate the musical practices and sounds they encountered.

The repeated and consistent mention of trumpets and drums in connection with Phra Narai's audiences and other appearances, mostly to the exclusion of other instruments, is conspicuous in the accounts. How did the French visitors understand the Siamese preference for these two instruments in royal audiences?[66] Turpin had a ready answer to that question: the tropical heat had prevented Siamese culture from developing beyond a relatively rudimentary state, the assumption being that drums are among the most primitive of musical instruments. Turpin drew on a number of firsthand sources, adding an interpretive layer of his own to place the travelers' experiences in a context that eighteenth-century readers of Buffon would have understood, namely, that climate had a determining effect on cultural development and refinement. Turpin claimed explicitly that "the laziness that the climate inspires" has suppressed "the flame of the arts and sciences" in Siam.[67] Of all the instruments, he wrote, "the noisiest are always preferred, such as the oboe, drums, trumpets, and fifes. None of the instruments on which one plays several voices are to their taste because they do not like that which is difficult. Thus, they affect a disdainful indifference for the harpsichord, the harp, and so on."[68] Asserting French cultural superiority, Turpin suggested that trumpets and drums were instruments of choice because they are loud and do not on their own allow for the complexities of polyphony, which were supposedly beyond the capabilities of the Siamese. Relying primarily on the firsthand accounts, and taking some distance from Turpin's armchair judgments, one way to account for the prominence of the trumpet and percussion instruments would be to recognize that these instruments can be heard at a greater distance than most others. Because their specific function as described in the travelers' accounts was to signal the king's actions and to command deference to the royal presence, their ability to be heard at a distance was crucial for royal audiences and excursions. Indeed, trumpets and drums had a similar function in Europe at that time, likely for similar reasons, and their use would have been immediately familiar to the French travelers.[69] It is therefore understandable that the French travelers

66. Miller and Chonpairot make the important point that "anything blown is called a flute or a trumpet. Since reeds are not normally seen, observers often do not distinguish them from flutes" ("History of Siamese Music," 64–65). This observation leads to the possibility that instruments unfamiliar to the European visitors were conflated.

67. Turpin, *Histoire civile et naturelle*, 133–34.

68. Turpin, *Histoire civile et naturelle*, 126.

69. As Arlette Farge has written about early modern France: "The sound of the trumpet was a sign that the king was giving an order, declaring war, peace or victory, or issuing a reproof. The sounds of injunc-

interpreted the Siamese uses of trumpets and percussive instruments as not having a musical purpose but, as was the case in France, as functioning as sonic signs, conveying a specific array of contextual meanings and messages associated with royal activities.

Despite the possible analogies between European and Siamese uses of these musical instruments, trumpets did not sound and drums were not struck every time Louis XIV made an appearance, but they do seem to have been for Phra Narai, judging from the travelers' accounts. I have insisted on the documentation of the soundscapes of royal audiences because it indicates that the French travelers understood that the measured sounds that punctuated them facilitated the involvement of both the participants and those observing the events from the outside by signaling their significance in a temporal frame, most importantly, the appearance of the monarch, which marked the formal opening of the audiences, and closure of the same as the king shuts his window. The notice the French took of these practices led them to adopt trumpets and drums for the 1686 audience with Louis XIV at Versailles. While misunderstandings and gaffes abound throughout the history of the French-Siamese relations, Louis François du Bouchet, the marquis de Sourches, documented this particularly successful instance of insightful cultural appropriation of Siamese customs: "The king gave their first audience to the ambassadors of the king of Siam. They were escorted by the duke de La Feuillade. . . . The Swiss guards were aligned on the steps up to the top of the marble staircase. [The ambassadors] ascended to the sound of trumpets and drums to imitate the practice of the king of Siam who never enters the royal audience chamber without this music."[70] Successful diplomatic hosts pay careful attention to cultural contexts and expectations, thereby creating a sense of welcome and a measure of familiarity for their guests. The information about Phra Narai's royal audiences brought back from Siam by the chevalier de Chaumont and the abbé de Choisy, notably the soundscapes that were part and parcel of them, resulted in the deliberate adaptation of a Siamese royal custom for the audience Louis XIV gave the Siamese delegation at Versailles. The French travelers' attention to the soundscapes of diplomacy during their audience with the Siamese king allowed them to create a similar sonic

---

tion issuing from the king and his representatives formed another language, one relayed by trumpets and a royal official" ("Sounds of Enlightenment Paris," 57). In his analysis of the soundscape of early modern Europe, David Garrioch has also indicated that both drums and trumpets held a particular symbolic and functional status because of their association with the crown, with war (a royal act), and with official pronouncements: "Trumpets were another official instrument, widely used for royalty and official announcements, in seventeenth- and eighteenth-century theatre[,] to announce gods and heroes, to herald punishments, and in some places the curfew, while the monopolies accorded to town criers served to protect the status not only of their announcements but also of the drums and horns they used" ("Sounds of the City," 17).

70. Bouchet, *Mémoires*, 1:436.

environment in Versailles for the Siamese delegation, taking a step toward mutual understanding between the two countries.

The commotion around Louis XIV shocked the Siamese delegation, according to Bénigne Vachet's account of the event. From the French descriptions of audiences with Phra Narai, it was clear that absolute silence reigned, and courtiers were all prostrate, forbidden even to set eyes on the king. Vachet describes the bewilderment of the Siamese visitors in the Hall of Mirrors, with regard both to the courtiers who continued their conversations in the presence of the king and to what they must have perceived as the courtiers' shocking physical demeanor and proximity to the royal person. The noise and confusion were such that one of those attending had to speak up so that the Siamese visitors would know that they were approaching the king amidst the throng of nobility jostling for attention: "Our Siamese visitors, who were accustomed to the profound respect and great silence that is kept in the presence of their king, were extremely surprised to hear muddled chatter and to see that everyone hastened to get close to the person of the king, some ahead of him, others following, and the largest number at his sides, such that when he was only five or six steps away from us we had to say, 'Here is the king!'"[71] The cultural conventions surrounding royal audiences with the two monarchs differed significantly. Phra Narai always appeared at a distance from, and physically above, all others. This vertical separation between the king and the nobility in particular was evident both on royal excursions, when he mounted a favorite elephant, and during royal audiences, when he made his appearance at a high window.[72] In these instances, following the signals of the trumpets and drums, the king appeared isolated in his high frame, surrounded by the prostrate Siamese nobility below

71. Launay, *Histoire de la mission de Siam*, 1:142.

72. Several accounts describe the contrivance devised to allow the chevalier de Chaumont to transmit Louis XIV's letter to Phra Narai while respecting the vertical hierarchy and distance required to separate the king from all others. Forbin notes that the letter was to be put in a golden chalice attached to a golden shaft, which Chaumont would then raise so that Phra Narai could reach it from his high perch. It is likely that Chaumont deliberately held the device a bit low, requiring the king to lean out of his royal aperture and to reach down to take the letter (*Mémoires*, 1:109). The lack of absolute respect for this vertical separation caused considerable difficulty for the first Siamese delegation to France in 1685 at a performance of Lully's *Roland*: "Les Siamois, qui ne savaient pas que le rang d'en bas fut [sic] le plus noble et le plus commode, furent se placer au plus haut pour n'avoir personne sur leur tête. A peine fûmes-nous assis, que les gardes s'aperçurent de leur erreur, et se mirent en devoir de nous faire passer plus haut. Les Siamois crurent qu'on leur faisait affront, et sans vouloir m'écouter, ils furent à pied comme des brutaux à l'hôtellerie où les carrosses nous attendaient, et revinrent à Paris" (The Siamese, who did not know that the lowest row was the most noble and convenient, seated themselves as high as they could so as not to have anyone above their heads. We were hardly seated when the guards realized their error and proceeded to place us higher. The Siamese thought they were being insulted, and without listening to me, they headed out on foot like brutes to the hotel where the carriages were waiting for us and returned to Paris (Launay, *Histoire de la mission de Siam*, 1:144).

and by a profound silence. The French travelers who prepared Versailles to welcome Kosa Pan and his delegation had encountered and remarked on these cultural differences, appearing most obviously in the sonic environment of royal audiences.

This contrast between silence and noise is the most significant divergence in the soundscapes of royal appearances between the two cultures. Tachard described a situation where the French were told to be quiet during the observation of an eclipse using scientific instruments the Jesuits had brought with them to Siam: "We were told to hold our tongues or to speak extremely quietly. . . . The respect they have for the king's person causes them to observe a profound silence everywhere he is."[73] Given the extreme difference between the courtly soundscapes of Versailles and Ayuttaya, the silence surrounding Phra Narai was palpable for the French travelers. During a royal excursion, Bouvet, too, underscored that what he noticed most of all was the extreme silence that reigned despite the huge numbers of people everywhere present: "What surprised me more was the multitude of people who lined the way . . . but above all the incredible silence that they kept everywhere, so much so that among this great confluence of people of all ages and nations not a single person was heard to spit or sneeze."[74] A similar account by the Dutchman Jeremias van Vliet of a royal excursion from earlier in the century concurs in pointing out the overwhelming silence, despite the presence of a massive throng of people: "The whole assembly did reverence to His Majesty with such silence that one could (after the instruments had stopped playing), in the midst of so many thousands of people, hear the birds singing above our heads, which is a seemingly fantastical matter but nevertheless true."[75] During the 1686 embassy, in contrast to Forbin's account of the absurdity the French saw in the Siamese mandarins' posture, the abbé de Choisy mentioned that he was pleased by his delegation's ability to hold their tongues and respect the hush that fell on their audience with Phra Narai: "The king appeared at a balcony, with the entire courtyard full of armed guards prostrate on the ground in profound silence. Even our entire French delegation contained ourselves very well and did not make a sound."[76]

Every account concurs in describing the royal events as taking place "in great silence," and Gervaise was surprised that "even when the king is not present they maintain a profound silence."[77] Gervaise also remarked that outside the palace three obligations were in effect everywhere the king ventured, the last and

73. Tachard, *Voyage de Siam*, 244.
74. Bouvet, *Voiage de Siam*, 118.
75. Quoted in Pombejra, *Siamese Court Life*, 96.
76. Choisy, *Journal du voyage de Siam*, 278.
77. Forbin, *Mémoires*, 1:151; Gervaise, *Histoire naturelle et politique*, 287.

perhaps most important being silence: "The first is that each person erects a hedge of rushes in front of his house high enough to prevent the king from being seen and from being seen by him when he passes. The second is to close the doors and windows immediately on hearing the fifes and drums that precede him. And third, to keep a profound silence until he has passed." An injunction inhibiting both vision and voice was in effect everywhere the king was present, and any sound was deemed an offense.[78]

As Corbin has reminded us, "Silence is not simply the absence of noise."[79] Silence carries with it a host of meanings, perhaps most notably in the seventeenth century the religious connotations associated with silence. Jacques-Bénigne Bossuet, who was bishop of Meaux at the time of the Siamese embassies, repeatedly emphasized in his sermons and other writings the importance of silence and, indeed, the need to listen to silence, for salvation: "Let us listen to the word that speaks to us in a profound and admirable silence. Let us lend the ear of our hearts to it."[80] These contemporary understandings of silence may have framed the astonishment the chroniclers acknowledged in remarking on the hush of respect that surrounded the Siamese king. Particularly in the case of Vachet, given the religious connotations associated with it, this attention to silence could have reinforced a lingering hope for Phra Narai's conversation.

The sounds and silences French travelers described provide additional information about the events they witnessed, what pleased them and what did not, and how they understood, or misunderstood, Siamese cultural practices. Unlike the descriptions of Siamese flora and fauna found in some of the travelers' accounts, the soundscapes described are largely human ones, providing insight into how the French travelers perceived the people of an extremely distant and foreign world. In other words, sonic environments are not passive entities: they have consequences because they are in many cases created by people, hold meanings for them, and provide an opportunity for understanding and engagement on the part of those who listen to them. Not only did the sounds the travelers heard sometimes astonish or repulse them, but the diplomats' reaction to the sounds and, indeed, engagement with them could either impede or further the diplomatic efforts they had traveled so far to undertake. When the French laughed at the prostrate Siamese courtiers, however quietly, sounds the French themselves made threatened to derail diplomatic efforts that were so long in the making. In the case of the Siamese music and theatrical performances they witnessed, the French heard sounds that reminded them of street

78. Gervaise, *Histoire naturelle et politique*, 293.

79. Corbin, *History of Silence*, 1.

80. Bossuet, *Elévations à Dieu*, 279. For more on seventeenth-century religious discussions of silence, see Corbin, *History of Silence*, 45–48.

performers or peasants, leading them to conclude that the Siamese were a relatively unsophisticated people. Sonic environments are a two-way street, and these cultural misunderstandings, driven both by sounds uttered and by sounds heard, were common and may have been unavoidable in many cases.

More intriguing were the instances in which some measure of shared understanding or aesthetic appreciation was achieved across cultural divides. In this light, the diplomatic framing of the Franco-Siamese embassies was considered so successful that when Tipû, the sultan of Mysore, sent a delegation to France in 1788, a French official argued that the ceremony with which they were received should match that offered to the Siamese delegations a century earlier.[81] Though the forms they took were different, the diplomatic rituals of the French and the Siamese were similar in their elaborateness and formality. During the elaborate Siamese river processions, for example, implicit comparisons with royal practices at Versailles may have provided common ground for the diplomats to appreciate the cultural traditions of their hosts. In other instances, as in the accounts of trumpets and drums used for royal audiences, an understanding of the sonic environments the travelers encountered laid the foundation for a successful adaptation of Siamese practice during the reception of the Siamese delegation at Versailles in 1686. The soundscapes the diplomats encountered revealed both stark differences and finer nuances that the diplomats either could not or chose not to appreciate or, on the contrary, that engaged them and helped further their goals for this particular diplomatic initiative within Louis XIV's efforts to transform France and the world.

DOWNING A. THOMAS is professor of French at the University of Iowa. He is author of *Music and the Origins of Language: Theories from the French Enlightenment* (1995) and *Aesthetic of Opera in the Ancien Régime, 1647–1785* (2002).

References

Arrest du conseil d'Etat du roi, portant suppression d'un ouvrage intitulé: Histoire civile et naturelle du royaume de Siam. Paris, 1772.

Berger, Robert W., and Thomas F. Hedin. *Diplomatic Tours in the Gardens of Versailles under Louis XIV*. Philadelphia, 2008.

Bloechl, Olivia. *Opera and the Political Imaginary in Old Regime France*. Chicago, 2017.

Bossuet, Jacques-Bénigne. *Elévations à Dieu sur tous les mystères de la religion chrétienne*. Paris, 1962.

Bouchet, Louis François du, marquis de Sourches. *Mémoires*. 13 vols. Paris, 1882–93.

Bouvet, Joachim. *Voiage de Siam*. Leiden, 1963.

Bull, Michael, ed. *The Routledge Companion to Sound Studies*. New York, 2019.

81. Martin, "Ambassades extraordinaires," 141.

Chaumont, Alexandre de. *Relation de l'ambassade du chevalier de Chaumont à la cour du roi de Siam*. The Hague, 1733.

Choisy, François-Timoléon de. *Journal du voyage de Siam*. Trevoux, 1741.

Corbin, Alain. *A History of Silence from the Renaissance to the Present Day*, translated by Jean Birrell. Cambridge, 2018.

Corbin, Alain. *Time, Desire, and Horror: Towards a History of the Senses*, translated by Jean Birrell. Cambridge, 1995.

Diderot, Denis, and Jean le Rond d'Alembert, eds. *Encyclopédie ou dictionnaire raisonné des arts et des métiers*. 28 vols. 1751–72; repr. Elmsford, NY, n.d.

Donneau de Vizé, Jean. *Suite du voyage des ambassadeurs de Siam en France*. Paris, 1686.

Donneau de Vizé, Jean. *Voyage des ambassadeurs de Siam en France*. Paris, 1686.

Farge, Arlette. "The Sounds of Enlightenment Paris." *Paragraph* 41, no. 1 (2018): 52–61.

Félibien, André. *Les fêtes de Versailles: Chroniques de 1668 et 1674*. Maisonneuve, 1994.

Forbin, Claude de. *Mémoires*. 2 vols. Amsterdam, 1748.

Garrioch, David. "Sounds of the City: The Soundscape of Early Modern European Towns." *Urban History* 30, no. 1 (2003): 5–25.

Gervaise, Nicolas. *Histoire naturelle et politique du royaume de Siam*. Paris, 1688.

Hamilton, Tom, and Nicholas Hammond, eds. "Soundscapes." Special issue, *Early Modern French Studies* 41, no. 1 (2019).

Hammond, Nicholas. *The Powers of Sound and Song in Early Modern Paris*. University Park, PA, 2019.

Irving, David R. M. "Lully in Siam: Music and Diplomacy in French-Siamese Cultural Exchanges, 1680–1690." *Early Music* 40, no. 3 (2013): 393–420.

Jacq-Hergoualc'h, Michel. "Les ambassadeurs siamois à Versailles le premier septembre 1686 dans un bas relief en bronze d'A. Coysevox." *Journal of the Siam Society* 72.0 (1984): 19–40.

Kerssenbrock-Krosigk, Dedo von. "Glass for the King of Siam: Bernard Perrot's Portrait Plaque of King Louis XIV and Its Trip to Asia." *Journal of Glass Studies* 49 (2007): 63–79.

Launay, Adrien. *Histoire de la mission de Siam, 1662–1811*. 3 vols. 1920; repr. Paris, 2000.

Leduc, Antoine. "Le canon offert à Louis XIV." In *Visiteurs de Versailles: Voyageurs, princes, ambassadeurs, 1682–1789*, edited by Daniëlle Kisluk-Grosheide and Bertrand Rondot, 162–63. Paris, 2017.

Le Guern, Philippe. "Sound studies: Sons de l'histoire et histoire des sons." *Revue de la Bibliothèque Nationale de France*, no. 55 (2017): 21–29.

Loubère, Simon de la. *Du royaume de Siam*. 2 vols. Paris, 1691.

Love, Ronald S. "Rituals of Majesty: France, Siam, and Court Spectacle in Royal Image-Building at Versailles in 1685 and 1686." *Canadian Journal of History / Annales canadiennes d'histoire* 31, no. 2 (1996): 171–98.

Martin, Meredith. "Ambassades extraordinaires et visiteurs des contrées lointaines." In *Visiteurs de Versailles: Voyageurs, princes, ambassadeurs, 1682–1789*, edited by Daniëlle Kisluk-Grosheide and Bertrand Rondot, 138–49. Paris, 2017.

Martin, Meredith. "Mirror Reflections: Louis XIV, Phra Narai, and the Material Culture of Kingship." *Art History* 38, no. 4 (2015): 652–67.

Martin, Meredith, and Gillian Weiss. *The Sun King at Sea: Maritime Art and Galley Slavery in Louis XIV's France*. Los Angeles, forthcoming.

Martin, Meredith, and Gillian Weiss. "'Turks' on Display during the Reign of Louis XIV." *L'esprit créateur* 53, no. 4 (2013): 98–112.

Ménestrier, Claude-François. *Des représentations en musique anciennes et modernes*. 1681; repr. Geneva, 1992.

Michel, Jean-Baptiste, et al. "Quantitative Analysis of Culture Using Millions of Digitized Books." *Science*, no. 6014 (2010): 176–82.

Miller, Terry E., and Jarernchai Chonpairot. "A History of Siamese Music Reconstructed from Western Documents, 1505–1932." *Crossroads: An Interdisciplinary Journal of Southeast Asian Studies* 8, no. 2 (1994): 1–192.

Morton, David. *The Traditional Music of Thailand*. Berkeley, CA, 1976.

Myers-Moro, Pamela. "Musical Notation in Thailand." *Journal of the Siam Society* 78, no. 1 (1990): 101–8.

Pan, Kosa. *The Diary of Kosa Pan: Thai Ambassador to France, June–July 1686*, edited by Michael Smithies, translated by Visudh Busyakul. Chiang Mai, 2002.

Pombejra, Dhiravat na. *Siamese Court Life in the Seventeenth Century as Depicted in European Sources*. Bangkok, 2001.

Scudéry, Madeleine de. *La promenade de Versailles*. Paris, 1669.

Tachard, Guy. *Second voyage du Père Tachard*. Amsterdam, 1689.

Tachard, Guy. *Voyage de Siam*. Amsterdam, 1687.

Thomas, Downing A. *Music and the Origins of Language: Theories from the French Enlightenment*. Cambridge, 1995.

Turpin, François Henri. *Histoire civile et naturelle du royaume de Siam*. Paris, 1771.

Van der Cruysse, Kirk. *Siam and the West, 1500–1800*, translated by Michael Smithies. Chiang Mai, 2002.

Vila, Anne C. *A Cultural History of the Senses in the Age of Enlightenment (1650–1800)*. London, 2014.

Welch, Ellen R. *A Theater of Diplomacy: International Relations and the Performing Arts in Early-Modern France*. Philadelphia, 2017.

Yamprai, Jittapim. "Richard-Michel de Lalande and the *Airs of Siam*." *Early Music* 41, no. 3 (2013): 421–37.

"It Is No Longer in Fashion—More's the Pity"

Reconsidering the Obsolescence of the Eighteenth-Century Vaudeville

JENNA HARMON

ABSTRACT   In a collected edition of his works, Charles Collé declared that "the vaudeville is thoroughly dead," "killed off" by the latest fad on Parisian stages, the *ariette*. However, this narrative is in tension with the appearance of *vaudevilles* across many forms of print media to the end of the eighteenth century. As a result, the print record presents a narrative different from the long-standing trope of the moribund vaudeville in the latter half of the eighteenth century. This article proposes that the story of the *vaudeville*'s demise is actually the effect of a simple but crucial conflation of two distinct song practices, both referred to as "vaudevilles," and traces this conflation to eighteenth-century musical dictionaries. Finally, it examines extratheatrical vaudevilles in novels, newspapers, and political songbooks, showing that the genre maintained relevancy in spite of narratives to the contrary.

KEYWORDS   vaudeville, eighteenth century, theater history, music history, song cultures

I n a 1768 edition of his collected society plays, the playwright Charles Collé included the following footnote to the list of characters for his *opéra-comique Joconde* (1757):

> In France, everything is a fad: as we know, the fad for vaudeville plays lasted for over forty years. For the last fourteen years, plays with *ariettes* have been in style. Will [the plays with *ariettes*] last as long as those they have killed off? The fickleness of the French when it comes to what pleases them would seem to make this an easy question to answer. In any case, as today the vaudeville is thoroughly dead, it occurred to me to rewrite *Joconde* and *Le Rossignol* in prose so that they better conform to the tastes of the present moment and do not seem old-fashioned. . . . Given the disgust with which modern music treats the melodies of the old vaudevilles, *Joconde* and *Le Rossignol* will perhaps benefit in the present moment from being put in prose. It's simple advice, which I give to those

French Historical Studies • Vol. 45, No. 2 (April 2022) • DOI 10.1215/00161071-9531968

who would like to give it a try. Their success would be even more certain in this moment if some musician, helped by a capable parodist, made these plays into plays with *ariettes*.[1]

In this footnote Collé claims that *vaudevilles* are "thoroughly dead" and "old-fashioned," having been "killed off" by the "new fad" for *ariettes*. He asserts that "modern music" treats not just *vaudevilles* but specifically their melodies "with disgust." For these reasons, Collé decided to update two of the pieces in the collected edition into exclusively spoken word plays, in the interest of making them more appealing for contemporary audiences. However, he acknowledges that if other playwrights wish to be more successful than even he, they should hire a musician to help them create a play with *ariettes*.

Collé paints a picture of two genres at war, the battle playing out not only on French stages but also on the printed page. Both *vaudeville* and *ariette* are vocal genres closely associated with the French comic theater tradition. A *vaudeville* is a type of contrafact, where well-known tunes are fitted with new lyrics, often with comedic or satirical results. Virtually any preexisting melody could serve as the basis for a *vaudeville*, from old folk melodies to opera airs. In print form, the chosen melody was indicated at the top of the new lyrics by a *timbre*, comprising the indicator "Air:," and followed by either the first line of the original song or its refrain (fig. 1).[2] Until the mid-eighteenth century, *ariette* referred to numbers with virtuosic singing in French opera, especially when it came to long melismas on particular vowel sounds. However, after the arrival of the Italian *bouffon* players in 1752, *ariette* shifted to refer to newly composed songs used in the French comic opera genre, *opéra-comique*. *Ariette* melodies were written to complement their text, advance the narrative, add more dimension to the singing character, or provide a mixture of all three.[3] While both genres share

1. Collé, *Théâtre de société*, 2:36. Duke University, Rubenstein Library Special Collections, 846.5 C697T: "Tout est de mode en France: celle des Pieces en Vaudevilles, s'est soutenue, pendant plus de 40 ans. Depuis près de 14 ans, les Pieces à Ariettes, ont la vogue. Vivront-elles aussi long-tems que celles qu'elles ont tuées? L'inconstances du François, dans ses plaisirs, paroît rendre cette question, facile à decider. Quoi qu'il en soit, comme le vaudeville est aujourd'hui totalement tombé, il étoit venu dans l'idée de refondre en Prose, Joconde & le Rossignol, pour se conformer au goût d'à present, & n'avoir pas l'air antique; . . . Vû le dégoût, que la musique moderne a jetté sur les airs des anciens Vaudevilles, Joconde & le Rossignol gagne-roient actuellement, peut-être, à être mis en Prose. C'est un simple avis, que l'on donne à ceux qui vou-droient en tenter l'essai. Leur succès seroit encore plus sûr dans ce moment-ci, si quelque Musicien aidé d'un Parodiste adroit, en faisoit des Pieces à Ariettes." At the time of Collé's writing, *ariettes* were a genre of vocal music most closely identified with comedic theater, coming especially out of the Italian tradition. This definition is further expanded below. All translations by the author unless otherwise indicated.

2. *Vaudevilles*, especially those written since 1750, have not attracted the same musicological attention as *ariettes*. For studies on *vaudeville* in the eighteenth century, see Martin, *Le théâtre de la foire*; Schneider, *Das Vaudeville*; Isherwood, *Farce and Fantasy*; and Harmon, "Made to Please."

3. For more on the role of the *ariette* in *opéras-comiques*, see Charlton, *Opera in the Age of Rousseau*; and Darlow, *Nicolas-Etienne Framery*.

common roots in the comic opera tradition, their melodies are an important point of differentiation, with *vaudevilles* using familiar tunes from a variety of sources and *ariettes* taking newly composed melodies.

If anyone was qualified to speak to the rise and fall of trends on the French stage, it was Collé, himself the author of many *opéras-comiques* and stand-alone *vaudevilles*.[4] As will be shown, he was far from the only person to share this account of the genre's demise, whose reverberations through time can be heard in modern histories of French vocal music. In the hundred-page-long "Opéra-Comique" chapter of his magisterial *Music in European Capitals*, Daniel Heartz devotes just eight and a half pages to *vaudevilles*, with the final sentence of this section reading: "[The living in harmony of *vaudevilles* and *ariettes*] became infrequent with the gradual disappearance of the former after the 1760s."[5] Mark Darlow puts it more strongly in his study of eighteenth-century lyric theater in France, stating that the *vaudeville* was "definitively replaced by the *ariette*" by the end of the 1750s.[6] Like the account that Collé offers, modern studies share this common narrative thread, where *vaudevilles* flourished roughly from the expulsion of the Italian players by Louis XIV in 1697 to the arrival of the Italian Bouffons in 1752, at which point the more sophisticated *ariette* supplanted them.

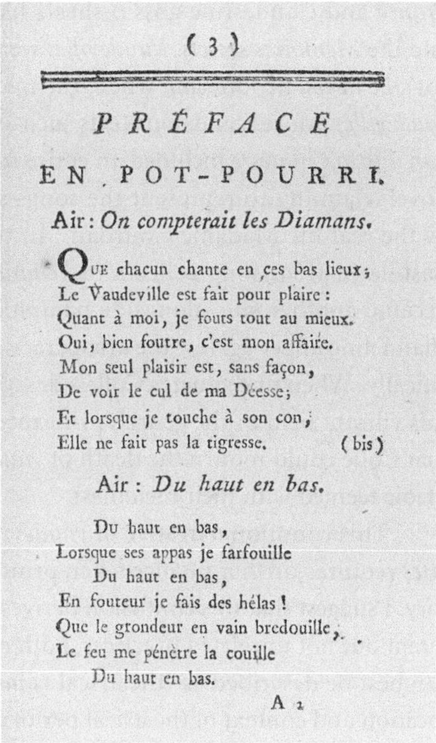

This diagnosis of *vaudeville*'s demise creates, however, an odd fit with an extensive print record in which *vaudevilles* continue to appear throughout the latter half of the eighteenth and into the first decades of the nineteenth centuries. They appeared in official, sanctioned newspapers such as the *Mercure de*

(3)

P R É F A C E

EN POT-POURRI.

Air: *On compterait les Diamans.*

QUE chacun chante en ces bas lieux;
Le Vaudeville est fait pour plaire :
Quant à moi, je fours tout au mieux.
Oui, bien foutre, c'est mon affaire.
Mon seul plaisir est, sans façon,
De voir le cul de ma Déesse;
Et lorsque je touche à son con,
Elle ne fait pas la tigresse.   (bis)

Air : *Du haut en bas.*

Du haut en bas,
Lorsque ses appas je farfouille
Du haut en bas,
En fouteur je fais des hélas !
Que le grondeur en vain bredouille,
Le feu me pénètre la couille
Du haut en bas.

A 2

FIGURE 1 "Que chacun chante en ces bas lieux / On compterait les Diamans." *Les fouteries chantantes* (1791). Bibliothèque Nationale de France.

---

4. Isherwood, *Farce and Fantasy*, 11.
5. Heartz, *Music in European Capitals*, 709.
6. Darlow, *Nicolas-Etienne Framery*, 81.

France and clandestine gossip sheets like the *Correspondance littéraire secrète* and the *Mémoires secrets*. *Vaudevilles* were included in novels, such Denis Diderot's *Le neveu de Rameau*, where the main character has entire monologues in *vaudevilles*. More scandalous texts such as the *Correspondance de Madame Gourdan dite la Comtesse* included an entire songbook of *vaudevilles* appended to the novel, claiming to represent the songs sung in the actual brothel maintained by the real-life Madame Gourdan.[7] In the decade leading up to the fall of the Bastille in 1789, song collections (*chansonniers*) made entirely of *vaudevilles* became another site, alongside pamphlets, cartoons, and satirical novels, for channeling anger against the aristocracy generally and the queen of France specifically. When one situates Collé's description of a moribund *vaudeville* within this vibrant field of the genre's print record, an incongruity emerges. How is it that Collé could mourn the death of *vaudeville* even as contemporaneous print media teemed with their melodies?

This common narrative of *vaudeville* practice ending with the rise of *ariettes* requires further nuance when print media are included in the genre's history. I suggest that this confusion derives from the conflation of two wholly different but not unrelated practices, both called *vaudeville*. One of these practices can best be described as "theatrical *vaudeville*," as it is most closely tied to the location and context of theatrical performance. Theatrical *vaudeville* was one of the defining features of early *opéra-comique*, with spoken dialogue alternating with sung *vaudevilles*, the selected melodies often adding ironic commentary to the events on stage. The other practice can best be described as "nontheatrical *vaudeville*," a stand-alone song practice that could be transmitted orally or through manuscript or print. Oral transmission of nontheatrical *vaudevilles* could theoretically happen anywhere a person cared to sing, but most surviving descriptions situate this mode of performance in the streets, particularly along the Pont Neuf of Paris.[8] In addition to singing their songs, many professional singers also sold printed or manuscript versions of *vaudevilles* at affordable prices. Once purchased, these written-down versions could then circulate again from hand to hand or through sung performance, demonstrating the unstable and diffuse modes by which nontheatrical *vaudevilles* moved through society. The mode of circulation and site of encounter differentiate the two versions of *vaudevilles*. While both theatrical and nontheatrical *vaudevilles* are contrafacts created from preexisting melodies, how individuals encountered them and the attendant associations suggest that they should be considered distinct.

7. An earlier edition of *Madame Gourdan* uses the title *La portfeuille de Madame Gourdan* (1783). This epistolary satire has been attributed to Théveneau de Morande. See Pia, *Les livres de l'enfer*, 160.

8. Darnton, *Poetry and the Police*, 84–89. For the close connection between singing and the Pont Neuf, see Isherwood, *Farce and Fantasy*, 1–9.

Given that Collé predominantly wrote for the theater, it is a perfectly logical response to think that this distinction was well known to Collé. In fact, it may seem both an obvious and minute point; as a theater writer, Collé was only ever talking about the death of theatrical *vaudeville*. However, this conflation of a specific theatrical practice with an entire genre has had profound historiographical consequences. Decoupling theatrical and nontheatrical *vaudevilles* allows for two primary interventions: to build on previous histories of the practice that have centered theatrical *vaudeville* as the primary practice of the genre and to call in French music scholars to hear musical material in nontraditional sites, such as novels and newspapers. As demonstrated earlier, historians of French music have primarily engaged with theatrical *vaudeville* but have typically not called attention to this distinction. This has produced a historiographical effect whereby theatrical *vaudeville* has become the default or perhaps only version of the practice, such that claims that the "*vaudeville* died," though only referring to the theatrical *vaudeville*, are applied to both practices. This conflation also has the side effect of limiting the archive to collections of works performed by the Opéra-Comique prior to their acquisition by the Comédie-Italienne in 1762 and materials related to their performance, such as reviews, administrative ledgers, or box office returns. If the theatrical *vaudeville* is the main practice and it falls out of favor after 1750, why would one think to go looking for them elsewhere? By clearly distinguishing printed *vaudeville* from theatrical *vaudeville*, I further nuance the history of this song practice by separating its fate from that of its theatrical twin and demonstrate to music scholars new potential sites of study.

If this definitional confusion between theatrical and nontheatrical *vaudeville* has led nontheatrical *vaudevilles* to be understudied among music historians, a slightly different confusion has arisen for a different group of scholars. French cultural historians have long been well aware of the importance of manuscript and printed *vaudevilles* but have typically treated them as poetic texts, not musical objects. Scholars such as Lynn Hunt and Chantal Thomas have pointed to the role of printed *vaudevilles* in shaping public opinion in the years leading up to and during the French Revolution.[9] However, their analyses did not extend to include the actual sound of these texts, almost always indicated by the timbres at the top of the new lyrics. Robert Darnton's *Poetry and the Police* represents one of the few cultural studies of nontheatrical *vaudeville* that engages with the actual melodies by including an "Electronic Cabaret," featuring Hélène Delavault performing the *vaudevilles* discussed throughout the study.[10]

9. See Hunt, "Political Pornography"; and Thomas, *Wicked Queen*.
10. Darnton, *Poetry and the Police*, 174–88. Laura Mason has also engaged with the inherent musicality of *vaudeville* texts, but she focuses primarily on what singing, particularly group singing, meant during the revolutionary years (*Singing the French Revolution*).

Whereas musicologists have typically missed nontheatrical *vaudevilles* because of their circulation in typically unmusical print locations, French cultural historians have often not engaged the presence of melody, as indicated by *timbre* at the beginning of most *vaudevilles*.

When looking to understand how a printed *vaudeville* might have been understood in its historical context, we see that the melody played an important role in how the text created meaning for an audience. *Vaudeville* melodies were contextually and affectively sticky, carrying references with them from previous contexts into the new ones in which they appear. These melodies were chosen not idly but with intention to produce specific effects or plays of meaning. This indexical strategy was used in both theatrical and printed *vaudeville* composition. In his study of the history of the tune "M. le Prévôt des Marchands," Philip Robinson speaks to exactly this close connection between the sound of a *vaudeville* and a listener's capacity to comprehend the full meaning of the song: "['M. le Prévôt des Marchands'] is . . . one of those vigorous airs which carries the weight of its connotations and references by the sheer force of its melody: it is enough, in Paris by the middle of the century, to identify this melody in order to comprehend the [references] that it carries, just as one today understands the meaning of 'La Marseillaise' or 'Sur le pont d'Avignon.'"[11] That this referential strategy appeared in both theatrical and nontheatrical *vaudevilles* suggests it is a core, definitional element of the practice. As such, to exclude consideration of the selected melody is to lose half of its meaning.

In giving *vaudevilles* a timbre, author-composers were expecting the melody to add to the overall meaning of the object, whether in print or aloud. Therefore, this article also encourages nonmusical scholars to consider melody as important a constituent of meaning as text. This need not mean a specifically musical analysis that considers rhythm, melodic contour, mode, or other musical elements (though it can, as I demonstrate in this study). But it does mean tracing, whenever possible, a melody's history from the countryside, urban streets, fairgrounds, or even the theater of the Royal Opera. Where a melody came from and the context(s) in which it was used worked in concert with newly written lyrics to produce meaning in *vaudevilles* such that the whole was much more than the sum of its parts.

This article dispels long-standing confusions in defining the eighteenth-century *vaudeville*, builds on existing narratives about its life and death, and demonstrates a methodology for more fully interpreting these texts. To accomplish this, I first turn to definitions of *vaudeville* ranging from 1752 to 1787. They show that from the 1750s to the 1760s *vaudeville* definitions hewed more closely

11. Robinson, "Les vaudevilles," 438–39.

to descriptions of nontheatrical *vaudeville*. From the 1770s onward definitions shift to focus on theatrical spaces, pitting *vaudevilles* against *ariettes*. Against this definitional background, and the common refrain that the *vaudeville* was "dead," I show how printed *vaudeville* flourished across print media and how taking their timbres into account as part of their analysis produces a more thorough accounting of how these objects were interpreted by their audiences. In doing so, I demonstrate the historiographical significance of what might seem like definitional nitpicking to argue that musical sound played a more significant role in the French literary imagination than has previously been considered.

Defining *Vaudeville*

The changing status of *vaudeville* in Paris's theatrical culture coincided with the rise of encyclopedias and dictionaries, including those on music and the theater. These texts demonstrate that definitions of *vaudeville* drifted from one resembling nontheatrical *vaudeville* to one closer to theatrical *vaudeville*. These shifts can be interpreted as the starting point for modern consolidation of what *vaudevilles* were, where they were performed, who performed them, and when they fell out of favor. Central to this interpretation is the infamous affair of the Italian Bouffons (*querelle des bouffons*), an intellectual debate from 1752 to the Italians' departure in 1754, in which a flurry of pamphlets debated the aesthetic merits of French lyric tragedies (*tragédie-lyrique*) and Italian comic opera while also trying to imagine what a possible future for *tragédie-lyrique* could be. One of the central threads of the *querelle* was the appeal of the *ariette*. While much of the focus of the debate centered on pitting the *ariette* against vocal writing typical of *tragédie-lyrique*, recent scholarship has shown that it was in France's comic theaters, and not the Royal Opera, that the strongest effects were felt.[12] While *vaudevilles* do not factor explicitly into the debate, the enthusiasm for the *ariette*'s capacity to produce a more cohesive dramatic whole and its rapid uptake by comic theater writers signal that *vaudevilles* silently stalked the margins of this debate.[13]

At the same time that these debates were occurring, the first few volumes of the *Encyclopédie* appeared, the most prominent example of larger Enlightenment projects for cataloguing and naming the world. The *Encyclopédie*'s primary editors, Jean le Rond d'Alembert and Denis Diderot, were also important contributors to the *querelle*, and even those involved with the *Encyclopédie* who did not contribute directly to the *querelle* would very likely have been aware of the

12. Doe, "French Opera at the Italian Theater," 33–34.
13. Gregory Higgins's work supports this "silent player" role for *vaudeville* in the decades leading up to the *querelle* ("Old Sluts and Dangerous Minuets").

various arguments rehearsed within it. When situating *vaudeville* within this larger debate, it becomes clear that it was *theatrical* vocal writing that was front of mind, and not songwriting more generally. This distinction had important consequences for those undertaking definitional projects—the aesthetic questions and concerns were only with theatrical *vaudevilles*, insofar as they stood in the way of the aesthetically superior *ariette*, making it important to pin down and codify that particular strain of the song practice. In doing so, however, the nontheatrical *vaudeville* was quietly erased from the conversation.

The connections among printed *vaudeville*, theatrical *vaudeville*, and *ariette* can be triangulated through the *querelle des bouffons*. To rehearse the many interpreted meanings of this intense debate would be beyond the scope of this article.[14] For our purposes, it is sufficient to know that the *querelle* was born of the arrival of the Italian Bouffon troupe (in fact, their second time in Paris) and their performance of an Italian comic opera, *La serva padrona*, on the stage of the Royal Academy of Music (or the Opéra), whose boards were typically devoted to the *tragedies-lyriques* of Jean-Baptiste Lully or Jean-Philippe Rameau. The performances were wildly successful, creating a sensation through Paris's cultural elite, who had grown weary of hearing the same operas by Lully or Rameau again and again. One of the more exciting aspects of the performance, beyond the novelty of seeing comedy performed at the Opéra, was the use of arias or, in French, *ariettes*. *Ariettes* were already a feature of French comic opera (*opéra-comique*), usually for one or possibly two voices, that follow a repetitive musical form of *aba* (or *da capo*, as the same music reappears to close the number, "go back to the start/head"). *Ariettes* were tuneful and melody driven, with the melodic writing composed specifically to suit the text and to contribute to the overall narrative. They contrast with *vaudevilles*, which were more typical for French comic opera at this time. By drawing on preexisting melodies, *vaudevilles* (both theatrical and not) are inherently self-referential and necessarily break the fourth wall, "constantly remind[ing] the audience that it is an act of artifice."[15] To avoid this distancing effect, composers and authors saw the *ariette* as a way to craft emotionally compelling, cohesive works. As the Collé quote at the opening of this article suggests, *ariettes* came to be accepted as the sound of the future, while the *vaudeville* was "old-fashioned." Such was the scale of these debates that the relative merits of *ariette* and theatrical *vaudeville* even served as the basis for an *opéra-comique*, *The Trial of Ariettes versus Vaudevilles*

14. For in-depth explorations of the political, philosophical, and aesthetic ramifications of the *querelle des bouffons*, see Blanning, *Culture of Power*; Charlton, "New Light on the Bouffons"; Verba, *Music and the French Enlightenment*; and Johnson, "Encyclopedists and the *Querelle des Bouffons*."

15. Darlow, "Vaudeville et distanciation," 52.

(1760). The *querelle* brought *vaudevilles* under scrutiny in a new way by inadvertently pitting them against Italianate *ariettes*, causing authors and cultural commentators to concentrate their focus on *vaudeville*'s specifically theatrical manifestations.

We can trace this shift to an exclusive emphasis on the theatrical *vaudeville* by following how definitions for the term changed over the two decades following the Italian Bouffons' arrival in 1752. Jacques Lacombe's *Portable Dictionary of the Arts* of 1752 defines *vaudeville* as "a type of song which typically includes elements of satire."[16] Further description of the genre appears in the definition for "song" (*chanson*), which includes a note to "see entry for 'Vaudeville,'" indicating that at least for Lacombe these two terms shared a level of interchangeability. Under "Song," Lacombe wrote, "There is nothing as free [*libre*] as this type of Poem. . . . Our French Poets could be considered the originators and exemplars of these small Poems where they demonstrate the joy, the lightness of spirit, and the sensitivity which shape the character unique to this Nation. See *Vaudeville*."[17] In these two entries, Lacombe makes no reference to a specific venue, or even to their melodies. Rather, he is most concerned with the satirical and poetic elements of these songs, which he suggests participated in the shaping of a specifically French national character. To better understand where one might hear *vaudeville* performed, one must travel to yet another entry, this time for "Opéra-Comique": "The merit of these short poems that are performed at the Opéra-Comique Theater [at the Saint-Germain fairgrounds] is found less in their consistency and ability to drive the plot, than in the choice of a subject which produce scenes that stand out, lighthearted performances, and *Vaudevilles* that demonstrate a refined and delicate sense of satire, with gay and amusing Airs."[18] From these definitions, we can infer several important characteristics about *vaudevilles*: they retained more or less the same qualities regardless of venue, those qualities were closely identified with comedy and lightheartedness, and those same qualities could even be seen as representative of a uniquely French character. In addition to an overall positive tone regarding *vaudevilles*,

16. "VAUDEVILLE, sorte de chansons [*sic*] qui renferme pour l'ordinaire quelques traits de satyre" (Lacombe, *Dictionnaire portatif des beaux-arts*, 672).

17. "CHANSON. Rien de plus libre que ce genre de Poésie. . . . Nos Poètes François peuvent être proposés comme les inventeurs & les modèles de ces petits Poèmes, où ils ont fait passer la gaieté, la legereté d'esprit, & la délicatesse qui forment le caractère propre de la Nation. *Voyez Vaudeville*" (Lacombe, *Dictionnaire portatif des beaux-arts*, 143–44). *Libre* also had connotations of slight inappropriateness or, at worst, libertinage.

18. "La mérite des petits Poèmes Dramatiques qu'on joue sur le Théâtre de l'*Opéra Comique* consiste moins dans la régularité & dans la conduit du plan, que dans le choix d'un sujet qui produise des scènes saillantes, des representations badines & des Vaudevilles d'une satyre fine & delicate, avec des Airs gais & amusans" (Lacombe, *Dictionnaire portatif des beaux-arts*, 456–57).

its theatrical manifestations did not primarily define the genre at this point, indicating that the full effects of the conflation were not yet manifest.

At the time Lacombe's definition appeared in 1752, *ariettes* were mostly associated with Italian comic opera, while *vaudeville* was the genre most closely associated with French comic opera. A necessary but subtle distinction to make at this point is that, by the 1750s, *vaudeville* was a vocal genre often used in French comic opera but was by no means exclusive to French comic opera in the way that *ariettes* came to be exclusive to *opéra-comique*. That is, *opéras-comiques* (and *comédies en vaudevilles*) used *vaudevilles*, sometimes even alongside *ariettes*.[19] *Vaudevilles* were brought in from the streets to lend "joy," "comedy," and "satire" (all quotes from Lacombe) to the fairground performances. The long struggle of the major theaters against the fairground vaudevillians bears out the popularity with audiences of choosing to adapt popular songs like *vaudevilles* for theatrical purposes. However, this separation between *opéra-comique* and *vaudeville*, where the latter genre becomes distinct from theatrical performance, changed following the success of the *bouffons*. As *ariettes* became the dominant vocal genre and, indeed, even started to define the genre of *opéra-comique*, attitudes started to change toward *vaudeville*. While *vaudeville* maintained a distinct identity from *opéra-comique* through the mid-1750s, the following decades saw the blurring of these distinctions.

Lacombe's dictionary entries for *vaudeville* and *chanson* make no reference to the fairground performances that featured them and praise their lighthearted sensibility and satire. However, after the 1750s, *ariettes* became the defining vocal genre for *opéra-comique*, and attitudes toward *vaudeville* began to shift noticeably in dictionary entries. By the 1760s the term *ariette* referred to a vocal work for one or two voices that appeared exclusively in an *opéra-comique* and whose melody was newly composed with the intention of complementing the libretto. Composers integrated *ariettes* fully into the story, functioning as diegetic music or "set" songs, in which the other characters on stage acknowledge that a musical performance is occurring.[20] In this way, they created a self-contained world on the stage, providing a sharp contrast to the playful ways in which *vaudevilles* allowed performers to provide metacommentary on the performance itself, or to break the fourth wall and speak directly to the audience.[21] The preference for *ariettes* in theatrical vocal writing is mirrored in dictionary

19. Charlton, *Grétry and the Growth of Opéra-Comique*, 5–6.
20. *Diegetic music* refers to music heard as music by the characters onstage. This is in opposition to *nondiegetic music*, which is music that only the audience hears and is unacknowledged by the characters onstage. See Neumeyer, "Diegetic/Nondiegetic."
21. Darlow, "Vaudeville et distanciation." For more on the stylistic development of the *ariette* in the mid-eighteenth century, see also Charlton, *Opera in the Age of Rousseau*.

entries from this period, such as the chevalier de Jaucourt's 1765 definitions in the *Encyclopédie*, and Jean-Jacques Rousseau's definition in his *Dictionnaire de musique* (1768). Before the *ariette*, there was no real need to differentiate between theatrical and nontheatrical *vaudevilles* in dictionaries because they functioned in much the same way. With the arrival of *ariettes*, however, theatrical *vaudevilles* now had something they were being measured against, with the fairground stage as the point of contact between the two genres.

The chevalier de Jaucourt's definition in the *Encyclopédie* reflects a growing ambivalence toward *vaudeville*, showing how perceptions among Paris's cultural elite had changed in the years since the *bouffons'* arrival.

> VAUDEVILLE, singular noun, masculine (*Poetry*). The *vaudeville* is a type of song, made to the tune of familiar airs, through which one can speak off-the-cuff, provided that the verses are sung, that they seem natural and have a little wit. . . . I believe, however, that our nation wins out over the others in the taste and number of *vaudevilles*; the inclination of the French for pleasure, satire, and often even an immoderate joyfulness, has made the French sometimes end even the most serious affairs with a *vaudeville*, once the affairs had begun to bore them; & this silliness sometimes consoles them when confronted with their actual unhappiness.[22]

Jaucourt, like Lacombe, writes that *vaudevilles* are witty, satirical, joyful, or lighthearted. Both even agree that there is something uniquely "French" about the *vaudeville*, whether it is their perceived contribution to the shaping of a national character or a knack for creating not only the most but the best *vaudevilles*. However, unlike Lacombe, whose enthusiasm for the genre is unalloyed, Jaucourt expresses a certain melancholic hesitation about the French enthusiasm for *vaudevilles*. Jaucourt represents the "French inclination" for the very qualities that Lacombe attributes to the *vaudeville* as evidence of a complacency, a desire to laugh in the face of problems rather than treat them seriously. Though Beaumarchais's *Marriage of Figaro* would not be written for another thirteen years, one can't help but hear a certain familiarity between Jaucourt's accusation that the French "end even the most serious affairs with a *vaudeville*" and *Figaro*'s famous last line: "Everything ends in song." While Jaucourt and Lacombe agree on the form of the *vaudeville* as a small song set to familiar melodies of a satirical character, Jaucourt introduces a new tone of disapproval not found in Lacombe.

22. "VAUDEVILLE, s. m. (*Poésie*.) le *vaudeville* est une sorte de chanson, faite sur des airs connus, auxquels on passe les négligences, pourvû que les vers en soient chantans, & qu'il y ait du naturel & de la saillie. . . . Je crois cependant que notre nation l'emporte sur les autres dans le goût & dans le nombre des *vaudevilles*; la pente des François au plaisir, à la satyre, & souvent même à une gaieté hors de saison, leur a fait quelquefois terminer par un *vaudeville* les affaires les plus sérieuses, qui commençoient à les lasser; & cette niaiserie les a quelquefois consolés de leurs malheurs réels" (Louis, "Vaudeville").

While Lacombe and Jaucourt shared definitional aspects, including familiar melodies and wit, Rousseau had a very different definition, calling into question whether *vaudevilles* should even be considered music at all. Rousseau's definition can be interpreted as the moment of epistemic break for *vaudevilles*, where nontheatrical *vaudeville* ceases to have musical status and becomes instead poetry. In his *Dictionnaire de musique*, Rousseau defines *vaudevilles* as:

> VAUDEVILLE. A type of song in couplets, typically occupied with playful or satirical subjects. . . . *Vaudeville* melodies are generally not musical. Since one only attends to the words, the Melody only gives the recitation a bit more emphasis; otherwise, in general, one finds neither taste, nor Song, nor Rhythm. The *Vaudeville* belongs exclusively to the French, and they are very biting, and very amusing.[23]

Rousseau overlaps with Lacombe and Jaucourt in acknowledging a sharpness to the comedy of and a unique Frenchness to *vaudevilles*. However, he deviates from them in saying that *vaudevilles* are "generally not musical" and that what others (such as Lacombe and Jaucourt) might have acknowledged as *vaudeville*'s musical qualities are really only structural devices for supporting the words. Rousseau's definition seems to be more clearly describing nontheatrical *vaudevilles* but, in denying them musicality, sets the modern precedent for interpreting them as poetry and not song.

On the other hand, when defining *ariettes*, Rousseau ascribes significant musicality to the genre: "Derived from Italian, this diminutive refers to 'short air'; but the meaning of this word has changed in France, and one now uses *ariette* to refer to large, single-movement pieces of music, typically rather gay and rhythmic, which one sings to the accompaniment of a symphony, and which are typically in the form of a rondeau (See Air, Rondeau)."[24] Even though Rousseau never mentions the fairgrounds in his definition for *vaudeville*, the contrasts between the two genres reflected in these definitions represent an emerging preference for *ariettes* and the eliding of "theatrical *vaudeville*" as the only kind under discussion. Rousseau's dictionary entries for *vaudeville* and *ariette*, then,

---

23. "VAUDEVILLE. Sorte de Chanson à Couplets, qui roule ordinarement sur des Sujets badin ou satyriques. . . . L'air des *Vaudevilles* est communément peu Musical. Comme on n'y fait attention qu'aux paroles, l'Air ne sert qu'à rendre la recitation un peu plus appuyée; du reste on n'y sent pour l'ordinaire ni goût, ni Chant, ni Mesure. Le *Vaudeville* appartient exclusivement aux François, & ils en ont de très piquants & de très-plaisants" (Rousseau, *Dictionnaire de musique*, 531–32).

24. "ARIETTE, s.f. Ce diminutif, venu de l'Italien, signifie proprement *petit Air*; mais le sens de ce mot est change en France, & l'on y donne le nom d'*Ariette* à des grands morceaux de Musique d'un movement pour l'ordinaire assez gai & marqué, qui se chantant avec des Accompagnemens de Symphonie, & qui sont communément en Rondeau. (Voyez Air, Rondeau.)" (Rousseau, *Dictionnaire de musique*, 34).

stand as an example of this subtle shift whereby nontheatrical *vaudevilles* effectively become poetry and *ariettes* rise to the status of a "piece of music."

Rousseau's definitions of *vaudeville* and *ariette* demonstrate how the introduction of *ariettes* into the musical theater landscape drew increased attention and scrutiny to theatrical *vaudevilles*, such that the term became synonymous with its theatrical manifestation. Later dictionary entries, such as that by composer J. J. O. de Meude-Monpas, show that by the 1780s this definitional shift was complete.[25] In his definition in *Dictionnaire de musique* of 1787, Meude-Monpas wrote:

> Vaudeville: Playful or satirical songs in couplets. Though many trace the origins of the *Vaudeville* to the days of Charlemagne, the more commonly accepted opinion is that they were created by a fuller named Basselin in the town of Vire, in Normandy. It is thought that because the villagers came to the valley in Vire to dance to these songs, the songs came to be called "*Vaux-de-Vire*," which over time became *Vaudeville*. Vaudeville melodies should be more primitive than impressive; the melodies should be easy to remember and have a quick cadence, such that each syllable is marked by a single note. It is no longer in fashion—more's the pity.[26]

In this entry Meude-Monpas offers the same origin story found in Lacombe's definition: *vaudeville* is an old genre hailing from Normandy, originated by a resident of Vire, and over time "Vaux-de-vire" became *vaudeville*. He provides descriptions of what a *vaudeville* should sound like: simple, easy-to-remember melodies delivered in a quick tempo and of a neumatic text setting, where each syllable of text is given a separate note.[27] Most intriguing is his definitive claim that *vaudeville* is no longer in fashion but that the loss is to be lamented (*tant pire*—essentially, "too bad"). Given the prevalence of printed *vaudevilles* at the time of Meude-Monpas's definition, we can see a full shift in definitional gravity toward the theatrical *vaudeville*, which had in fact long disappeared from the *opéra-comique* stages by this period. As such, Meude-Monpas's 1787 definition

---

25. Little is known about the chevalier de Meude-Monpas. Eileen Southern has determined that he "served as a musketeer in the service of Louis XVI of France and went into exile with the onset of the turmoil of the Revolution. He studied music in Paris with Pierre La Houssaye and François Giroust" (*Biographical Dictionary*, 271).

26. "VAUDEVILLE, s. m. Chansons à couplets d'un genre badin ou satyrique. Quoiqu'on fasse remonter l'origine du *Vaudeville* jusqu'au temps de Charlemegne; l'opinion la plus ordinaire, c'est qu'il fut inventé par un certain *Basselin*, Foulon à Vire en Normandie; et come, pour danser sur ces chants, on s'assembloit dans le Val de Vire, ils furent appellés, dit-on, *Vaux-de-Vire*; puis, par corruption, *Vaudeville*. L'air du Vaudeville doit être naïf plutôt que brillant: il doit être d'un chant facile à retenir, et d'une marche rapide, afin que chaque syllable soit marquee par chaque note. Il n'est plus guères de mode: tant pire" ([J.J.O], *Dictionnaire de musique*, 208–9).

27. This is in contrast to melismatic text setting, where a single syllable is sung on many notes.

of *vaudeville* demonstrates that elite discussion of *vaudeville* focused on its theatrical manifestation, where *ariettes* had thoroughly triumphed over the older *vaudeville*.

Dictionary entries from the period 1750–80 demonstrate two shifts in attitudes toward *vaudeville*, both instigated by the growth in popularity of *ariettes* in 1752. The first shift is one in valence: early definitions of *vaudeville*, such as that offered by Lacombe, are generally positive, praising its lighthearted and satirical qualities. After the introduction of *ariettes*, this valence becomes more negative. For Jaucourt, *vaudevilles* are a potentially dangerous form of escapism, allowing the French people to sing away and laugh at their problems rather than taking action against the root causes. For Rousseau, *vaudevilles* lack taste and basic musical appeal. Instead, *ariettes* represent all that *vaudevilles* are not for Rousseau: musical, rhythmic, an equal meeting of melody and text. That the two genres are so clearly in dialogue with each other in Rousseau's dictionary demonstrates the second shift: definitions of *vaudeville* are really definitions of *theatrical vaudeville* and not *vaudevilles* writ large. By the time Meude-Monpas wrote in the late 1780s, this shift was so complete that he could mourn that *vaudevilles* "are no longer at all fashionable" despite their ubiquity across print genres not related to musical theater. Though both Collé in the 1750s and Meude-Monpas in the 1780s lamented the death of *vaudevilles*, nontheatrical *vaudeville* was alive and well in novels, newspapers, and song collections to the end of the century.

From Stage to Page: *Vaudeville*'s "Afterlife" in Print

Far from disappearing, from the mid-eighteenth century onward *vaudeville* underwent an important transformation from a genre strongly identified with live performance on the lyric stage to one found increasingly on the printed page. The printed page emerged as a primary home for the *vaudeville* during a period when printing in general exploded in both production and consumption. Statistically more people across the socioeconomic spectrum owned more books than they had in previous centuries, and presses were eager to keep up with demand.[28] Alongside the historically ubiquitous religious texts, periodicals like the *occasionels* and early newspapers disseminated reports of local and foreign events. The emergence of the novel as a new, popular genre has been interpreted as a force for changing Enlightenment conceptions of leisure and individual subjectivity and producing a new relationship between authors and readers.[29]

28. For statistical breakdowns by class in France on book ownership over time, see Chartier, *Cultural Uses of Print*, 183–239.
29. Wittman, "Was There a Reading Revolution?," 297–98; Darnton, "Readers Respond to Rousseau."

Printed plays were also popular items, to the extent that from the seventeenth to the eighteenth century playwrights frequently wrote with not just a stage performance in mind but also an eye to the printed life of the play after opening night. During the eighteenth century the time between a play's performance run and the text's publication grew shorter and shorter, to the point that the text began to precede opening night.[30] It also became common to own plays that one might never see performed, calling into question distinct lines between performing and reading.[31] In each of these genres, one can find examples of printed *vaudevilles* after their alleged demise in the 1750s. Though *vaudevilles* appeared less frequently on the theatrical stage, they could be found throughout many of the print materials that proliferated during this period.

The movement of *vaudeville* to the printed page after a long association with the theater raises questions about the role of performance in nontheatrical *vaudevilles*: to what extent were they still performed? As a printed text with no formal musical notation, are they "songs" or are they "poetry"? That printed *vaudevilles* still included a *timbre* suggests that melody was a functional element in how they constructed meaning and how audiences interpreted them. To support this claim, I turn to the work of the theater historian Julie Stone Peters, who offers the concept of "provisional theatricality" for understanding how performance was always at the center of printed plays in the eighteenth century, even when they were never intended to be performed, as in closet dramas: "The aspiration to authorial hermeticism (via the printed text) was challenged from the beginning by playbooks that celebrated their provisional theatricality, that insisted on their own currency and implied their own extinction."[32] Here Peters claims that printed playbooks explicitly played with their generic ambiguity (could they be performed? should they?) and "insisted on their own currency"— namely, live performance. Like the printed play, *vaudevilles* also insisted on a currency unique to them: melodies (*timbres*). In his writing in the genre, Roger Chartier describes printed songs as one of the few print genres of the century that "presupposed a mediating voice between the written word and the hearer."[33] Unlike the printed playbook, where the mediating voice is predominantly a spoken one, in *vaudevilles* the melody invoked by the *timbre* is the vehicle for the mediating voice, and it is this perpetual "silent singing" which creates its "provisional musicality." Printed playbooks, therefore, offer a useful interpretive model for approaching printed *vaudevilles*, which exist in a related provisional state of performance implied by the inclusion of the timbre or melodic citation.

30. Peters, *Theatre of the Book*, 59–60, 74.
31. Peters, *Theatre of the Book*, 74; Darnton, "Readers Respond to Rousseau," 254–55.
32. Peters, *Theatre of the Book*, 61.
33. Chartier, *Cultural Uses of Print*, 229.

Vaudevilles demonstrated a "provisional musicality" through the inclusion of a melodic citation and required that the musical mediating voice be considered in any interpretation of a printed *vaudeville*. Compelling examples of the celebration of *vaudeville*'s "provisional musicality" can be found in printed novels in the latter half of the eighteenth century. Perhaps the most famous example of a novelist consciously playing with this provisional musicality is Denis Diderot in his *Le neveu de Rameau* (1761–62), where the nephew of the famous composer frequently bursts into long strings of *vaudevilles* in his discussions with the novel's protagonist, "MOI." In his analysis of this work, Scott Sanders argues that readers would not merely have read these passages in the novels but would actually have *heard* them. Sanders situates the reading of *vaudevilles* within "a matrix of sensibility," where "mnemonic lyrics activate aural memory, thereby stimulating a physical (kinaesthetic) imagination in the reader."[34] In *Le neveu* specifically, Sanders argues that Diderot's deployment of *vaudevilles* functioned as a demonstration of the *philosophe*'s materialist philosophy, whereby responses (in this case, memory and emotions) could be elicited from the human body through the application of external stimuli (the reading of *timbres*). Though *Le neveu* is unique in its heavy reliance on *vaudevilles* as a central narrative and affective device, it is a useful example for how *vaudevilles* could be taken up in print while still holding on to melody as a functional element.

Whereas *Le neveu* incorporated *vaudevilles* directly into the narrative, *Madame Gourdan* demonstrates a different way novels used the provisional musicality of *vaudevilles*: by incorporating them to invoke the imagined sounds of a particular setting, to bolster the novel's authenticity. The *Correspondance de Madame Gourdan dite la Comtesse* (1784) was originally printed anonymously but has since been attributed to the infamous hack writer of Paris's Grub Street Théveneau de Morande.[35] *Madame Gourdan* purports to be the authentic correspondence of the famed madam Marguerite Gourdan, who maintained one of Paris's most elite and exclusive brothels at 12 Rue Saint-Sauveur. The title page advertises a "collection of Songs for use at the Dinners hosted at the home of Madame Gourdan" that is appended to the end of the volume, though *vaudevilles* also appear throughout the main body of the text, with many of Gourdan's fictional correspondents incorporating *vaudevilles* into their letters. If one of the central arguments for *vaudeville*'s lack of appeal on the theatrical stage was its interruption of the fourth wall, in *Madame Gourdan* vaudeville is mobilized in the service of creating a more immersive, fully realized world. This further bolsters the novel's "authenticity gambit," giving readers the ability to construct the

34. Sanders, "Sound and Sensibility," 243–44.
35. Darnton, *Literary Underground*, 25.

imagined world of Gourdan's brothel, conjuring up not only sights but also sounds and offering an opportunity for readers to re-create for themselves the same musical activities that took place at the brothel, whether real or imagined. While on the stage *vaudevilles* were seen as disrupting narrative cohesion, on the printed page in a novel like *Madame Gourdan vaudeville* worked to create an absorptive reading experience whereby readers could actually hear the songs referenced.

Though *vaudevilles* had largely disappeared from the theater by the 1770s, they continued to appear in printed texts, with melodies still a central element of an audience's experience given the assumption of a mediating voice. In addition to novels, newspapers also included *vaudevilles*, setting the stage for the political satire that proliferated in the 1780s and early 1790s. Rather than "keeping up with the times," however, the melodies most often used were those that had been in circulation since the 1720s and 1730s, if not earlier.[36] Periodicals emerged from the earlier practice of *nouvelles à la main*, manuscript reports of the events (and salacious gossip) at court that were copied and sent to subscribers. In an effort to crack down on the slander that circulated clandestinely around the country in this form, the crown gave privileges to three journals, among them the *Mercure de France*, provided they stuck to the party line dictated from Versailles.[37] The *Mercure* was a literary review journal, one of the most popular and authoritative periodicals of the Old Regime. New issues of the *Mercure* came out once a week, and in addition to essays on new literary works, it included *pièces fugitives*, a genre that included ephemera such as light verse, word puzzles, riddles, and *vaudevilles*. As one of France's more or less official journals, the *Mercure* would rarely have printed material that mocked the royal family, whether openly or through oblique references. This sets its contents apart from the *Correspondance secrète* and the *Mémoires secrets*, which trafficked primarily in gossip and rumor. Collectively published between 1762 and 1790, these scandal sheets compiled all of the news and gossip Paris and Versailles generated, spreading political news and art reviews while documenting cases of sexual impropriety, both real and rumored.[38] In addition to traditional prose

---

36. The Theaville: Base de Donnés Théâtre et Vaudeville project offers an interactive list displaying *vaudeville* titles in descending order of popularity based on the number of times a specific *timbre* appeared among 306 identified *vaudevilles* within 110 plays from 1709 to 1790. When filtering for the period 1750–90, the top three most popular melodies, "Un capucin à barbe blonde," "Grand duc de Savoie à quoi penses-tu," and "Voulez-vous savoir qui des deux," have an earliest publication date of 1717–21. These three melodies far outstrip the others on the list. The third most popular melody, "Voulez-vous savoir qui des deux," is used more than twice as often as the fourth most popular melody, "Ton himer est Catherine." See "L'air à la mode," *Théaville: Base de donnés théâtre et vaudeville*, www.theaville.org/kitesite/index.php?r=lab %2Fvaudevilles-pop&annee_ini=1750&annee_fin=1790.

37. Darnton, *Devil in the Holy Water*, 317–20.

38. For more on these journals, see Merrick, "Sexual Politics and Public Disorder."

reports, these journals also included *vaudevilles*, sometimes penned by the journal's contributors or submitted anonymously. For example, of the first eight issues of the *Correspondance secrète* in 1775, four featured at least one, more often two, *vaudevilles* per issue. Many centered on various political dramas, such as the reinstatement of the Paris Parlement following their mismanagement under Chancellor Maupeou.

Satirical, politically focused songs are juxtaposed with *vaudevilles* on more frivolous matters, such as Madame du Barry's efforts to humiliate a perceived rival, Madame Bêche, who managed to catch the eye of "one of our young princes." The prince and Madame Bêche were found in a compromising position in "one of the rooms of Versailles, at the moment when he was pressing this woman in a most lively and energetic manner," and the episode gave rise to the included *vaudeville* (fig. 2).[39] That the woman's name was related to *bêcher*, "to dig," was perhaps too good a pun to let pass by. Though a *timbre* for this *vaudeville* is not given, a note immediately following the *vaudeville* suggests that the author has "left [the reader] in the middle of singing," suggesting that the *vaudeville*'s refrain ("C'est là que le trop heureux . . . ") was enough to conjure the melody, even if it can no longer be identified. While novels incorporated *vaudevilles* to create a reading experience that engaged all the senses, newspapers incorporated them to launch pointed political critiques and satire, using the melody of the *timbres* to impart additional meanings through reference to earlier versions of the song.

The appearance of *vaudevilles* in gossipy newspapers critiquing the government and aristocracy set the stage for entire song collections, or *chansonniers*, devoted to antimonarchical *vaudevilles*, such as *Les fouteries chantantes* of 1791. While the *Correspondance secrète* is full of satirical commentary on political events in the form of *vaudevilles*, after the fall of the Bastille in 1789 *vaudevilles* took on a new level of political invective. This was especially the case when it came to the loathed queen of France, Marie-Antoinette. The queen was surrounded by enemies who often turned, anonymously, to the press to air their suspicions and grievances. Emerging from these smear campaigns is the political *chansonnier Les fouteries chantantes, ou les récréations priapiques des aristocrats en vie*, par la muse de libertins* (1791), which consisted entirely of *vaudevilles*. The primary objective of *Les fouteries chantantes* was to offer up the imagined sexual lives of the aristocracy, clergy, and monarchist politicians to general scorn. A

---

39. "Madame Bêche, who is the wife of one of the king's musicians, has recently eclipsed Madame du Barry. . . . Not long ago, in one of the rooms of the Palace of Versailles, one of our young princes was caught pressuring this woman, in a most ardent and forceful manner, to accede to his advances. The celebrity that Madame Bêche has accrued through these adventures provided the inspiration for these couplets, whose author is suspected to be a person of rank" (Metra, *Correspondance secrète*, 38).

des falles du château de *Verfailles*, au moment où il preffoit cette femme de la maniere la plus vive & la plus énergique de répondre à fes feux. La célébrité que ces aventures ont procurée à Madame *Béche*, donne quelque intérêt à ces couplets dont l'auteur eft foupçonné un perfonnage diftingué.

* 1.
Qu'il eft heureux, notre ami Bêche,
Ah! qu'il poffede un joli bien!
Moulin, four, preffoir, chaffé & pêche
A fon fief il ne manque rien.
C'eft-là que le trop heureux Bêche
Comblé des faveurs du deftin,
Vit content & bêche, bêche
Vit content & bêche fon jardin.

2.
Sous deux jolis Rochers d'albâtre,
L'amour aiguife tous fes traits;
Une butte en amphithéâtre
Couronne un Vallon toujours frais;
C'eft-là que le trop &c.

3.
Un galant bofquet, de fon ombre
Couvre un joli petit château,
Dont l'entrée eft étroite & fombre,
Mais l'amour y tient fon flambeau;
C'eft-là, &c.

4.
Une pompe à fimple fculpture
Dont l'amour conduit le travail,

Fait jaillir une fource pure
Dans une conque de corail.
C'eft-là que puife l'ami Bêche
Pour arrofer foir & matin
Le terrein qu'il bêche, bêche, beche
Le terrein qu'il bêche en fon jardin.

5.
Mais ce jardin où regne Flore,
Où brille la rofe & le lys,
On ne l'a vu produire encore
Que des fleurs & jamais des fruits?
Redouble d'ardeur, ami Bêche,
Il faut que Pomone ait fon tour:
Force coups de bêche, bêche, bêche
Force coups de bêche nuit & jour.

6.
Je n'ai qu'ébanché la peinture
Des beautés du petit château.
Que j'en ferois d'après nature
Un fidele & charmant tableau!
Mais l'amour ne permet qu'à Bêche
L'accès de ce réduit divin,
Et lui feul en bêche, bêche, bêche
Et lui feul en bêche le jardin.

Puifque je vous mets en train de chanter, je vais vous ajouter 4 couplets qui ont le mérite du moment, & celui de l'impromptu. A un des derniers Bals de l'Opéra, le Duc de *Nivernois* fut agacé par une femme habillée en Boulangere; les attraits qu'elle laiffa voir en fe démafquant, infpirerent à ce Seigneur aimable qui s'eft autant diftingué dans les affaires d'Etat que dans celles d'efprit & de goût, ces couplets agréables & délicats. Ils fe chantent fur l'air : *dans ma Cabane obfcure, du devin de Village.*

1.
Charmante Boulangere,
Qui des dons de Cerès
Sais d'une main légere
Nous faire du pain frais;
Des biens que tu nous livres
Pourquoi nous rejouir?
Ah! quand ta main fait vivre,
Tes beaux yeux font mourir.

2.
De ta peau blanche & fine
J'admire la fraîcheur;
C'eft la fleur de farine
Dans toute fa blancheur.
Que j'aime la tournure
Des petits pains au lait,
Que la belle nature
A mis dans ton corçet !

De

FIGURE 2 Detail from *Correspondance secrète*, Feb. 25, 1775. Bibliothèque Nationale de France.

combination of visual and musical portraits works together to craft fictionalized versions of these individuals that tautologically confirm what their political enemies suspected all along. Through a series of *vaudevilles* whose subject matter and language are worthy of Rabelais, a justificatory narrative emerges for why these public figures should be reviled.

Melody plays a crucial role in imbuing these brief stories with dense meaning through intertextual reference to contemporary *opéra-comique* and familiar folk tunes. One particular *vaudeville*, "Fouteries précieuses et bien chère, ou un collier pour foutre un con," revisits the infamous Diamond Necklace Affair of 1785, involving Marie-Antoinette, the striving courtier Cardinal Louis de Rohan-Soubise, and the con artist Jeanne la Motte (rendered in the *vaudeville* as "La Mothe"). By the time *Les fouteries chantantes* was published in 1791, public opinion had long been firmly turned against the queen, but five years after the fact, the Diamond Necklace Affair was still a relevant cultural touchstone worthy of inclusion in this collection. Readers of *Les fouteries chantantes* would have been well acquainted with all of the case's sensational details from the many trial briefs published during and after the case. These texts helped fuel the surge of anti–Marie-Antoinette pamphlets that offered fanciful and often sexually explicit depictions of what it was thought *really* happened the night Rohan and the queen "met."[40] "Fouteries précieuses" belongs in this tradition.

In this version of events, to set up a liaison with the queen Rohan seeks out la Motte, who is all too eager to help. The language is unclear as to whether Rohan has sex with the actual queen or merely thinks he has, but in the end the queen takes pity on him and blames the whole affair on la Motte. The accompanying portrait of Rohan contains the events of the *vaudeville* in miniature: a young man wearing the skullcap of a cardinal on both his head and back approaches a reclining nude woman, whose torso creates the subject's forehead and whose bent knee creates a nose (fig. 3).

"Fouteries précieuses" is a reminder that perhaps not every *timbre* was chosen with equal amounts of care, that considerations like performative pleasure may have factored into these choices as well. The bawdy content of this *vaudeville* is enhanced by the selection of the *timbre* "Quand la mer rouge apparut," in which a character named Grégoire, upon seeing the Red Sea, believes that it is made of wine and that he must drink it up. The intertextual resonances are less strong in this instance, but the rhythmic motifs of the *timbre*'s refrain create opportunities for pleasurable delivery and punning. The melodic line primarily outlines tonic triads in the major mode, with short four-bar phrases. Most

40. Examples of these pamphlets can be found in Fleischmann, *Les pamphlets libertins*. For more on the various trial briefs and their impact, see Maza, "Diamond Necklace Affair."

notable, and perhaps most fun to sing, in "Quand la mer rouge apparut" are the "hiccups," where the first word of the closing couplet is split into two syllables, each of which is repeated three times at the same pitch. This is followed by a diminution in the repetitions, bringing the syllables closer together before uniting them into a recognizable word (measures 13–15). The result is a breathless delivery, with no obvious space for a singer to draw breath except in short gasps, mimicking the hiccupping speech of a drunk. Breaking the words down into syllables also creates opportunities for punning or for singers to dwell on double entendres. The author of "Fouteries précieuses" seems not to have taken advantage of the second of these linguistic possibilities, instead lacing the *vaudeville* with obscenity. Rather than creating puns, the repetition of nonsense sounds like "qua" or "fla" offers a form of silly

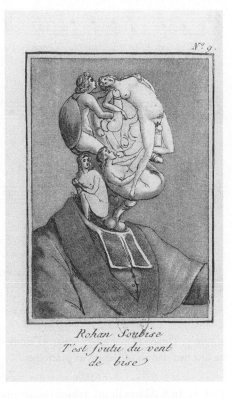

FIGURE 3 Caricature of Cardinal Rohan. *Les fouteries chantantes* (1791). Bibliothèque Nationale de France.

pleasure, as silly as a cardinal successfully seducing a queen. Through this process, the *timbre* participates in the creation of a fantasy version of both the cardinal and the queen (fig. 4).

In the latter half of the eighteenth century, *vaudevilles* shifted from being more or less equally circulated on and off stage to circulating primarily in print media. While it is reasonable to think that the loss of the live singing voice would evacuate *vaudeville* texts of their musicality, we can turn to theater studies to contextualize how readers may have responded to seeing a performance genre in print on the page. Both Julie Stone Peters and Roger Chartier propose the assumption of a mediating voice for printed plays and printed *vaudevilles*, respectively, meaning that the melodies cited by the *timbre* at the top of a *vaudeville* continued to "sound" for readers even apart from live performance. Such an interpretation is supported by Scott Sanders's analysis of Diderot's *Le neveu de Rameau*, in which the titular character's frequent musical outbursts are not just a technique for character development but were, in fact, "audible" for

FIGURE 4 "Quand la mer rouge apparut." Edition created by the author, using the text from the first two stanzas of "Fouteries précieuses."

readers. In looking at additional examples of printed, nontheatrical *vaudevilles* from the period after 1750, we see further evidence of both how melody was heard from these texts and how melody played an important role in a reader's interpretation of the text's meaning.

Through these examples and textual readings, I have sought to demonstrate the contradiction between these histories of the *vaudeville*'s death after 1750 and an extensive print record that suggests otherwise. What is at stake for musicologists in the conflation of the two genres is the erasure of an entire musical practice that took place away from established theaters. Instead, it played out across the pages of gossip columns or, somewhat more speculatively, on the streets and in the homes of readers. That narrative also paints a more deceptively unified picture of attitudes toward *vaudevilles* than is actually preserved in texts such as musical dictionaries. It may seem a subtle distinction, but by decoupling nontheatrical from theatrical *vaudeville*, the history of the genre itself changes substantially. If the theatrical stage and the page represent *vaudeville*'s two homes, the arrival of *ariettes* signaled *vaudeville*'s turning off the lights in its theater home and moving in full time to its home on the printed page. Not a death at all, this shift instead represents a proliferation of the genre beyond the printed song sheets sold by street singers, revealing an entire new archive of previously unconsidered musical sources.

For nonmusicologists, my hope is that this work demonstrates the importance of considering the *vaudeville* as a musical object and not a poetic text, understanding that the melodies selected by *vaudeville* authors were not idle choices but carried important interpretive implications for readers. Collections of printed *vaudeville* melodies reveal a continued investment in the *sound* of the *vaudeville*, not just its connections with satire and witty verse, though these aspects can be found as well. In newspapers and journals, *vaudevilles* appear as another means of relating information about life under the Old Regime, recalling the singers of the Pont Neuf who would write and sell songs that capitalized on the week's gossip, only to move on to the next topic the following week. When appearing in novels, they created depth to the imaginary world crafted by the author, as in *Le neveu*'s madly virtuosic performances, or the songs that were imagined to follow dinner at one of Paris's most famous brothels. Such musical reading in otherwise literary contexts encouraged readers to engage a mediating voice in their reading practices. The post-1750 *vaudeville* may have been thought an object out of time, but its ongoing presence on the printed page reveals a genre that still held a powerful capacity to produce meaning long after its disappearance from the stage.

JENNA HARMON is lead researcher at Mentor Collective. Her doctoral research focused on the intersections of sexuality and vernacular song in eighteenth-century France.

Acknowledgments

The author thanks the anonymous reviewers and editors of *French Historical Studies* for their encouraging and helpful feedback on earlier versions of this article. She also thanks Drew Edward Davies, Scott Paulin, Ryan Dohoney, and Sarah Maza for their input and guidance on earlier stages of this project. Research for this article was conducted with the support of a Fulbright Fellowship, and the author thanks Pierre Frantz for his sponsorship and hospitality at the Centre d'Etude de la Langue et la Littérature Française 16e–18e Siècles.

References

Blanning, T. C. W. *The Culture of Power and the Power of Culture: Old Regime Europe*. Oxford, 2002.

Charlton, David. *Grétry and the Growth of Opéra-Comique*. Cambridge, 1986.

Charlton, David. "New Light on the Bouffons in Paris (1752–1754)." *Eighteenth Century Music* 11, no. 1 (2014): 31–54.

Charlton, David. *Opera in the Age of Rousseau: Music, Confrontation, Realism*. Cambridge, 2012.

Chartier, Roger. *The Cultural Uses of Print in Early Modern France*, translated by Lydia G. Cochrane. Princeton, NJ, 1987.

Collé, Charles. *Théâtre de société*. Vol. 2. The Hague, 1768.

Darlow, Mark. *Nicolas-Etienne Framery and Lyric Theatre in Eighteenth-Century France*. Oxford, 2003.

Darlow, Mark. "Vaudeville et distanciation dans l'opéra-comique des années 1750." In *La "Querelle des Bouffons" dans la vie culturelle française du XVIIIe siècle*, edited by Andrea Fabiano, 47–52. Paris, 2005.

Darnton, Robert. *The Devil in the Holy Water, or The Art of Slander from Louis IV to Napoleon.* Philadelphia, 2010.

Darnton, Robert. *The Literary Underground of the Old Regime.* Cambridge, MA, 1982.

Darnton, Robert. *Poetry and the Police: Communication Networks in Eighteenth-Century Paris.* Cambridge, MA, 2010.

Darnton, Robert. "Readers Respond to Rousseau: The Fabrication of Romantic Sensitivity." In *The Great Cat Massacre and Other Episodes in French Cultural History*, 215–56. New York, 1985.

Doe, Julia. "French Opera at the Italian Theater (1762–1793): *Opéra-Comique* and the Development of National Style in France." PhD diss., Yale University, 2013.

Fleischmann, Hector. *Les pamphlets libertins contre Marie-Antoinette.* Orthez, 2011.

Harmon, Jenna. "Made to Please: Vaudeville and Obscene Parisian Media, 1750–1793." PhD diss., Northwestern University, 2019.

Heartz, Daniel. *Music in European Capitals: The Galant Style, 1720–1780.* New York, 2003.

Higgins, Gregory. "Old Sluts and Dangerous Minuets; or, The Underlying Musical Tensions of the Querelle des Bouffons." *Eighteenth-Century Studies* 45, no. 4 (2012): 549–63.

Hunt, Lynn. "Political Pornography and the French Revolution." In *The Invention of Pornography: Obscenity and the Origins of Modernity, 1500–1800*, edited by Lynn Hunt, 301–40. New York, 1993.

Isherwood, Robert. *Farce and Fantasy: Popular Entertainment in Eighteenth-Century Paris.* New York, 1986.

[J.J.O], chevalier de Meude-Monpas. *Dictionnaire de musique dans lequel on simplifie les expressions et les définitions mathématiques et physiques qui on rapport à cet art. . . .* Paris, 1787.

Johnson, James H. "The Encyclopedists and the *Querelle des Bouffons*: Reason and the Enlightenment of Sentiment." *Eighteenth-Century Life* 10, no. 2 (1986): 12–27.

Lacombe, Jacques. *Dictionnaire portatif des beaux-arts ou abregé de ce qui concerne l'architecture, la sculpture, la peinture, la gravure, la poésie, et la musique. . . .* Paris, 1752.

Louis, chevalier de Jaucourt. "Vaudeville." In *Encyclopédie, ou dictionnaire raisonné des sciences, des arts et des métiers, etc.*, edited by Denis Diderot and Jean le Rond d'Alembert. University of Chicago ARTFL Encyclopédie Project, Autumn 2017 ed., edited by Robert Morrissey and Glenn Roe. encyclopedie.uchicago.edu.

Martin, Isabelle. *Le théâtre de la foire: Des tréteaux aux boulevards.* Oxford, 2002.

Mason, Laura. *Singing the French Revolution: Popular Culture and Politics, 1787–1799.* Ithaca, NY, 1996.

Maza, Sarah. "The Diamond Necklace Affair, 1785–1786." In *Private Lives, Public Affairs: The Causes Célèbres of Prerevolutionary France*, 167–211. Berkeley, CA, 1993.

Merrick, Jeffrey. "Sexual Politics and Public Disorder in Late Eighteenth-Century France: The *Mémoires Secrets* and the *Correspondance Secrètes*." *Journal of the History of Sexuality* 1, no. 1 (1990): 68–84.

Metra, Louis-François. *Correspondance littéraire secrète.* Feb. 25, 1775.

Neumeyer, David. "Diegetic/Nondiegetic: A Theoretical Model." *Music and the Moving Image* 2, no. 1 (2009): 26–39.

Peters, Julie Stone. *Theatre of the Book, 1480–1880: Print, Text, and Performance in Europe.* Oxford, 2000.

Pia, Pascal. *Les livres de l'enfer: Bibliographie critique des ouvrages érotiques dans leurs différentes éditions au XVIe siècle à nos jours*. Paris, 1998.

Robinson, Philip. "Les vaudevilles: Un médium théâtrale." *Dix-huitième siècle*, no. 28 (1996): 431–47.

Rousseau, Jean-Jacques. *Dictionnaire de musique*. Paris, 1768.

Sanders, Scott. "Sound and Sensibility in Diderot's 'Le Neveu de Rameau.'" *Music and Letters* 94, no. 2 (2013): 237–62.

Schneider, Herbert, ed. *Das Vaudeville: Funktionen eines multimedialen Phänomens*. Hildesheim, 1996.

Southern, Eileen. *Biographical Dictionary of Afro-American and African Musicians*. Westport, CT, 1982.

Thomas, Chantal. *The Wicked Queen: The Origins of the Myth of Marie Antoinette*, translated by Julie Rose. New York, 1999.

Verba, Cynthia. *Music and the French Enlightenment: Reconstruction of a Dialogue, 1750–1764*. Oxford, 1993.

Wittman, Reinhard. "Was There a Reading Revolution at the End of the Eighteenth Century?" In *A History of Reading in the West*, edited by Guglielmo Cavallo and Roger Chartier, translated by Lydia G. Cochrane, 285–306. Amherst, MA, 1999.

Mobilizing Historicity and Local Color in *Fernand Cortez* (1809)
Narratives of Empire at the Opéra

ANNELIES ANDRIES

ABSTRACT   This article interrogates why the creators of Napoleonic opera, specifically of Gaspare Spontini's *Fernand Cortez* (1809), were so eager to publicize their source-based method for representing history. The article frames this eagerness in broader developments toward historical realism in nineteenth-century France and its epistemological claims, namely, that history provides true knowledge about the past. These epistemological claims are foundational to how historians and artists sought to mobilize historicity and local color to champion narratives of empire as founded on the supposedly transhistorical process of civilization. In *Fernand Cortez* these mobilizations revised eighteenth-century skepticism toward sixteenth-century colonialism into a narrative of imperial success that the government hoped would garner support for Napoléon's Spanish campaign. Ultimately, the emphasis on historicist detail undermined the opera's specific propagandistic message, but it did provide a model that popularized and disseminated general ideologies about empire and civilization beyond France's intellectual circles.

KEYWORDS   Napoleonic opera, historiography, historicism, local color, narratives of empire

We are happy to note that there are few dramatic works . . . where history is
more faithfully followed than in this opera.
—Libretto preface to *Fernand Cortez ou la conquête du Mexique*

With these lines, the libretto preface drew attention to the historical research that had gone into producing Gaspare Spontini's newest opera, *Fernand Cortez ou la conquête du Mexique* (*Hernán Cortés or the Conquest of Mexico*), which premiered at the Paris Opéra on November 28, 1809.[1] The opera depicts an important episode in the Spanish colonization of the Americas: the

---

1. In the early nineteenth century the Aztec Empire was generally referred to as Mexico and its inhabitants as Mexicans. Therefore, throughout this article, I use *Mexican* as a synonym for *Aztec* when translating nineteenth-century documents.

French Historical Studies • Vol. 45, No. 2 (April 2022) • DOI 10.1215/00161071-9531982
Copyright 2022 by Society for French Historical Studies

siege and fall of the Aztec capital, México-Tenochtitlan, in 1521 at the hands of the Spanish conquistador Hernán Cortés and his soldiers. The libretto, written by Etienne de Jouy and Joseph-Alphonse Esménard, is structured around two well-known historical events. Act 1 depicts the moment when Cortés burned his fleet to defy the Aztecs' demand that he leave their shores and to rob his mutinous soldiers of the means to return to Spain. Act 3 opens with the massacre at the Great Temple—a Spanish intervention during an Aztec sacred festival in which most of the participants were slaughtered (allegedly to prevent a human sacrifice).[2] But it is not just the plot that reflects the imprint of history. The set and costume designs, some of the musical instruments, and possibly even the choreography were based on historical sources.

While this article details how these sources were used, its principal aim is to examine why the artists producing *Fernand Cortez* thought fidelity to history so important to their work. In particular, I explore the ideological significance of a source-based methodology in the construction of historical knowledge and local color. This shift in methodology has most often been discussed in relation to the later ascendency of a "new school" of historiography in the 1820s, represented perhaps most iconically by the German historian Leopold von Ranke but also connected to French historians such as Augustin Thierry and François Guizot.[3] Musicologists such as Anselm Gerhard, Sarah Hibberd, and Mark Pottinger have pointed out that this "new school" shared a mode of historical narration with a French opera genre that arose in the 1820s: *grand opéra*.[4] Since the genre's attention to historical fidelity in the visual, musical, and narrative representation of a plot's historical era and place was well publicized, *grand opéra* is thought to have become a more conspicuous vehicle for this new approach to history than other operatic genres. Moreover, scholars have linked the genre's investment in a historicist representation, which allowed a work to present multiple "safe," less propagandistic readings that appealed to a wide variety of audiences, to the increasing urbanization and the emergence of more democratic forms of government in 1820s France.[5]

---

2. Historians largely agree that the massacre was not motivated by a desire to prevent human sacrifices. The Aztec accounts indicate that their precious ritual vestments had aroused the greed of the Spanish. See Roa-de-la-Carrera, "Francisco López de Gómara," 40–41; and Lockhart, *We People Here*.

3. See, e.g., Reizov, *L'historiographie romantique française*, 11; Bann, *Clothing of Clio*, 8–53; and den Boer, "Historical Writing in France," 184–87.

4. Gerhard, *Urbanization of Opera*, 71–76; Hibberd, *French Grand Opera*; Pottinger, *Staging of History in France*. The connections among historiography, the novel, and various theatrical genres are also discussed in Samuels, *Spectacular Past*.

5. The importance of "safe" readings that had a wide appeal in *grand opéra* is highlighted in Hibberd, *French Grand Opera*, 7–8, 180; and Hallman, *Opera, Liberalism, and Antisemitism*, 298–301.

Yet, modes of historical representation that claimed a certain historical fidelity by featuring source research antedate the cultural and political developments of the 1820s. Following in the footsteps of Hayden White, Stephen Bann has connected this mode to the mid-eighteenth-century emergence of new ideas about historical verisimilitude and fidelity, which not only affected history writing but also went hand in hand with "the increasingly expert production of pseudohistorical forgeries" such as James Macpherson's Ossianic poetry.[6] In the same period, historical fidelity became a hot topic in theatrical production and its discourse as well: theaters rivaled one another publicizing their "faithful" engagement with history and historical sources, and critics eagerly discussed whether productions realized this ambition.[7] The Opéra, which thought itself the premier theater of France (and, by extension, of Europe), could not be seen to fall behind: from the late 1760s onward it started to embrace this new theatrical trend.[8] By the Napoleonic era (1799–1815) most operas were based on historical subject matter from antiquity and beyond rather than mythological subjects (see appendix). Perhaps more important, the Opéra's artists and management proudly trumpeted the fact that these plots were based on historical sources and presented in a historicized manner—meaning they were located in a historically specific time and place.[9] *Fernand Cortez* in particular became the early nineteenth-century standard-bearer of these ambitions and has therefore been mentioned as a precursor to later *grand opéra*.[10] Yet, as I will discuss, Spontini's work underscores how this historicist mode of representation in opera emerged earlier than the urbanizing and democratizing processes of the 1820s and was embroiled in Napoléon's imperialist politics.

A particular artistic technique to convey this historicist mode of representation was the use of what late eighteenth-century artists and critics started to

6. Bann, *Clothing of Clio*, 14, 2.

7. For a broader discussion of the increasing engagement with historicist representations, see Frantz, *L'esthétique du tableau*, 97–98; and Charlton, *Grétry and the Growth of Opéra Comique*, 233–37.

8. Henri Rossi identifies *Ernelinde, princesse de Norvège* (1767) as the earliest French historical opera (*Opéras historiques français*, 15). Mark Darlow has demonstrated that parts of the plot and the set designs for *Nepthé* (1789) were based on historical sources (*Staging the Revolution*, 235–40).

9. This historicized representation was even adopted in Ossianic and biblical plots, which today would more likely be categorized as legendary or mythological, such as *Ossian ou les bardes* (1804). See Andries, "Uniting the Arts to Stage the Nation," 167–75. To champion their historicist representation, many early nineteenth-century libretti included prefaces that identified the historical sources and events the plots drew on. Historical images also frequently inspired costume and set designs. Publications such as Jean-Charles Levacher de Charnois's *Recherches sur les costumes et sur les théâtres de toutes les nations, tant anciennes que modernes* (1790, repr. 1802) exploited the demand for historically researched materials. While I have found little evidence of the Opéra and its artists publicly communicating their efforts beyond libretto prefaces, they may have done so informally, since it is an item repeatedly discussed in reviews and other critical writings.

10. See Charlton, *Cambridge Companion to Grand Opera*, 5–6; Döhring and Henze-Döhring, *Oper und Musikdrama*, 117–19; Gerhard, "*Fernand Cortez* und *Le Siège de Corinthe*"; and Mungen, "Wagner, Spontini, und die Grand Opéra."

call "local color" (*couleur locale*).[11] This term was used to convey how the temporal (and at times geographical) distance of a plot was conveyed on a visual, textual, and musical level—a representational method required by the aforementioned new attitudes toward historical verisimilitude that had also found their way to the theater.[12] This emphasis on representing the "distance" did not prevent these works from losing their educational and political function. Indeed, in her work on historical theater in Berlin around 1800, Katherine Hambridge has pointed to the mediating function of local color.[13] After all, the historicist project was not as easily achievable in theater and opera as in writing or painting, because the former combined different arts: while costume and set designers could precisely copy historical objects and images (though this does not mean they always did or that their sources were historically accurate), such fidelity was not possible for composers or librettists. The latter artists were often short of historical source material, for speech and music are ephemeral, and often no notated music was available for a specific time period and region. In addition, it was paramount that the historical events and sounds be molded to fit contemporary theatrical conventions; after all, audiences were less likely to accept speech or music that sounded completely out of the ordinary. Therefore, Hambridge argues, local color "mediated between the twin imperatives of historical difference and familiarity."[14] Contemporary, "modern" harps, for instance, were used to represent any variety of ancient plucked string instruments, whether aeolian harps or lyres.[15]

Because of these problems with historical fidelity, musicologists have at times dismissed historicist local color as a mere decorative surface effect or a fetish of the French theatrical landscape around 1800.[16] However, an emphasis on mediation and attendant concerns about intentional or unintentional

11. See Malakis, "First Use of *Couleur Locale*."

12. According to several scholars, local color was used to represent a different approach to history: see Charlton, *Grétry and the Growth of Opéra Comique*, 233–36; Frantz, *L'esthétique du tableau*, 97–98; and Samuels, *Spectacular Past*, 3–5.

13. See Hambridge, "Performance of History." This function also shines through in David Charlton's discussion of André Grétry's use of local color in his *opéras comiques* of the late 1770s and 1780s (*Grétry and the Growth of Opéra Comique*, 172).

14. Hambridge, "Performance of History," 19.

15. For instance, modern harps were used in abundance to convey a fourth-century bardic local color in Jean-François Le Sueur's *Ossian ou les bardes*. See Andries, "Uniting the Arts to Stage the Nation," 169.

16. One of the earliest instances of this criticism is found in Victor Hugo's well-known preface to *Cromwell* (1827). Several scholars have since sided with Hugo. Moreover, the aesthetic estimation of local color is implicated in music scholarship's ambivalent relationship with exoticism and Orientalism. Already in 2011 Jonathan D. Bellman pointed out that Orientalist features of a musical work are often brushed off as merely "decorative." Because of local color's assumed aesthetic superficiality, Gerhard advocated a shift of focus to "couleur" or "tinta," a broader, supposedly more unifying compositional technique used to express the drama's atmospheric and psychological weight. See Hugo, *Cromwell*; Bellman, "Musical Voyages and Their Baggage," 418; and Gerhard, *Urbanization of Opera*, 163–64.

inaccuracies or even revisionisms ignores that the artists of *Fernand Cortez* attributed significant importance to their work's historical fidelity, as the above-cited excerpt from the libretto preface makes clear. Taking this engagement with historicity seriously, I propose that the enthusiasm for historically researched local color in *Fernand Cortez* was at least in part fueled by the epistemological claims that come with this mode of historical narration—what Kalle Pihlainen has recently called "narrative truth."[17] Source-based representations gave the historical representations an aura of scientific truth value, of providing true knowledge.

This was, however, knowledge not just about a specific historical event but also about events' underlying "transhistorical processes," that is, processes recognized to function throughout history independent of time or place. I am borrowing transhistoricity as a concept from current curatorial practices in which objects are thematically related across various times and geographical boundaries in museum exhibitions.[18] The concept facilitates a connection between the particular time and place of a historicist representation and the generality of historical narrative constructions. These transhistorical processes made it easier to use history for education purposes because they formulated narratives that were validated in the specificity of historical episodes but simultaneously applicable to different historical times and places, including the present.

In this article, I show how the historicist representation and use of local color in *Fernand Cortez* activated transhistorical narratives of empire and thus cast this opera as a tool for propagating early nineteenth-century French imperialism. These narratives were based on the popular notion that humanity was progressing toward an ever more civilized state—a topic of intense intellectual debate in the eighteenth and nineteenth centuries, which was also widely invoked at the time as a justification for European imperialism and colonialism, including Napoléon's own military campaigns.[19] While previous discussions of historicism and local color in opera and theater around 1800 have largely examined their connection to nation building, my approach here casts a wider net, examining their impact on sustaining contemporary French narratives of empire.[20]

17. Pihlainen, *Work of History*, 1–14.

18. The concept is elaborately discussed in Wittocx et al., *Transhistorical Museum*; see esp. Setari, "Notes on Transhistoricity."

19. According to Stuart Woolf, the term *civilization* was used in Britain and France from the 1760s on as a typical characteristic of European societies, giving them license to propagate this characteristic across the world ("Europe and Its Historians," 323–24). This connection among civilization, Europe, and imperialism is found in several eighteenth- and early nineteenth-century texts, of which several are excerpted in von Kulessa and Seth, *L'idée de l'Europe au siècle des Lumières*.

20. On connections of local color to ideas of nation building and nationalism in early nineteenth-century Europe, see Hambridge, "Performance of History," 19; and Samuels, *Spectacular Past*, 46–47.

I first explore how the source-based method of historical representation and narration was used to connect various examples of imperialism. A brief survey of institutional French historiography around 1800 highlights the discipline's growing enthusiasm for source research entwining with its propagation of narratives of empire—characteristics found in both nationalist and Orientalist historiographical projects. Then I turn to narratives about the "conquest" of the Americas related to *Fernand Cortez*, showing how the opera interweaves different historical processes of "civilization" to amplify the plot's imperialist message: the conquest of the Aztec Empire (1521), the campaign in Egypt and Syria (1798–1801), and Napoléon's Peninsular War started in 1808 with more covert reference to Charlemagne and his medieval empire. Local color and claims of historicity were specifically mobilized to interweave these events; I favor *mobilization* here over the term *mediation* for its more conspicuous political and militaristic overtones.

While these mobilization efforts may effectively propagate more abstract transhistorical notions of empire, at the end of the article I discuss their weakness when it comes to providing propaganda for a specific political enterprise, in this case Napoléon's Spanish campaign. The superimposition of various imperial endeavors in *Fernand Cortez* created uncertainty about exactly how this transhistorical process was to be mapped onto the present; the confusion was heightened by the opera featuring Spanish conquistadores as the civilizers while in 1809 the Spanish were supposed to be the ones subjected to French civilization efforts. Still, the multivalence of this transhistorical message facilitated the continued popularity of this opera following the fall of the Napoleonic Empire. More broadly, the opera provided a model for narrating the civilizing process across time and space that would continue to be used in other operatic, theatrical, and historical texts of the nineteenth century.

Historicity and Historiography of Empire

The decades straddling 1800 in France were marked by a lively and ever more popularized interest in historical sources and artifacts. An often-cited indicator of this popularization is the emergence of the modern public museum, with the opening of the Louvre and the Musée Nationale des Monuments Française in 1793 and 1795, respectively.[21] In addition to museums, France also saw a marked rise in the establishment of learned societies, some with the explicit intent of studying history and historical sources.[22] Both the museums and the intellectual

---

21. On the emergence of the public museum, see McClellan, *Inventing the Louvre*. On the rhetoric concerning historical verisimilitude in the museum, see Bann, *Clothing of Clio*, 77–92.
22. See Lentz, *Quand Napoléon inventait la France*.

societies indicate that studying and exhibiting historical objects were activities profoundly entwined with politics, education, and above all, propagating France's intellectual and cultural prestige. This was clearly the aim of the Institut de France, one of France's most prestigious intellectual institutions. Founded in 1795, it was considered a living counterpart to the *Encyclopédie* as it brought together (and expanded on) the intellectual disciplines previously divided among the royal *académies*.[23] Its foundational decree proclaimed that "its aim is to perfect the sciences and the arts through uninterrupted research, the publication of its discoveries, and correspondence with foreign learned societies. . . . These scientific and literary endeavors serve the general utility and glory of the Republic."[24]

The writing of history was one of the Institut de France's intellectual endeavors. Initially, the discipline was part of the second class, dedicated to the moral and political sciences (the first class covered the natural sciences, and the third, literature and arts). This division already gestured toward history's entwinement with political and educational matters. The second class was populated in part with prominent political figures, such as Emmanuel Joseph Sieyès and Jean-Jacques-Régis de Cambacérès, who became Napoléon's fellow consuls in 1799. At the same time, its members included important historians such as Louis-Pierre Anquetil, the author of the newest *Histoire de France* (first published in 1805), and Pierre-Charles Levesque, who taught history at the Collège de France from 1791 until his death in 1812.[25] The intertwining became slightly less overt in 1803, when Napoléon reformed the Institut de France and gathered disciplines that strongly relied on researching and interpreting historical sources in the "class of history and ancient literature," which also encompassed Oriental languages, philosophy, legislation, and ancient geography.[26] The historiography discussed in this class was not limited to French national history but also included ancient history and histories of foreign regions and countries, such as China and Egypt.

The attitude toward history writing at the Institut de France can be gleaned from the *Rapport historique sur les progrès de l'histoire et de la littérature ancienne depuis 1789 et sur leur état actuel* (*Historical Report on the Progress of History and Ancient Literature since 1789 and on Their Present State*), commissioned by Napoléon in 1802 but published in 1810.[27] The document substantiates

23. On the foundation of the Institut de France, see Beale, "Academies to Institut."

24. The decree was reprinted in the *Almanach nationale de France*, 445.

25. *Almanach nationale de France*, 450. Despite its popularity throughout the nineteenth century, Anquetil's *Histoire* was criticized by Augustin Thierry, a representative of the "new school" of the 1820s, for being too anecdotal and devoid of source research. On Anquetil's profile as a historian, see Whitehead, "Revising the Revisionists."

26. See *Almanach impériale*, 577.

27. Dacier, *Rapport historique*.

that historiography was a French prestige project and thus entwined with nationalist and imperialist ambitions. Since the document was addressed to Napoléon, the sycophantic tone of the opening sections is unsurprising. The first address by Levesque described the emperor as the savior of modern history from revolutionary destruction and more generally justified this reverence by claiming that history's main goal was to "one day celebrate with dignity the greatest of reigns and the greatest of nations."[28] Later on, the link is made to Charlemagne as one of the first French monarchs to employ historians to record the history of his empire.[29] The second address by the historian Bon-Joseph Dacier commended Napoléon "for surrounding himself with all the Enlightenment's intellectual activities, for embracing at a glance all human knowledge, for appreciating it in its entirety and diversity, and for judging its utility for the happiness and prosperity of the great society of mankind."[30] Thus Dacier connected Napoléon's patronage of this discipline to justifications for his imperialist ambitions, as he extended the boundaries of France through myriad military campaigns.

The body of the *Rapport historique*, which consists of a brief overview of French historiography and evaluations of historical writings, is a witness to the increasing estimation of historical fidelity. It highlights that in the eighteenth century, when "history was most cultivated in France," authors distinguished themselves by "engaging their readers through their style" and by their "greater respect for the truth than most of their predecessors."[31] The combination of these two qualities has led some historians to regard these claims of "truth" with skepticism and to dismiss them as largely a mode of rhetoric.[32] Despite differing from our modern approach to historical information, the *Rapport historique* still corroborates that source research lent credence to historical writing. After all, important criteria for praising works were evidence of extended source research; a balanced, calm, and impartial approach to these sources; and detailed information being used to uncover the transhistorical causes of important events.[33] In contrast, anecdotes intended to amuse readers, overt political bias, and impassioned narratives that vilified one political party were regularly criticized.[34] The authors regretted, for instance, that the aforementioned Anquetil had turned more toward the anecdotal than the instructional in his later works, including

28. Dacier, *Rapport historique*, 2.
29. Dacier, *Rapport historique*, 168.
30. Dacier, *Rapport historique*, 3–4.
31. Dacier, *Rapport historique*, 171.
32. See, e.g., Reizov, *L'historiographie romantique française*, 15–19.
33. See, e.g., the reports on modern history (i.e., since the fall of the Roman Empire): Dacier, *Rapport historique*, 204–21.
34. Dacier, *Rapport historique*, 214–17.

the *Histoire de France*, but they praised the rigorously researched earlier writings, such as his *L'esprit de la Ligue* (1767).[35]

Political ideology was, of course, not absent. In light of my focus on narratives of empire, it is worthwhile to spotlight the evaluation of two histories of Charlemagne. The authors found fault with Gabriel-Henri Gaillard's *Histoire de Charlemagne* (1782), inasmuch as Gaillard denounced "war and conquest . . . in the hope of bringing general peace to Europe by way of his writings."[36] Though written before Napoléon's rise to power, Gaillard's narrative was now out of favor for it went directly against France's imperialist "war and conquest." Moreover, Charlemagne was considered one of the earliest heroes of French history and one of the figures on which Napoléon liked to model himself.[37] The report's ideological tone is further supported by the praise for Dietrich Hermann Hegewisch's *Geschichte der Regierung Kaiser Karls der Grossen* (*History of the Reign of Emperor Charlemagne*, 1777); a French translation was published in 1791. Despite Hegewisch's being a "Saxon," he considered Charlemagne's subjugation of his people and their conversion to Christianity necessary because it delivered them from their "ferocious turbulence" and "bloodthirsty superstition."[38] This discussion thus upheld the notion not only that it was France's (historical) duty to spread the principles of civilization (and Christianity) it had nurtured in its own borders but also that the subjugated populations benefited and would eventually be grateful for being conquered.

Even when the Institut de France was not merely a governmental puppet and actively opposed governmental interference, history as practiced at this institution was conceived as a profoundly political discipline.[39] The members of the class of history and ancient languages still included many prominent politicians, such as Napoléon's brother Joseph and Charles Maurice de Talleyrand-Périgord, who despite France's turbulent political climate held influential governmental positions almost continuously from the 1780s until the 1830s. While invested in source research, how historians constructed narratives from these sources was strongly influenced by the notion that historiography, at least in part, raised good French citizens. And as Matthew d'Auria has recently shown, many of the narratives that throughout the nineteenth century informed

35. Dacier, *Rapport historique*, 211.
36. Dacier, *Rapport historique*, 208.
37. See Dwyer, *Citizen Emperor*, 150–52.
38. Dacier, *Rapport historique*, 209.
39. This opposition was especially clear in 1810 with the decennial prize competition, which was to honor the best works of the previous ten years in various disciplines. While the Institut de France's members served as jury, they had not nominated all the works that Napoléon favored, which led to much controversy; eventually no prizes were ever awarded. See Seth, "L'Institut et les prix littéraires"; and Grigsby, "Classicism, Nationalism, and History."

historians' concept of what a good French citizen was were rooted in eighteenth- and early nineteenth-century writings.[40]

Yet, while many authors have focused on nation building through national history, a similar function was also performed by Orientalist historiographical projects in which source research was similarly used to lend credence to "narrative truths." Perhaps the most renowned example is the historical and scientific output of Napoléon's Egyptian and Syrian campaign (1798–1801), which Edward Said argued marked the emergence of modern French-British colonialism.[41] On this campaign, Napoléon had taken thirty-five intellectuals who formed the Institut d'Egypte. They were hired to advise the government and "propagate the Enlightenment" and to study the country's fauna, flora, geography, history, music, and so on.[42] Their efforts resulted in the monumental, multivolume publication *Description de l'Egypte*, of which the first volumes were published in 1809, the year *Fernand Cortez* premiered. Its introduction shows the intersection of the scientific activities (including source research) and ideology. It stated that Napoléon's campaign aimed "to ease the condition of the inhabitants and to obtain for them all the advantages of a perfected civilization," and it asserted that "one cannot attain this goal without the continuous employment of the sciences and arts."[43] While the Egyptian campaign ultimately failed, these research activities allowed France, according to Said, to exercise an intellectual form of control over Ottoman Egyptian culture and its history; it was "the very model of a truly scientific appropriation of one culture by another, apparently stronger one."[44] Historical and scientific research sanctioned by an institution is again constructed as providing epistemological criteria for a transhistorical narrative that justifies empire. It is exactly this fusion of a source-based historical representation with Orientalist and exoticist tropes that is used to strengthen this narrative in *Fernand Cortez*.

Historicist Narratives of Empire in *Fernand Cortez*

It has long been known that the artists creating this opera were eager to display their historical research. As early as 1874, the archivist and librarian Théodore de Lajarte (1826–90) uncovered a letter indicating that the scene painters for *Fernand Cortez* sought historically accurate illustrations of sixteenth-century Mexico, its inhabitants, and the Spanish conquistadors to reproduce this setting in

---

40. D'Auria, *Shaping of French National Identity*.
41. Said, *Orientalism*, 42–43.
42. Lentz, *Quand Napoléon inventait la France*, 265.
43. Fourier, *Description de l'Egypte*, vi.
44. Said, *Orientalism*, 42–43.

the sets with greater fidelity.[45] Several of the costume designs were inspired by a single scholarly source, *The History of Mexico*, a 1787 English translation of Francesco Saverio Clavigero's *La historia antigua de México* (1780).[46] The resemblances between the costume designs for the production by François-Guillaume Ménageot and the *History of Mexico*'s illustrations are remarkable. Some figures are reproduced almost exactly—down to details of posture and facial features— while others are clad in outfits and armor from the *History of Mexico* (see figs. 1–5). Clavigero's book may even have supplied material for the sets. While the one design tentatively associated with *Fernand Cortez* does not offer a clear resemblance, the book may have provided a template for the Aztec zodiac calendar detailed in descriptions for an act 1 ceiling curtain.[47]

The *History of Mexico* is also the likely source for the most peculiar detail of the opera's musical historicism: the score features an *ayacachtli* (see figs. 6– 7).[48] The *ayacachtli*, spelled *ajacaxtli* in Spontini's autograph manuscript score as in Clavigero's *History of Mexico*,[49] is a gourd-shaped rattle known in Europe from publications on the Americas, some dating back to the sixteenth century, as a prototypical indigenous Mesoamerican instrument.[50] Originally, Spontini had intended the instrument to serve as a pervasive sonic marker of the Aztecs, used in several numbers, including in the Mexican March in act 1 when the Aztecs first arrive on the stage.[51] However, the instrument is crossed out in most

45. Report from Mitoire, guard of the storage facilities of the Menus-Plaisirs, the organization responsible for royal festivities and theater, to Picard, directeur de l'Académie Impériale, May 17, 1809, Archives Nationales à Paris, AJ[13] 92. Lajarte's discovery is mentioned in Charlton, *Cambridge Companion to Grand Opera*, 5.

46. Clavigero, *History of Mexico*. A stamp on the first page of the book now held at the Bibliothèque Nationale de France shows that it was indeed part of Napoléon's Bibliothèque Impériale and may thus have been the volume found by the Opéra's artists.

47. Report from Mitoire to Picard, June 16, 1809, Archives Nationales à Paris AJ[13] 92. The zodiac signs are also described in a review of *Le publiciste*, Nov. 30, 1809. The critic's contention that M. Humboldt had delivered the images for the zodiac and the plants is likely erroneous but points to the reviewer's interest in validating the accuracy of this staging element.

48. While there are similarities between the naming and depiction of the instrument, the costume of the dancer seems not directly based on Clavigero's *History of Mexico*. It is possible that inspiration was taken from the illustrations by I. Van Beecq for Antonio de Solís's *Histoire de la conquête du Mexique ou de la Nouvelle Espagne*, a source cited in the libretto preface of *Fernand Cortez*. In these illustrations the Aztec dancers are depicted with feather loin and head garments (de Solís, *Histoire de la conquête du Mexique*, 275, 290).

49. Spontini, "Fernand Cortez," 1:331–35, Paris, Bibliothèque-Musée de l'Opéra A418 i; Clavigero, *History of Mexico*, 398.

50. The earliest European source to mention an *ayacachtli* is Bernardino Sahagún's *Historia general de Las Cosas de Nueva España* (ca. 1577), also known as the Florentine Codex. Publications about extra-European exploration were the most prominent source for descriptions of non-European music in the seventeenth and eighteenth centuries. See Irving, "Comparative Organography in Early Modern Empires." On the *ayacachtli* specifically, see also Stevenson, *Music in Aztec and Inca Territory*, 34–36.

51. Originally, every act of the opera contained a march or a dance that featured this instrument. Spontini, "Fernand Cortez," 1:331–35, 3:266–90, 5:291–99, Bibliothèque-Musée de l'Opéra A418 i–v.

FIGURE 1 Engraving of a "Mexican Priest" and a "Mexican Warrior,"
from Clavigero's *History of Mexico*, 1787. Courtesy Bibliothèque
Nationale de France.

FIGURE 2 Engraving of "A Common Sacrifice," from Clavigero's
History of Mexico, 1787. Courtesy Bibliothèque Nationale de France.

FIGURE 3 Engraving of "Shields," from Clavigero's *History of Mexico*, 1787. Courtesy Bibliothèque Nationale de France.

FIGURE 4 Ménageot's costume designs for a "Mexican Sacrificial Priest" and a "Priest" in *Fernand Cortez*, based on the engravings of a "Mexican Priest" and "A Common Sacrifice" (figs. 1–2), ca. 1809. Courtesy Bibliothèque-Musée de l'Opéra.

FIGURE 5 Ménageot's costume designs for "Mexican Soldiers and Officers" in *Fernand Cortez*, based on the engravings of a "Mexican Warrior" and "Shields" (figs. 1 and 3), ca. 1809. Courtesy Bibliothèque-Musée de l'Opéra.

places, possibly because of its rather small sound and limited carrying power. It seems that at the premiere it featured in only one Aztec dance, the only number in the printed score in which the instrument appears.[52] In this number, a dancer beats the instrument onstage so that its function as an Aztec marker is also realized visually.[53] No evidence indicates that such an instrument had previously appeared on a European stage.[54] Until then, composers had largely resorted to imitating historical or exotic sounds with standard Western instruments rather than by reconstructing indigenous instruments. Consequently, the efforts to include the *ayacachtli* are another testament to the artists' unprecedented engagement with historical sources.

The libretto also proudly advertised the production's adherence to historical sources. The preface claimed that "the most trustworthy historians have furnished us with all the principal events and all the important characters (except for

52. Spontini, *Fernand Cortez*, 226.

53. Because of its limited appearance and visual rather than aural effect, Alessandro Lattanzi describes the *ayacachtli* in *Fernand Cortez* as "another example of the Parisian fetishism for *couleur locale*" and "a surface exoticism" ("Spontini's Panoply," 52).

54. Michael V. Pisani claims that this is the very first "attempt to use any indigenous American instruments in a European musical composition" (*Imagining Native America in Music*, 43).

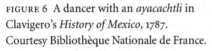

FIGURE 6 A dancer with an *ayacachtli* in Clavigero's *History of Mexico*, 1787. Courtesy Bibliothèque Nationale de France.

FIGURE 7 Ménageot's costume design for a dancer with *ayacachtli*, ca. 1809. Courtesy Bibliothèque-Musée de l'Opéra.

Alvare [Cortez's brother])."[55] Any adjustments made to the original historical events seemed merely to align the libretto with the expected dramatic conventions, and some were justified by reference to historical fidelity. The excision of the Aztec emperor Montezuma, for instance, happened because "history, by stigmatizing the shameful weakness of this prince, did not allow us to present him onstage in a dramatic manner."[56] In this quote, the librettists suggest they prefer cutting characters over portraying them in a manner violating historical accounts.

Indicating the similarity between libretto and historical circumstances is the reason for a lengthy quotation ascribed to Antonio de Solís's *Histoire de la conquête du Mexique ou de la Nouvelle Espagne* (*History of the Conquest of Mexico or New Spain*, 1691).[57] The quote supports the claim that the relationship

55. De Jouy and Esménard, *Fernand Cortez*, 4–5.
56. De Jouy and Esménard, *Fernand Cortez*, 5.
57. This is the first French translation of Antonio de Solís's original Spanish *Historia de la conquista de México* (1684).

between Cortez and the character of Amazily was modeled on Cortés's romance with Doña Marina, his historical Aztec mistress. Since this quotation offers a key to understanding the narrative of empire underlying the opera's use of historical sources, it is worth quoting in full:

> This historian [de Solís] says that of the twenty women given to Cortés by the chief from Yucatán, this general [Cortés] immediately noticed the superior genius of one of them. He had her educated and baptized as *Marina* (we have named her *Amazily*). It seems that geniuses of a superior order stimulated each other. Cortés and Marina liked each other from the very first moment and then bound themselves to each other with the most tender love. Cortés, who quickly recognized the extent of his lover's intelligence and strength of character, made her his advisor and translator, and considerably benefitted from his relationship with this young American: twice she saved his life, risking her own; and because among heroic souls, a taste for pleasure often goes hand in hand with a passion for glory, they fell in love and from their union a son was born, named *Martín Cortés*, who Philip II [of Spain] invested with the title of knight of St. Jacques.[58]

Given all the effort spent on the historicist representation of *Fernand Cortez*, it may come as a surprise that this quotation is a fabrication. Even though it sounds historical, it neither cites nor paraphrases any text from de Solís's *Histoire de la conquête du Mexique*. De Solís's study focuses on Doña Marina's role as a translator and negotiator in Cortés's campaigns. He only briefly mentioned that the conquistador had approached her with "manners that purity would not have allowed" and as a result had a son with her—behavior that his fellow historians, so he claimed, had criticized as "unbridled passion."[59] The libretto's quotation, in contrast, cleanses the historical figures of these less savory aspects and makes them more suitable as operatic heroes. Because altering events and characters in light of contemporary theatrical and moral conventions was a common practice, and one already admitted to in the libretto preface with regard to Montezuma, this deception is especially surprising.

While one may suggest that the artists were merely seeking historical verisimilitude, I argue that the semblance of historical accuracy achieved by this fabricated quote was needed to uphold the epistemological claims about the opera's narrative of empire. The narrative's essence is even encapsulated in the quotation itself: Cortés/Cortez undertakes the project of civilizing Marina/Amazily through education, religious conversion, and compassion. This project elevates the previously "uncivilized" other to a level comparable to that of the "civilized" self, and the relationship between the two becomes mutually beneficial and

58. De Jouy and Esménard, *Fernand Cortez*, 5–6.
59. De Solís, *Histoire de la conquête du Mexique*, 138–39.

leads to a union (their son, Martín Cortés). This narrative is also neatly reproduced in the opera itself, where the confrontation between the Aztecs and the Spanish conquistadors ultimately results in a final celebration of the "union of two worlds."[60] It is no accident that a major agent in this unification is Marina/Amazily, the person who supposedly could testify to the benefits of the imperialist civilizing mission. Besides the visual and musical local color in the production, the quotation in the introduction, as long as its fabricated nature is not revealed, could thus underscore the transhistorical narratives of civilization and empire.

Narrating the Conquests of the Americas

Establishing this "narrative truth" was important for the reception of *Fernand Cortez*, because Napoléon's government hoped to use the opera to garner support for another imperial campaign: the Peninsular War.[61] This war started following the abdication of the Spanish king Charles IV in favor of Ferdinand VII in March 1808. The French government, however, did not recognize Ferdinand as the new sovereign and instead installed Napoléon's brother, Joseph.[62] This decision caused violent uprisings in Madrid and elsewhere in Spain, which French troops brutally suppressed. In the summer of 1808, Ferdinand VII decided to launch a military campaign against the new government the French installed in Bayonne, where his forces ultimately clashed with the armies of Napoléon.[63]

From Bayonne the emperor reportedly wrote a letter to Joseph Fouché, minister of police at the time, to commission an opera that would create public support for this war.[64] It is unclear who decided on the topic for the opera, but it was likely chosen in the hope of evoking a parallel between Cortés's conquest of the Aztec Empire and Napoléon's Spanish campaign.[65] After all, as a

---

60. De Jouy and Esménard, *Fernand Cortez*, 62.
61. For more on the Peninsular War, see Esdaile, *Peninsular War*.
62. Esdaile, *Peninsular War*, 37.
63. Esdaile, *Peninsular War*, 38–39.
64. See Madelin, *Les mémoires de Fouché*, 259. The authenticity of the memoirs of Fouché has been challenged, since they were first published after Fouché's death. Yet Louis Madelin's preface suggests that even though the narrative may have been fabricated, the information is based on existing notes by Fouché. With regard to *Cortez*, correspondence between Fouché and the librettist Esménard from May 1808 suggests that the minister of police was indeed involved in the opera's creation. See Libby, "Gaspare Spontini," 109–10.
65. Conflicting narratives exist in the anecdotal notes by de Jouy, one of the opera's librettists, that accompanied the 1817 revision of *Fernand Cortez* and Adolf Bernhard Marx's records of conversations with Spontini that variously attribute the choice of plot either to de Jouy or to Napoléon. Yet de Jouy's memoirs and the above-mentioned correspondence between Fouché and Esménard suggest that the government tasked the librettists with finding a plot that would fit the political situation. Libby, "Gaspare Spontini," 108–10.

governmentally funded institution subject to censorship, the Opéra regularly featured works that had a propagandistic tone, if not always as closely paralleling political realities as this one.[66] Moreover, one of Napoléon's censors, Esménard, was specifically asked to collaborate on this libretto. While the Opéra and its artists were silent on this parallel between the plot and the Spanish campaign, the official reading was clearly recognized by several critics. For instance, Lucien Geoffroy wrote in the *Journal de l'Empire* that "one should observe that while the Spanish conquerors justly opposed the abominable sacrifices [of the Aztecs], the Inquisition was authorizing similar ones in their country, for burning people is not less barbarous than slitting their throats. Hail to the hero of humanity [Napoléon], who is destroying this horrible desecration of a clement, peaceful, and charitable religion."[67] French public opinion was starting to oppose Napoléon's incessant warfare and likely motivated this operatic propaganda campaign.[68] Still, the government profited from a well-established image of Spain as a society on the fringes of Europe and civilization, "a barbarous and inhospitable land," as one revolutionary publication called it.[69] While the actual reasons for Napoléon's Peninsular War are complex,[70] officials frequently used the imperialist narrative that it was a country in need of civilizing, especially when it came to its religious practices.[71]

As Sarah Hibberd has demonstrated, recasting his Spanish campaign as a religious war fitted with Napoléon's politics of presenting himself as the savior of Catholicism.[72] These politics had started when he reconciled France with the Catholic Church in the 1801 Concordat, and they were enforced in 1806 when the emperor instituted official celebrations for St. Napoléon on his birthday, August 15.[73] The emperor may even have taken his inspiration from Spanish history itself; since 1493 Spanish monarchs had been allowed to carry the title "Rex Catholicissimus" (Ferdinand VII was still addressed as such) and used the title to justify their sponsorship of the Inquisition and colonial exploits in the New World and elsewhere.[74]

To imbue the conquest of the Americas with a positive imperialist message, it was necessary to change the narrative. Eighteenth-century intellectuals,

---

66. An elaborate discussion of Napoléon's use of the Opéra and its repertoire for political ends is given in Chaillou, *Napoléon et l'Opéra*.

67. *Journal de l'Empire*, Nov. 30, 1809.

68. Dwyer, *Citizen Emperor*, 273.

69. Bourdon, *Recueil des actions heroïques et civiques*, 17–18. Quoted in Dwyer, *Citizen Emperor*, 273.

70. The different causes of the war are elaborately described in Esdaile, *Peninsular War*, 1–36.

71. On the perception of religious differences between French conceptions of Catholicism and those of the Mediterranean regions during the Napoleonic Wars, see Clarke, "Encountering the Sacred."

72. Hibberd, "'L'épique en action.'"

73. Dwyer, *Citizen Emperor*, 212–15.

74. On the entwining of Catholicism with Spain's colonial projects, see van Oss, *Catholic Colonialism*, xi–xii. A brief overview of the Inquisition is given in Tarver and Slape, *Spanish Empire*, 113–16.

such as Jean-Jacques Rousseau and Denis Diderot, often used this conquest to debate the merits and abuses of empire building, especially through colonialism and its attendant atrocities and religious extremism.[75] This debate also informed theater works such as Voltaire's *Alzire, ou les américains* (*Alzire, or the Americans,* 1736), which denounced the aggressive colonialist who seeks to dominate indigenous peoples and to force them into subjugation.[76] Since Voltaire, similar approaches had been taken in two works loosely based on his tragedy: Pierre-Joseph Candeille's *Pizarre, ou la conquête du Pérou* (*Pizarro, or the Conquest of Peru*), a *tragédie lyrique* (1785), with a libretto by Charles-Pierre Duplessis, and a melodrama of the same title by René-Charles Guilbert de Pixérécourt, which premiered in 1802.[77] The latter also features a "benevolent" colonialist mediator as a figure that allows for a narrative supporting imperialism. This is also the case with Etienne-Nicolas Méhul's opera *Cora* (1791) with a libretto by Valadier, in which the Incan title character is in love with the Spanish mediator. She seems to support a more positive image of Spanish imperialism by proclaiming that "everything is changed in these climates: everything has softened, our morals, our virtues, our courage, [we are] less ferocious in battle and more humane after a victory."[78] Still, a handful of good Spanish characters had not redeemed the unfavorable light in which the conquest of the Americas had usually been portrayed on Parisian stages.[79]

According to *Fernand Cortez*'s librettists, the main culprit of Cortés's bad reputation among the Parisian audiences was not a play or an opera but Jean-François Marmontel's popular novel *Les Incas, ou la destruction de l'empire du Pérou* (*The Incas, or the Destruction of the Empire of Peru,* 1777).[80] While this novel, like the theatrical pieces, focused on Spanish atrocities during the colonization of Peru, it also featured lengthy episodes in chapters 6–8, in which two Aztec refugees related the fall of their empire, thus casting Cortés's conquest in the same light as Pizarro's.[81] The librettists claimed, though, that equating the two Spanish conquistadors was a mistake:

75. See Muthu, *Enlightenment against Empire.*
76. Sanchez, "Voltaire et sa tragédie américaine Alzire," 20.
77. Duplessis, *Pizarre, ou la conquête du Pérou*; Pixérécourt, *Pizarre ou la conquête du Pérou.*
78. Valadier, *Cora,* 3.
79. Of these versions, only Candeille's *Pizarre,* performed at the Opéra a few times in 1785 and 1791, was referenced in reviews of *Cortez.* See *Journal de l'Empire,* Nov. 30, 1809; and *Journal de Paris,* Dec. 1, 1809. Jürgen Maehder has demonstrated that the libretto of *Fernand Cortez* was instead closely related to various eighteenth-century Italian *opere serie* ("Die Darstellung der Conquista Mexicos").
80. De Jouy and Esménard, *Fernand Cortez,* 3. Marmontel's novel had also been the source for Méhul's *Cora,* performed a total of five times during 1791. This opera seems to have been entirely forgotten by the premiere of *Cortez,* for the librettists and critics only reference Marmontel's *Les Incas.* On *Cora,* see Bartlet, "Etienne-Nicolas Méhul and Opera," 194–214.
81. The librettists' criticism of Marmontel's *Les Incas* was another of their deceptions. As Dennis Libby has shown, it had been a prominent model for the libretto of *Cortez.* Marmontel had also based his

Cortés, a Spanish nobleman gifted with all the qualities that make a hero, had to fight in his prodigious expedition, against obstacles that only he could have surmounted. With a strong army of *seven hundred men, eight cannons, and seventeen horses*, he conquered an immense empire defended by a nation of warriors whose ferocious morals and cruel superstitions weaken the sympathy that one would usually feel for those with unhappy courage.[82]

These qualities, they argued, set Cortés apart from Pizarro, who supposedly had many more military resources available and faced a peaceful, unarmed nation, which he brutally exterminated.[83]

By claiming that their portrayal of Cortez was based on historical sources, the librettists thus "corrected" the Enlightenment version of the conquest of the Americas. They highlighted that Cortés had "truly" been a heroic man and the Aztecs were uncivilized barbarians unworthy of the audience's sympathy. Under the cloak of historicity, the artists not only made their Cortez into a more typical operatic character—the benevolent ruler—but also mobilized this historical episode to align Cortés's conquest with Napoléon's imperialist projects. The preface states that this historical episode "proves with the greatest brilliance what the courage, perseverance and indomitable will of a *great man* can achieve."[84] This mention of a "great man" is almost certainly an implicit reference to Napoléon; after he became emperor, he regularly styled himself Napoléon Le Grand, probably after Charlemagne, whose imperialist projects, as we have seen, were a well-worn topic of historiography discussed at the Institut de France around this time.[85]

The link between Cortés and Napoléon was made more explicitly in other writings of the time. In 1808, a certain P. Roure published the epic poem *La Cortésiade ou le Nouveau monde en douze chants* (*The Cortesiad or the New World in Twelve Cantos*).[86] The poem is preceded by an "Hommage à Napoléon le Grand," glorifying the emperor's endeavors to end oppression and bring

---

plot on the historical accounts of Antonio de Herrera and de Solís, the two histories cited in the libretto preface of *Fernand Cortez*. Marmontel's version closely resembles the events as played out—and further compressed—in the opera. Moreover, the names Amazili and Telasco first crop up in his novel, where they are a young Incan couple rather than Cortés's Aztec mistress and her brother. Because of these connections, Libby has suggested that Marmontel's novel was a more direct source than the actual historical works of de Solís and de Herrera ("Gaspare Spontini," 124–27).

82. De Jouy and Esménard, *Fernand Cortez*, 3.

83. De Jouy and Esménard, *Fernand Cortez*, 4.

84. De Jouy and Esménard, *Fernand Cortez*, 3 (emphasis mine). The link was made more explicitly in the printed score, which was dedicated to the queen of the two Sicilies, meaning Julie Clary, the spouse of Joseph I, king of Spain. Moreover, the dedication specifically states that through his "conquests" the "great man" had made Paris "the capital of the world" (Spontini, dedication in *Cortez*).

85. On Napoléon modeling himself on Charlemagne, see Dwyer, *Citizen Emperor*, 150–52.

86. Roure, *La Cortésiade*.

freedom to the world.[87] The poem, as promised on the title page, is "enriched with historical and geographic notes, and notes concerning natural history," thus reflecting the tendency to validate narratives by showing off historical research.[88] It is uncertain whether Roure knew of the opera *Fernand Cortez* when writing his text. Yet this poem demonstrates that the creators of this opera were not the only ones eager to revise the historiography of the conquest of the Americas to exploit its political expediency in 1808, when Napoléon embarked on his Spanish campaign, as well as to appeal to French pride in the country's historical and scientific activities.[89]

Mobilizing Musical Local Color

The alignment between historical episodes of civilization and present-day imperialism was also present in how Spontini crafted the musical opposition between the Spanish conquistadores and the Aztecs. Of course, instances of historically "accurate" local color in music—even when very freely interpreted—were limited and would have been undesirable. As mentioned earlier, the *ayacachtli* was in all likelihood used in only one dance at the opera's premiere and served more as a visual than a musical marker of otherness. Similarly, the only instance of identifiably Spanish-flavored local color appears but a few pages later, when the Spanish cavalry charge is accompanied with triplets evoking the typical rhythm of a bolero, a reference picked up by at least one critic.[90] More generally, the score is permeated with musical idioms that at first sight have little to do with historically researched local color. Yet these idioms had familiar associations with other narratives of empire for the opera's first audiences, more specifically the recent Egyptian and Syrian campaign.

In the Mexican March—the music heard when the Aztecs first arrive onstage—Spontini replaced the crossed out *ayacachtli* with a triangle.[91] At the time, the triangle was commonly associated with the *alla turca* style, a highly popular, stylized manner of depicting exotic characters in the eighteenth and early nineteenth centuries, especially Ottomans.[92] The Mexican march in *Fernand*

87. Roure, *La Cortésiade*, vi–vii.

88. While the appearance of footnotes in an epic poem may surprise modern readers, it may have been unremarkable to Roure's contemporaries. After all, epic poems were considered valuable sources of historical information. For example, in the 1780s the French archaeologist Jean-Baptiste Le Chevalier had used Homer's *Iliad* to locate and excavate the site of Troy (Le Chevalier, *Voyage dans la Troade*).

89. Népomucène Louis Lemercier's *Christophe Colomb*, a *comédie historique* about the 1492 voyage to the Americas, also highlights the progressive scientific ideas that allowed Columbus to succeed in his journey and how religious extremists opposed him. The play was first performed at the Odéon on March 7, 1809, only a few months before the premiere of *Fernand Cortez*.

90. *Le publiciste*, Nov. 30, 1809.

91. Spontini, "Fernand Cortez," 1:331–35, Bibliothèque-Musée de l'Opéra A418 i.

92. On *alla turca* in eighteenth-century opera, see Locke, *Musical Exoticism*, 110–23; Locke, *Music and the Exotic*, 299–323; and Hunter, "'Alla Turca' Style." Thomas Betzwieser (*Exotismus und "Türkenoper"*)

FIGURE 8 *Fernand Cortez*, act 1: the beginning of the Mexican March. Courtesy Bibliothèque Nationale de France.

Cortez (fig. 8) contains several features typical of this style. Its harmony is simple, merely alternating between dominant and tonic chords, and the melody uses many semitone figurations. The march's short repetitive motives, dotted rhythms, and abrupt dynamic accents give the piece a percussive character that is further

and Larry Wolff (*Singing Turk*) have discussed at length how the portrayal of Ottoman characters is connected to eighteenth-century political ambitions in France and the Habsburg Empire, respectively.

FIGURE 8 (continued)

underlined when the cymbals, bass drum, and triangle chime in. Such *alla turca* features, musicologist Ralph P. Locke contends, constitute "a complex of generally noisy sonic materials," and throughout the eighteenth century this association with noise had generally dehumanized or ridiculed Ottoman and other exotic characters.[93]

93. Locke, *Musical Exoticism*, 110.

The composer's intentional creation of a "noisy" musical idiom is even more conspicuous in the act 3 opening chorus, "Enchaînons, frappons les victimes" ("Let us enchain, beat the victims"). This chorus depicts the Aztecs as they are readying themselves to commit that most contemptible act: human sacrifice (specifically of Cortez's brother, Alvaro, and his men). The scene starts as a soft rumble in the low strings and timpani, with the tempo indicated as *allegro feroce marcato*, a ferocious, marked, and quick tempo—*feroce* is an unusual addition to a tempo indication (fig. 9). Then, after four measures, a loud *fortissimo* call in the horns, trumpets, and trombones announces the beginning of the sacrificial rite. Following the call, the tam-tam, bass drum, and side drum—the loudest instruments then available in operatic orchestras—join in, and above this noisy tapestry the violins foreshadow the chorus's first theme. This theme displays many of the distinctive features of Spontini's Aztec music and, like the Mexican march, makes some allusions to the *alla turca* idiom: a simple harmonic accompaniment and a melody with chromatic ornamentations that circles around semitones. Its dotted rhythms, staccato markings, and plethora of accents give the music an aggressive, percussive quality. Throughout the chorus, the themes prioritize rhythm over lyricism: the repetition of notes and short motives and the small range prevent the melodic material from developing and expanding.

The text setting adds to the repetitive impression of this chorus. The entire number is based on just four eight-syllable lines:

Enchaînons, frappons les victimes,	Let us enchain, beat the victims,
Répandons leur sang odieux;	Let us spill their odious blood;
Nos fureurs sont trop légitimes;	Our furor is all too legitimate;
Nous vengeons l'empire et les dieux.	We avenge our empire and our gods.[94]

The series of imperatives—"enchaînons, frappons, . . . répandons"—and the short sentence structures made it easy for the composer to break down the text into single words and small phrases that are frequently repeated. Whereas the first theme sets the whole poetic text once, subsequent thematic sections feature several repetitions of either parts or the entirety of the text. This textual repetition, combined with the percussive musical setting, turns the Aztecs' exclamations into an oppressive sonic tapestry that enacts the violence and bloodlust expressed in the lyrics.

The opening of act 3 elicited significant consternation in the press, with several critics indicating that Spontini had created the impression that the Aztec's music was barbarous, bordering on "noise." The reviewer of the *Courrier de l'Europe* declared that "these are the songs of barbarians, which says it all. Here, the composer became completely Mexican, because there is such torment

94. De Jouy and Esménard, *Fernand Cortez*, 47.

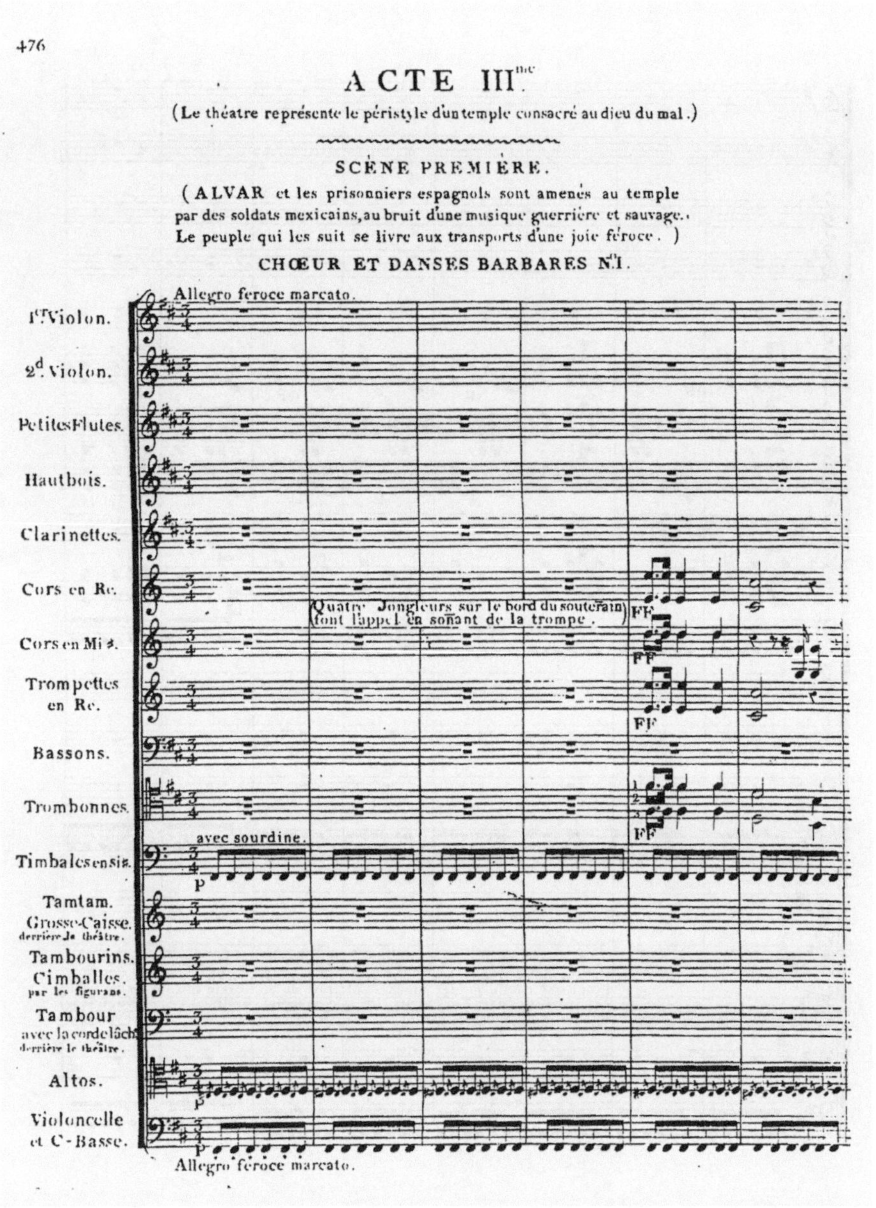

476
ACTE IIIme
(Le théatre représente le péristyle d'un temple consacré au dieu du mal.)
SCÈNE PREMIÈRE.
(ALVAR et les prisonniers espagnols sont amenés au temple
par des soldats mexicains, au bruit d'une musique guerrière et sauvage.
Le peuple qui les suit se livre aux transports d'une joie féroce.)
CHŒUR ET DANSES BARBARES N°1.
Allegro feroce marcato.
1er Violon.
2d. Violon.
Petites Flutes.
Hautbois.
Clarinettes.
Cors en Ré.
Quatre Jongleurs sur le bord du souterain font l'appel en sonant de la trompe.
Cors en Mi♭.
Trompettes en Ré.
Bassons.
Trombonnes.
avec sourdine.
Timbales en si♭.
Tamtam.
Grosse-Caisse.
derrière le théâtre.
Tambourins.
Cimballes.
par les figurans.
Tambour
avec la corde lâche
derrière le théâtre.
Altos.
Violoncelle et C-Basse.
Allegro feroce marcato.
FF
p

FIGURE 9 *Fernand Cortez*, act 3: the opening of the Aztec chorus "Enchaînons, frappons les victimes." Courtesy Bibliothèque Nationale de France.

and musical movement in the orchestration, which undoubtedly reflects the [dramatic] situation, but tires out even the most undaunted contemplator and his ear."[95] Many critics similarly complained about the barbarity expressed in

95. *Courrier de l'Europe*, Dec. 3, 1809.

FIGURE 9 (continued)

these and other Aztec choruses; the impression was sometimes so strong that it affected the assessment of the entire score as mere noise.[96]

96. One critic grumbled that "from start to end it is really such frightful noise that one cannot leave without a headache" (*Allgemeine musikalische Zeitung*, Feb. 21, 1810).

FIGURE 9 (continued)

One possible explanation for the critics' visceral reaction is that Spontini had simply outdone any of his predecessors and contemporaries in imagining a kind of music that drastically deviated from contemporary norms. The excess of Spontini's music became very conspicuous when reviewers compared it to other so-called barbarous choruses, such as those of the Scythians in Christoph

Willibald Gluck's *Iphigénie en Tauride* (1779), an opera still performed at the time.[97] Even though Gluck used some of the same instruments (piccolo, cymbals, and side drum) and a similar syllabic, strongly accentuated text setting, the Scythian choruses are shorter, have more conventional harmonic language and more lyrical melodies, and avoid incessantly repetitive motives.[98]

Spontini's Aztec music did not come across as wholly invented, though; even though the above-quoted critic may have meant the remark that "the composer became completely Mexican" as scorn, it does give the impression that he thought Spontini had captured some essence of what "Mexican music" may have sounded like. It is indeed possible that Spontini had taken inspiration from Clavigero's *History of Mexico*, which highlighted the prominence of percussive instruments in Aztec music, such as the *huehuetl* and *teponazli*. Clavigero described the *huehuetl* as a three-foot-tall drum and the *teponaztli* as another drum that comes in different sizes, but the sound of the largest one "is so loud that it may be heard at the distance of two or three miles." Moreover, he specified that the Aztec's "singing was harsh and offensive to European ears, but they took so much pleasure in it themselves, that on festivals, they continued singing the whole day."[99]

Such ethnographic descriptions did not have to go together with assumptions of barbarism. Musicologist Olivia Bloechl has argued that there was a continuous tension between representations of "race" and "exoticism" that on the one hand sought to gain control over the Other and on the other hand reflected Enlightenment fascination in Europe with "primitive" cultures unsoiled by the influences of modern, scientific society.[100] However, the latter representations were hardly estranged from discourses of power; as Vanessa Agnew highlights, this fascination could still result in the exploitation of so-called primitive cultures as scientific test subjects.[101] These tensions are clear in Clavigero's book itself, whose depiction of indigenous Mesoamericans is entirely in line with the Enlightenment's "noble savage": it includes criticism of the violent intervention by the Spanish but simultaneously accentuates that Aztec practices were regarded as uncivilized.[102] Yet Spontini's noisy, oppressive music leaves no room for this

---

97. The opera was performed at least twice a year from 1800 to 1808, with a total of forty-one performances for these years. Performance data have been collected from the *Journal de l'Opéra* (gallica.bnf.fr/ark: /12148/cb426079139/date.r=Journal+de+Paris).

98. According to Libby, this resulted in the contemporary judgment that Gluck's Scythian choruses had the "force of brevity, clarity, and simplicity" ("Gaspare Spontini," 152–54).

99. Clavigero, *History of Mexico*, 398.

100. See Bloechl, "Race, Empire, and Early Music."

101. See Agnew, "Music's Empire." On the politics of power behind pre-nineteenth-century descriptions of non-European music, see also Irving, "Comparative Organography in Early Modern Empires."

102. The encounter between the Spanish and the Aztecs is detailed in the second volume of Clavigero's *History of Mexico*. This volume is not held at the Bibliothèque Nationale de France, so it may not have

tension: it is the opposite of the more common musical representation of the "noble savage" in French opera, with simple but highly melodious music.[103]

Crucially, with his noisy musical idiom and invocation of *alla turca* style, Spontini instead superimposed onto the Aztec music an association with the Ottoman Empire, the nation against which Napoléon had undertaken his Egyptian and Syrian campaign in 1798. The aforementioned *Description de l'Egypte*, which began publication the same year *Fernand Cortez* premiered, also included a discussion of Ottoman Egyptian music, clearly affirming its inferiority compared to Western music.[104] Its author, Guillaume André Villoteau, a member of the Opéra's chorus, had joined the campaign's scientific team as the music specialist. He had studied theoretical treatises and recorded many detailed accounts of its music in his notebooks, but the *Description de l'Egypte* provided space only for simplified and generalized reports, leading to very prejudiced viewpoints.[105] For instance, he described Egyptian music as "splitting our ears with forced, hard, and baroque modulations, ornaments that reveal an extravagant and barbarous taste, and all this performed by rude, nasal, and badly intoned voices, accompanied by instruments whose sounds are either thin and muted or shrill and piercing."[106] His response to this music shows some similarities to that of a reviewer of Spontini's opera, who judged one of the Aztec choruses as "too barbarous, . . . one hears a little flute that pierces the ears, and that produces a repulsive effect rather than a frightening one."[107] It is significant that in both instances the music is described as *barbarous*, an adjective commonly used for nations and people considered to be in need of civilization.

The musical enactment of the Aztecs' assumedly uncivilized nature was set in great relief in the opening of act 3, where the Aztec music alternates with music by the Spanish prisoners awaiting sacrifice. The latter music appealed to France's revolutionary imagination, as well as its Catholic identity. The first piece, "Le brave est au-dessus des caprices du sort" (The brave one is above the whims of fate), is a solo for Cortez's brother, Alvaro, with choral response. Its text invokes revolutionary values such as brotherhood and a willingness to die for the fatherland, while musically it references the end of the *Marseillaise*. The

---

been part of Napoléon's Bibliothèque Impériale, and the artists involved in creating *Cortez* may thus not have known about it.

103. On the representation of the "noble savage" in French opera at the time, see Andries, "Uniting the Arts to Stage the Nation," 169–75.

104. See Leoni, "Western Middle-East Music Imagery."

105. Leoni, "Western Middle-East Music Imagery," 177–78.

106. Villoteau, "De l'état actuel de l'art musical en Egypte," 614–15. The original French is quoted in Leoni, "Western Middle-East Music Imagery," 180–81.

107. *Petites affiches*, Dec. 14, 1809.

second piece is an a cappella trio for Alvaro and two of his compatriots, which specifically connects sentiments of patriotism with the idea of a religious war. It reminded reviewers of François-Joseph Gossec's unaccompanied trio "O salutaris hostia" (1784), a hymn for the Feast of Corpus Christi.[108] In 1794 this trio had been turned into the revolutionary "Hymne à la liberté," providing a clear example of how religious music was mobilized for the republican national cause,[109] and in 1803 it was used in the popular pasticcio oratorio *Saül*, sung by the Levites safeguarding the Holy ark against ungodly invaders.[110] The national and religious associations from the trio further enhanced how musical local color was mobilized to revise history; namely, it suggested that Cortés had indeed waged a religious war to abolish barbaric religious superstition and civilize its Aztec population and that Napoléon had the same goal when invading Spain.

Failed Mobilizations: The Problem of Historical Contingency

Despite all the efforts to imbue *Fernand Cortez* with a political message about civilization through imperialism, the work famously failed to fulfill its intended propagandistic purpose. French musicologist Jean Mongrédien has argued that some of the praise for Cortez's victories in the opera libretto ended up being perceived as "an affront to Napoléon," since the Peninsular War had not led to victory; subsequently, performances were suspended.[111] The reality may have been more complex. The first performance run was interrupted due to an illness of Caroline Branchu, the soprano cast as Amazily.[112] Still, *Fernand Cortez* was not the hoped-for success. In addition, with public opinion becoming increasingly hostile toward Napoléon's imperial projects in the 1810s and with the French army's atrocities in Spain and Egypt gaining publicity, the silent disappearance of *Fernand Cortez* from the Opéra's repertoire in 1812 may well have been politically motivated.[113]

108. Gossec, "O salutaris hostia," Bibliothèque Nationale de France MS-1484.

109. Gossec and Caron, "Hymne à la liberté." The use of this hymn is one of myriad examples that demonstrate how the revolutionary cults, such as the Cult of the Supreme Being, were built on religious practices, despite the strong rhetoric of dechristianization. See Tallett, "Dechristianizing France"; and Aston, "Impact of the Revolution."

110. De Chédeville and Deschamps, *Saül*, 18. The trios in *Saül* and in *Fernand Cortez* were performed by the same singers, which may have strengthened the connection between the two numbers.

111. Mongrédien, *French Music from the Enlightenment to Romanticism*, 59–60. The same information is given again without specific documentary references in Chaillou, *Napoléon et l'Opéra*, 233.

112. This was noted in the *Allgemeine musikalische Zeitung*, Feb. 21, 1810; and *L'ambigu*, Mar. 10, 1810.

113. The final performance on January 24, 1812, roughly coincided with a turning point in the Spanish campaign: on January 19 Arthur Wellesley, First Duke of Wellington, had breached the French defense wall between Portugal and Spain by winning the border fortress Ciudad Rodrigo. In recent histories of the Napoleonic Wars this event tends to be regarded as the first sign of the collapse of the French Empire, which

In a short biography of Spontini from 1840, the failure of the political message was ascribed to Spontini's music, in particular the aforementioned a cappella trio:

> [Spontini] had painted the Spanish character with so many beautiful colors, notably in the admirable *trio of the Spanish prisoners*, the first example of a trio without accompaniment, in which the exaltation of patriotism and faith stands out to such a high degree that the result ended up being diametrically opposed to the intentions of the emperor. He wanted to draw the attention to Spain, and thanks to Spontini's opera, every night one could admire the pride, courage, and fanaticism of the Spanish whose sons were the only ones to hold their heads upright against him in the middle of a subjugated Europe, and led by the least intrepid individuals, they made the eagles retreat for the first time.[114]

The music indeed provided a complicated referential framework. It created a clear opposition that could be read in light of imperialist ideology: on one side, an uncivilized population that produced barbarous music verging on noise; on the other, a civilized nation that expressed itself in a more conventionally lyrical manner, with gestures toward contemporary patriotic and religious music. There was, however, room for interpretation as to how this general imperialist framework was to be applied to the contemporary situation. After all, the choruses amalgamated references to various historical and contemporary empires: the Aztec Empire, the Ottoman Empire, the sixteenth-century Spanish kingdom of Castille and Aragon (then ruled by Charles I, who also was the Holy Roman Emperor), and France's republican/imperial ambitions since the 1789 revolution. Audiences could easily have read the prisoners' expressions of patriotism as Spanish and as an incentive to support their resistance against Napoléon and the brutality of his armies; after all, *Fernand Cortez* gloriously portrayed Spain's history as a bringer of civilization.[115] Moreover, the historically researched details of this operatic production and the claims in the libretto preface gave credence to this portrayal of sixteenth-century Spanish civilization efforts as faithful to historical accounts.

This uncertainty about how the narrative of empire was to be applied to contemporary situations was perhaps even a result of Napoléon's own use of

---

was later accelerated by the annihilation of Napoléon's Grand Armée in the disastrous Russian campaign of 1812–13. See Esdaile, *Peninsular War*, 380; and Bell, *First Total War*, 293.

114. De Loménie, *Galerie des contemporains illustres*, 24–25.

115. It is noteworthy that by 1809 allusions to revolutionary music were increasingly problematic; as the emperor was ever more criticized for his authoritarian rule, his reputation as the "son of the Revolution" had been called into question since 1807. Moreover, "La Marseillaise" had largely been supplanted by Méhul's "Chant du départ" and the song "Veillons au salut de l'Empire" in the official music scene. Dwyer, *Citizen Emperor*, 255–56; Tulard, *Napoléon et Rouget de Lisle*, 46–49.

history throughout his career. Christopher Prendergast has argued that Napoléon was the man of the moment, who believed in the pragmatics of action and
often cherry-picked from history what seemed most useful at a specific moment.
The present thus became contingent on "the often unpredictable and uncontrol-
lable temporality of intention, deed and outcome."[116] Choosing Hernán Cortés
as an example may have seemed opportune in the summer of 1808, when the
Spanish campaign had just started and Napoléon intended to stamp out the
protest quickly. However, an opera was not—and could not be—the work of a
moment; it usually took at least a year to produce. Moreover, successful operas
would be performed during multiple seasons in a continuously changing political climate. Thus, even though the censorship bureau had approved *Fernand
Cortez*, claiming that "it is unnecessary to present to his majesty an analysis of
this work, for he knows its beautiful conception, its noble and pure style, and
the happy allusion to a hero, which excites admiration," there was no guarantee
that these allusions would remain as opportune months or years later.[117] The
politically fraught context of the period between November 1809 and January
1812 when *Cortez* was performed may have made audiences eager to find ways of
silent resistance, misreading what the censors had deemed the opera's "happy
allusions."

The failed mobilization of *Fernand Cortez* is also reminiscent of a larger
problem of seeking uniformity among diversity across space and time within
Napoléon's politics of empire. In an excerpt from Emmanuel de Las Cases's
Mémorial de Sainte-Hélène, the author detailed how Napoléon reflected on his
imperialist vision in 1816, claiming that he had sought "the interests, happiness
and well-being of the European association" by binding satellite states to one
legal code and a uniform currency and measuring system.[118] Yet, as Biancamaria
Fontana has shown, Napoléon's version of imposed uniformity was also identified as a problem in contemporary anti-imperialist critique, for it was linked
to ideas of monarchical absolutism and the centralization of an empire that
stamped out "local differences and regional specificities."[119] These ideas pervaded Benjamin Constant's *De l'esprit de la conquête et de l'usurpation dans leurs
rapports avec la civilisation européenne* (*On the Spirit of Conquest and Usurpation
and Its Connections to European Civilisation*, 1814), in which modern imperialism
is characterized by an artificially imposed uniform rule, fueled by greed and

116. Prendergast, *Napoleon and History Painting*, 76.
117. Censorship report on *Fernand Cortez*, Nov. 28, 1809, Archives Nationales à Paris F²¹ 969.
118. Las Cases, *Mémorial de Sainte-Hélène*, 285.
119. Fontana, "Napoleonic Empire and the Europe of Nations," 124.

covered by a mantle of grand ideological statements.[120] Napoléon's government was diagnosed as despotic because it suppressed individuality, whereas maintaining the individuality of persons and regions was what had guarded ancient empires against despotism and made them thrive.[121] An imposed uniform reading would have been necessary for *Fernand Cortez* to serve its propagandistic purpose, yet opera in general does not lend itself to such practices, and the unprecedented attention to historical detail in the staging of this opera had emphasized the particularity of the Aztec Empire. By superimposing different historical episodes, *Fernand Cortez* provided a multiplicity of readings that allowed for both pro- and anti-imperial interpretations, as well as understandings not related to ideologies of empire.

While *Fernand Cortez* failed as an instrument of Napoleonic propaganda, it did not fail as an operatic work or in validating and disseminating the "narrative truth" of its transhistorical message about civilization and empire. It was one of a handful of operas revived after the fall of Napoléon in 1815 and was preserved in the repertoire at the Opéra until the mid-nineteenth century, and later in other places. It could serve as a model for staging the transhistorical process of humanity's progress toward an ever more civilized state and Europe/the West as the bringer of said civilization (whether through imperial force or not). As such, it continued an ideology that would remain omnipresent in historiography and theatrical works throughout the nineteenth century. More important, it showed the ideological work that can be achieved by local color and historicist representations in validating and disseminating the "narrative truth" of this transhistorical process.

. . .

This article has examined the intertwining of historiography, Orientalism/exoticism, and theater in promulgating narratives of empire and how a source-based representational method was mobilized for this purpose. It has highlighted how the librettists' seemingly innocuous claim to have "faithfully" followed history needs to be taken seriously to understand how the emphasis on historically researched local color was thought to serve the ideological work that the censors and government expected historical opera to do during the Napoleonic era— even if, in the end, that ideological work was not entirely successful. This era is a transitional one in the changing approaches to historical narration; while marked by an increased interest in a source-based reconstruction, history

---

120. Constant, *De l'esprit de la conquête et de l'usurpation*, 192–96. See also Fontana, "Napoleonic Empire and the Europe of Nations," 124–25.

121. Constant, *De l'esprit de la conquête et de l'usurpation*, 56–59, 95 (on the benefits of maintaining individuality within empires), 171 (on Napoléon's despotism).

simultaneously maintained its subservience to contemporary political leaders and their ideological projects.

The parallels in the developments of historical narration described in this article did not stop after the Napoleonic era. As many scholars have noted, the fall of the supposedly all-powerful Napoléon and his empire in 1815 had a considerable effect on how history was conceptualized by the "new school" of historians in the 1820s.[122] The 1817 revision of *Cortez* neatly shows this reconceptualization, which included a change of focus from individual heroism to man's subjectedness to historical circumstances and the tensions between various social groups (whether defined by class or ethnicity).[123] In 1809 the opera had opened with prominent displays of Cortez's leadership skills, as he burned his fleet to defy the Aztecs and his own mutinous soldiers. In the 1817 revision this display of political leadership was shortened and relegated to act 2.[124] Instead, the conflict between the two nations—the Spanish conquistadors and the Aztecs—became the focal point of the dramaturgy. The aforementioned, original act 3 scenes in which the Aztecs prepare to sacrifice the Spanish prisoners were now moved to the opening of the work. Another confrontation between the Spanish and the Aztecs largely took up the new final act.[125] The result of this revision is that the plot, rather than showcasing the heroism of Cortez, focused on the conflict between two nations and their people.[126] Introduced at the beginning of the opera, the particular historical circumstances, rather than the hero's personal ambitions, are cast as a motivator for Cortez's actions—a dramaturgy often found in later *grand opéra*.[127] Moreover, Maria Birbili has argued that the revised plot structure is more ethnographically informed and presents a more historically accurate version of colonial politics than the earlier version with its focus on the heroic conquistador.[128] Because these 1817 changes to *Cortez* antedate Thierry's famous *Lettres sur l'histoire de France* of 1820, which advocates a turn from monarchs to the masses as the focal point of historiography

122. See Reizov, *L'historiographie romantique française*, 11.

123. See Reizov, *L'historiographie romantique française*, 5–8.

124. See de Jouy, *Fernand Cortez*.

125. Act 3 of the 1817 revision also featured at its opening a highly abbreviated version of the scene between Amazily and Cortez, which in 1809 had taken up the entire second act.

126. Such changes also gave more independence to the chorus representing the crowd enacting some of the historical forces that propel the action. On the chorus's growing independence, see Gerhard, *Urbanization of Opera*, 82–90.

127. Scholars have also noticed that in other early nineteenth-century theatrical genres authors tended to turn away from attributing the actions of an individual to heroic, personal motivations and instead considered them at least partly guided by larger historical forces. See Hibberd, *French Grand Opera*, 15–16; and Gerhard, *Urbanization of Opera*, 101.

128. While Birbili's observations are valid ("Caught in Transition"), I would argue that the different political situation in France after 1815 was a more stringent motivation for de Jouy's revisions. It is true, however, that de Jouy was critical of colonialism, and Ayumi Kubo has argued that this is perceptible in both the 1809 and the 1817 libretti for *Cortez* ("Librettos of Etienne de Jouy," 59–66).

and which is often taken as a kind of manifesto for the new historiographical school, it is unclear whether it was the page that influenced the stage or the other way around.

This further points to the symbiotic relationship between more intellectual and more entertaining representations of history; after all, Kalle Pihlainen has recently emphasized that the "work of history," or how historical meaning is constructed through narrating with historical sources, is not solely the domain of scholarly historiographical works but encompasses a multiplicity of literary, theatrical, and other genres engaging with sources.[129] Opera seems a particularly fruitful object for examining this construction. Because this genre combines different arts, it allows for narratives to be presented in visual, musical, and textual ways and to interact with a multiplicity of historical sources in its production. Moreover, as opera was a prestigious export product, works like *Fernand Cortez* traveled to various theaters around Europe and sometimes even globally,[130] and their narratives were also disseminated among wide layers of society through theatrical parodies, sheet music, reviews in the press, and so on—a topic that certainly merits its own separate discussion. The transhistorical narratives embedded in opera thus had the potential to circulate widely far beyond the reach of many intellectual histories. For now, this article has shown that the "reading together" of theatrical pieces and historiography can enhance our understanding of the political work that historicism and local color did in the Napoleonic era, whether that work consisted of spreading and popularizing particular notions about history or of showing how history is conceived to be applicable to the present.

ANNELIES ANDRIES is assistant professor in musicology at Utrecht University. With Clare Siviter (University of Bristol), she guest-edited a special issue of the *Journal of War and Culture Studies*, titled "Theatrical Encounters during the Revolutionary and Napoleonic Wars" (2021). She is author of "Uniting the Arts to Stage the Nation: Le Sueur's *Ossian* (1804) in Napoleonic Paris," *Cambridge Opera Journal* (2019).

Acknowledgments

For their generous and insightful comments, the author thanks Gundula Kreuzer, Sarah Hibberd, Rebekah Ahrendt, Marco Ladd, Maarten Noorduin, the editors and three anonymous reviewers of *French Historical Studies*, and the editors of this special issue. The archival research for this article was supported by the Eugene K. Wolf Travel Grant from the American Musicological Society and a dissertation research grant from the Whitney and Betty MacMillan Center for International and Area Studies at Yale. All translations are the author's unless otherwise noted.

129. Pihlainen, *Work of History*, 95–97.

130. A concise overview of the European premieres of *Fernand Cortez* is given in Loewenberg, *Annals of Opera*, k. [col.] 612–13. In the 1830s Spontini's works, including the overture of *Fernand Cortez*, were also performed in New Orleans. See Levine, *Highbrow/Lowbrow*, 91.

APPENDIX: Repertoire of Newly Composed Operas That Premiered at the Paris Opéra, 1799–1815

May 5, 1800 [15 floréal an VIII]	*Hécube*	Score: George Granges de Fontenelle Libretto: Jean-Baptiste-Gabriel-Marie de Milcent
October 10, 1800 [18 vendémiaire an IX]	*Les Horaces*	Score: Bernardo Porta Libretto: Nicolas-François Guillard
April 12, 1801 [22 germinal an IX]	*Astyanax*	Score: Rodolphe Kreutzer Libretto: Jean-Elie Bénédo Dejaure
May 4, 1802 [14 floréal an X]	*Sémiramis*	Score: Charles-Simon Catel Libretto: Philippe Desriaux
September 14, 1802 [27 fructidor an X]	*Tamerlan*	Score: Peter von Winter Libretto: Etienne Morel de Chédeville
March 29, 1803 [8 germinal an XI]	*Proserpine*	Score: Giovanni Paisiello Libretto: Nicolas-François Guillard (after Philippe Quinault)
August 9, 1803 [21 thermidor an XI]	*Mahomet II*	Score: Louis Jadin Libretto: Georges Saulnier
February 10, 1804 [20 pluviôse an XII]	*Le connétable de Clisson*	Score: Bernardo Porta Libretto: Etienne Aignan
July 10, 1804 [21 messidor an XII]	*Ossian ou les bardes*	Score: Jean-François Le Sueur Libretto: Paul Dercy and Jacques-Marie Deschamps
April 15, 1806	*Nephtali ou les Ammonites*	Score: Félix Blangini Libretto: Etienne Aignan
August 19, 1806	*Castor et Pollux*	Score: Peter von Winter Libretto: Pierre-Joseph Bernard
October 23, 1807	*Le triomphe de Trajan*	Score: Louis-Luc de Persuis Libretto: Joseph Esménard
December 16, 1807	*La vestale*	Score: Gaspare Spontini Libretto: Etienne de Jouy
March 21, 1809	*La mort d'Adam*	Score: Jean-François Le Sueur Libretto: Nicolas-François Guillard
November 28, 1809	*Fernand Cortez*	Score: Gaspare Spontini Libretto: Etienne de Jouy and Joseph Esménard
March 23, 1810	*La mort d'Abel*	Score: Rodolphe Kreutzer Libretto: François-Benoît Hoffman

(*Continued*)

APPENDIX (*Continued*)

August 9, 1810	*Les bayadères*	Score: Charles-Simon Catel
		Libretto: Etienne de Jouy
April 16, 1811	*Sophocle*	Score: Vincenzo Fiocchi
		Libretto: Etienne Morel de Chédeville
December 17, 1811	*Les Amazones*	Score: Etienne-Nicolas Méhul
		Libretto: Etienne de Jouy
September 15, 1812	*Jérusalem délivrée*	Score: Louis Luc de Persuis
		Libretto: Pierre-Marie-François Baour-Lormain
April 6, 1813	*Les Abencérages*	Score: Luigi Cherubini
		Libretto: Etienne de Jouy
August 10, 1813	*Médée et Jason*	Score: Georges Granges de Fontenelle
		Libretto: Jean-Baptiste-Gabriel-Marie de Milcent
May 30, 1815	*La princesse de Babylone*	Score: Rodolphe Kreutzer
		Libretto: Louis-Jean-Baptiste-Etienne Vigée

Note. This repertoire list includes all evening-length operas, generally in the genre of the *tragédie lyrique*, performed at the Opéra, even if libretti and scores often gave different genre names. The Opéra's repertoire also included shorter one- or two-act operas, opera-ballets, ballets, oratorios, and patriotic and propagandistic pieces, as well as many revivals of older compositions.

References

Agnew, Vanessa. "Music's Empire." In *Enlightenment Orpheus: Music's Power in Other Worlds*, 73–120. Oxford, 2008.

Almanach impériale. Paris, [1805].

Almanach nationale de France. Paris, [1795].

Andries, Annelies. "Uniting the Arts to Stage the Nation: Le Sueur's *Ossian* (1804) in Napoleonic Paris." *Cambridge Opera Journal* 31, nos. 2–3 (2019): 153–87.

Anquetil, Louis-Pierre. *Histoire de France*. 14 vols. Paris, 1805.

Aston, Nigel. "The Impact of the Revolution on Religious Life and Practice." In *Religion and Revolution in France, 1780–1804*, 211–57. London, 2000.

Bann, Stephen. *The Clothing of Clio: A Study in the Representation of History in Nineteenth-Century Britain and France*. Cambridge, 1984.

Bartlet, M. Elisabeth C. "Etienne-Nicolas Méhul and Opera during the French Revolution, Consulate, and Empire: A Source, Archival, and Stylistic Study." PhD diss., University of Chicago, 1982.

Beale, Georgia. "Academies to Institut." *Consortium on Revolutionary Europe* 1972: 110–27.

Bell, David. *The First Total War: Napoleon's Europe and the Birth of Warfare as We Know It*. Boston, 2007.

Bellman, Jonathan D. "Musical Voyages and Their Baggage: Orientalism in Music and Critical Musicology." *Musical Quarterly* 94, no. 3 (2011): 417–38.

Betzwieser, Thomas. *Exotismus und "Türkenoper" in der französischen Musik des Ancien Régime: Studien zu einem ästhetischen Phänomen.* Laaber, 1993.

Birbili, Maria. "Caught in Transition: Exoticism in Gaspare Spontini's *Fernand Cortès.*" In *Opera, Exoticism, and Visual Culture,* edited by Hyunseon Lee and Naomi Segal, 13–30. Oxford, 2015.

Bloechl, Olivia. "Race, Empire, and Early Music." In *Rethinking Difference in Music Scholarship,* edited by Olivia Bloechl, Melanie Lowe, and Jeffrey Kallberg, 77–107. Cambridge, 2015.

Bourdon, Léonard. *Recueil des actions heroïques et civiques des républicains français,* no. 1. Paris, an II [1793–94].

Chaillou, David. *Napoléon et l'Opéra: La politique sur la scène, 1810–1815.* Paris, 2004.

Charlton, David, ed. *The Cambridge Companion to Grand Opera.* Cambridge, 2003.

Charlton, David. *Grétry and the Growth of Opéra Comique.* Cambridge, 1986.

Clarke, Joseph. "Encountering the Sacred: British and French Soldiers in the Revolutionary and Napoleonic Mediterranean." In *Militarized Cultural Encounters in the Long Nineteenth Century: Making War, Mapping Europe,* edited by Joseph Clarke and John Horne, 49–73. Cham, 2018.

Clavigero, Francesco Saverio. *The History of Mexico: Collected from Spanish and Mexican Historians, from Manuscripts and Ancient Paintings of the Indians. . . .* London, 1787.

Constant, Benjamin. *De l'esprit de la conquête et de l'usurpation dans leurs rapports avec la civilisation européenne.* N.p., 1814.

Dacier, Bon-Joseph. *Rapport historique sur les progrès de l'histoire et de la littérature ancienne depuis 1789 et sur leur état actuel.* Paris, 1810.

Darlow, Mark. *Staging the Revolution: Cultural Politics and the Paris Opéra, 1789–1794.* Oxford, 2012.

D'Auria, Matthew. *The Shaping of French National Identity: Narrating the Nation's Past, 1715–1830.* Cambridge, 2020.

de Chédeville, Etienne Morel, and Jacques-Marie Deschamps. *Saül.* Paris, 1803.

de Jouy, Etienne. *Fernand Cortez, ou la conquête du Mexique.* Paris, 1817.

de Jouy, Etienne, and Joseph-Alphonse Esménard. *Fernand Cortez, ou la conquête du Mexique.* Paris, 1809.

De Loménie. *Galerie des contemporains illustres par un homme de rien, no. 111: Spontini.* Paris, [1840].

Den Boer, Pim. "Historical Writing in France, 1800–1914." In vol. 4 of *The Oxford History of Historical Writing,* edited by Stuart Macintyre, Juan Maiguashca, and Attila Pók, 184–203. Oxford, 2011.

de Solís, Antonio. *Histoire de la conquête du Mexique ou de la Nouvelle Espagne.* Paris, 1691.

Döhring, Sieghart, and Sabine Henze-Döhring. *Oper und Musikdrama im 19. Jahrhundert.* Laaber, 1997.

Duplessis, Charles-Pierre. *Pizarre, ou la conquête du Pérou.* Paris, 1785.

Dwyer, Philip. *The Citizen Emperor: Napoleon in Power.* New Haven, CT, 2013.

Esdaile, Charles. *The Peninsular War: A New History.* London, 2002.

Fontana, Biancamaria. "The Napoleonic Empire and the Europe of Nations." In *The Idea of Europe: From Antiquity to the European Union,* edited by Anthony Pagden, 116–28. Cambridge, 2001.

Fourier, Joseph, ed. *Description de l'Egypte ou recueil des observations et des recherches qui ont été faites en Egypte pendant l'expédition de l'armée française.* Vol. 1. Paris, 1809.

Frantz, Pierre. *L'esthétique du tableau dans le théâtre du XVIIIe siècle.* Paris, 1998.

Gerhard, Anselm. "*Fernand Cortez* und *Le Siège de Corinthe*: Spontini und die Anfänge der Grand Opera." *Atti del terzo congresso internazionale di studi Spontiniani* 1985: 93–111.

Gerhard, Anselm. *The Urbanization of Opera: Music Theater in Paris in the Nineteenth Century,* translated by Mary Whittall. Chicago, 1998.

Gossec, François-Joseph, and Caron. "Hymne à la liberté." Paris, [1794].

Grigsby, Darcy. "Classicism, Nationalism, and History: The Prix Décennaux of 1810 and the Politics of Art under the Post-revolutionary Empire." PhD diss., University of Michigan, 1995.

Hallman, Diana R. *Opera, Liberalism, and Antisemitism in Nineteenth-Century France: The Politics of Halévy's "La Juive."* Cambridge, 2002.

Hambridge, Katherine. "The Performance of History: Music, Identity, and Politics in Berlin, 1800–1815." PhD diss., University of Cambridge, 2013.

Hibberd, Sarah. *French Grand Opera and the Historical Imagination.* Cambridge, 2009.

Hibberd, Sarah. "'L'épique en action': *Fernand Cortez* and the Aesthetic of Spectacle." Paper presented at the Annual Conference of the Royal Music Association, London, Sept. 5, 2016.

Hugo, Victor. *Cromwell.* Paris, 1836.

Hunter, Mary. "The 'Alla Turca' Style in the Late Eighteenth Century: Race and Gender in the Symphony and the Seraglio." In *The Exotic in Western Music,* edited by Jonathan Bellman, 43–73. Boston, 1998.

Irving, David R. M. "Comparative Organography in Early Modern Empires." *Music and Letters* 90, no. 3 (2009): 372–98.

Kubo, Ayumi. "The Librettos of Etienne de Jouy (1807–1829): A Difficult Career during the Napoleonic and Restoration Eras." PhD diss., King's College London, 2013.

Las Cases, Emmanuel de. *Mémorial de Sainte-Hélène ou journal où se trouve consigné, jour par jour, ce qu'a dit et fait Napoléon durant dix-huit mois.* Vol. 5. Paris, 1823.

Lattanzi, Alessandro. "Spontini's Panoply: The Sound of Martial Music and the Clamour of War in *Fernand Cortez.*" In *Oper und Militärmusik im "langen" 19. Jahrhundert: Sujets, Beziehungen, Einflüsse,* edited by Achim Hofer, 25–61. Würzburg, 2020.

Le Chevalier, Jean-Baptiste. *Voyage dans la Troade, ou tableau de la plaine de Troie dans son état actuel.* Paris, an VII [1798–99].

Lemercier, Népomucène Louis. *Christophe Colomb.* Paris, 1809.

Lentz, Thierry, ed. *Quand Napoléon inventait la France: Dictionnaire des institutions politiques, administratives et de cour du Consulat et de l'Empire.* Paris, 2008.

Leoni, Stefano. "Western Middle-East Music Imagery in the Face of Napoleon's Enterprise in Egypt: From Mere Eurocentric Exoticism, to Very Organized Orientalistic Ears." *International Review of the Aesthetics and Sociology of Music* 38, no. 2 (2007): 171–96.

Levacher de Charnois, Jean-Charles. *Recherches sur les costumes et sur les théâtres de toutes les nations, tant anciennes que modernes.* Paris, 1790, repr. 1802.

Levine, Lawrence. *Highbrow/Lowbrow: The Emergence of Cultural Hierarchy in America.* Cambridge, MA, 1988.

Libby, Dennis. "Gaspare Spontini and His French and German Operas." PhD diss., Princeton University, 1969.

Locke, Ralph P. *Musical Exoticism: Images and Reflections.* Cambridge, 2009.

Locke, Ralph P. *Music and the Exotic from the Renaissance to Mozart.* Cambridge, 2015.

Lockhart, James. *We People Here: Nahuatl Accounts of the Conquest of Mexico.* Eugene, OR, 2004.

Loewenberg, Alfred. *Annals of Opera, 1597–1940.* London, 1978.

Madelin, Louis. *Les mémoires de Fouché.* Paris, 1945.

Maehder, Jürgen. "Die Darstellung der Conquista Mexicos im Übergang von der Opera seria des Settecento zur Oper des Empire." In *Spontini und die Oper im Zeitalter Napoleons*, edited by Detlef Altenburg, Arnold Jacobshagen, Arne Langer, Jürgen Maehder, and Saskia Woyke, 157–88. Sinzig, 2014.

Malakis, Emile. "The First Use of *Couleur Locale* in French Literary Criticism." *Modern Language Notes* 60, no. 2 (1945): 98–99.

Marmontel, Jean-François. *Les Incas, ou la déstruction de l'empire du Pérou*. Vol. 2. Paris, 1777.

McClellan, Andrew. *Inventing the Louvre: Art, Politics, and the Origin of the Modern Museum in Eighteenth-Century Paris*. Cambridge, 1994.

Mongrédien, Jean. *French Music from the Enlightenment to Romanticism, 1789–1830*, translated by Sylvain Frémaux. Portland, OR, 1986.

Mungen, Anno. "Wagner, Spontini, und die Grand Opéra." In *Richard Wagner und seine "Lehrmeister": Bericht der Tagung am musikwissenschaftlichen Institut der Johannes-Gutenberg-Universität Mainz, 6./7. Juni 1997: Egon Voss zum 60. Geburtstag. Schriften zur Musikwissenschaft*, edited by Christoph Hellmut Mahling and Kristina Pfarr, 129–44. Mainz, 1999.

Muthu, Sankar. *Enlightenment against Empire*. Princeton, NJ, 2003.

Pihlainen, Kalle. *The Work of History: Constructivism and a Politics of the Past*. Abingdon, 2019.

Pisani, Michael V. *Imagining Native America in Music*. New Haven, CT, 2005.

Pixérécourt, René-Charles Guilbert de. *Pizarre ou la conquête du Pérou*. Paris, an XI [1802].

Pottinger, Mark A. *The Staging of History in France: The Characterization of Historical Figures in French Grand Opéra during the Reign of Louis Philippe*. Saarbrücken, 2009.

Prendergast, Christopher. *Napoleon and History Painting: Antoine-Jean Gros's "La Bataille d'Eylau."* Oxford, 1997.

Reizov, Boris. *L'historiographie romantique française, 1815–1830*. Moscow, 1962.

Roa-de-la-Carrera, Cristián. "Francisco López de Gómara and *La Conquista de México*." In *Chimalpahin's Conquest: A Nahua Historian's Rewriting of Francisco Lopez de Gomára's "La Conquista de México,"* edited by Susan Schroeder, Anne J. Cruz, Cristián Roa-de-la-Carrera, and David E. Tavárez, 35–49. Stanford, CA, 2010.

Rossi, Henri. *Opéras historiques français, 1767–1989*. Paris, 2019.

Roure, P. *La Cortésiade, ou le Nouveau monde, poème en 12 chants, enrichi de notes historiques, géographiques et d'histoire naturelle sur le Nouveau monde*. Paris, 1808.

Said, Edward. *Orientalism*. New York, 1978.

Samuels, Maurice. *The Spectacular Past: Popular History and the Novel in Nineteenth-Century France*. Ithaca, NY, 2004.

Sanchez, Jean Pierre. "Voltaire et sa tragédie américaine *Alzire* (1736)." *Caravelle*, no. 58 (1992): 17–37.

Setari, Nicola. "Notes on Transhistoricity: Between Art Theory and Curatorial Practice." In Wittocx et al., *Transhistorical Museum*, 24–36.

Seth, Catriona. "L'Institut et les prix littéraires." In *L'empire des muses: Napoléon, les arts et les lettres: Littérature et politique*, edited by Jean-Claude Bonnet and Jean-Claude Berchet, 111–31. Paris, 2004.

Spontini, Gaspare. *Fernand Cortez, ou la conquête du Mexique*. Paris, 1809.

Stevenson, Robert Murrell. *Music in Aztec and Inca Territory*. Berkeley, CA, 1968.

Tallett, Frank. "Dechristianizing France: The Year II and the Revolutionary Experience." In *Religion, Society, and Politics in France since 1789*, edited by Frank Tallett and Nicholas Atkin, 1–28. London, 1991.

Tarver, H. Micheal, and Emily Slape, eds. *The Spanish Empire: A Historical Encyclopedia*. Vol. 1. Santa Barbara, CA, 2006.

Thierry, Augustin. *Lettres sur l'histoire de France pour servir d'introduction à l'étude de cette histoire*. Paris, 1820, repr. 1827.

Tulard, Jean. *Napoléon et Rouget de Lisle: "Marche Consulaire" contre "Marseillaise."* Paris, 2001.

Valadier. *Cora*. Paris, 1791.

Van Oss, Adriaan C. *Catholic Colonialism: A Parish History of Guatemala, 1524–1821*. Cambridge, 2002.

Villoteau, Guillaume André. "De l'état actuel de l'art musical en Egypte, ou relation historique et descriptive des recherches et observations faites sur la musique en ce pays." In Fourier, *Description de l'Egypte*, 607–846.

Von Kulessa, Rotraud, and Catriona Seth, eds. *L'idée de l'Europe au siècle des Lumières*. Cambridge, 2017.

Whitehead, Barbara. "Revising the Revisionists: Louis-Pierre Anquetil and the Saint Bartholomew's Day Massacre." In *Politics, Ideology, and the Law in Early Modern Europe: Essays in Honor of J. H. M. Salmon*, edited by Adrianna E. Bakos, 159–73. Rochester, NY, 1994.

Wittocx, Eva, Ann Demeester, Peter Carpreau, Melanie Bühler, and Xander Karskens, eds. *The Transhistorical Museum: Mapping the Field*. Amsterdam, 2018.

Wolff, Larry. *The Singing Turk: Ottoman Power and Operatic Emotion on the European Stage from the Siege of Vienna to the Age of Napoleon*. Stanford, CA, 2016.

Woolf, Stuart. "Europe and Its Historians." *Contemporary European History* 12, no. 3 (2003): 323–37.

Napoleonic Commemoration on the Operatic Stage

The Retour des Cendres *and Halévy's* La Reine de Chypre

DIANA R. HALLMAN

ABSTRACT   The *retour des cendres*, the commemorative return of Napoleon's remains in 1840, represented an important gesture of Napoleonic restoration in the July Monarchy, along with the creation of monuments, paintings, histories, plays, and encomiums to the defeated emperor. The monarchy's commemoration expanded to the stage of the Paris Opéra in 1841 with the appearance of *La reine de Chypre*, the five-act grand opera by Fromental Halévy and Henri de Saint-Georges, which reverberated with sonic, visual, literary, and political allusions to the Napoleonic legend and overt references to the ceremonial return of the emperor's ashes, including its use of the *grandes trompettes* from Napoléon's cortege and Invalides service. In its historical reframing of Catarina Cornaro's early fifteenth-century rise to power in Cyprus and defiance of Venetian tyranny, the nostalgic portrayal of exiled French chevaliers, particularly the dying king Lusignan, evoked France's fallen hero as it joined in the dynamic reshaping of imperial memory.

KEYWORDS   Napoleon, July Monarchy, commemoration, Opéra, Paris

T he *retour des cendres*, the return of Napoléon's remains from Sainte-Hélène to France in 1840, represented an important gesture of Napoleonic restoration in the July Monarchy, along with the creation of monuments, paintings, histories, plays, and encomiums to the defeated emperor. In 1841, Napoleonic commemoration expanded to the stage of the Paris Opéra (Académie Royale de Musique) with the appearance of *La reine de Chypre*, the five-act grand opera by French composer Fromental Halévy and librettist Henri de Saint-Georges. In the opera's poignant portrayal of exiled French warriors within a theatrical reframing of Catarina Cornaro's early fifteenth-century rise to power in Cyprus and defiance of Venetian tyranny, it engaged in the memorialization of France's fallen hero through an intertextual mix of sonic, visual, literary, and political allusions to the Napoleonic legend, as well as overt links to the ceremonies of

French Historical Studies • Vol. 45, No. 2 (April 2022) • DOI 10.1215/00161071-9531996
Copyright 2022 by Society for French Historical Studies

the *retour*. Amid the July Monarchy's assertive reclamations of national memory, the Paris Opéra stage functioned as a metaphorical museum: through the facade of a distant time and place so characteristic of French grand opera, the exiled French hero Lusignan of *La reine* appears as Napoleonic cipher, alongside other historical-allegorical figures that would play significant roles in Louis-Philippe's historical projects intended to glorify the nation but also appease political divisions within it. In the opera's final act, this hero—slowly dying in his island exile—joins the icon of the crusader, his romantic rival and fellow exile Gérard, who dons religious-warrior emblems of a chevalier of Rhodes (originally Malta) and leads the victorious battle of the Cypriots over the Venetians. Their beloved Cypriot queen, now portrayed as a Joan of Arc figure, joins Gérard in the opera's culminating scene to pledge loyalty to the dying Lusignan and to "his God, his king, his liberty!"

Although *La reine de Chypre* can be viewed simply as a captivating theatrical tale of tragic love and rivalry set against events and conflicts of a remote history in an exotic setting, one that absorbed medievalist trends coursing through French plays, operas, and novels of the 1820s and 1830s, it also engages with history as political opera. Like many French grand operas—works in four or five acts created for the Paris Opéra stage and characterized in part by opulent spectacle, historically researched costumes, extended choral or polychoral scenes, innovative orchestration, and melodramatic endings—*La reine* reverberated with contemporary sociopolitical implications.[1] Although the genre had long been viewed in the twentieth century as a spectacle-driven art designed primarily to entertain the ascendant bourgeoisie of the July Monarchy—a description solidified by William Crosten in 1948[2]—Jane Fulcher shifted the scholarly focus to the art form's deeper political import in *The Nation's Image: French Grand Opera as Politics and Politicized Art* (1987). In her emphasis on the Opéra's participation in political discourse under Louis-Philippe, more nuanced and malleable than in revolutionary theatrical works that had served as "explicit ideological propaganda," Fulcher questioned "how the image of the Opéra and the repertoire changed in a continuing process of subtle adaptation" within a shifting political context and "how the works themselves reacted back on this context and helped to influence political perceptions."[3] Other authors enhanced her

---

1. Following Daniel Auber's *La muette de Portici* of 1828, the genre of French grand opera largely developed within the July Monarchy, although important new works were completed after 1848, including Giacomo Meyerbeer's *Le prophète* (1849) and *L'Africaine* (1865) and Giuseppe Verdi's *Don Carlos* (1867). The genre rivaled Italian opera in popularity in European musical capitals throughout the nineteenth century and influenced Wagnerian and Russian opera. For more on the genre's characteristics and social-political significance, see Fulcher, *Nation's Image*; Charlton, *Cambridge Companion to Grand Opera*; and Hibberd, *French Grand Opera*.

2. Crosten, *French Grand Opera*; Fulcher, *Nation's Image*.

3. Fulcher, *Nation's Image*, 4, 8–9.

pursuit of political meanings in French grand opera, including Nicholas White, who wrote in *The Cambridge Companion to Grand Opera* that "grand opera often constructs history in terms of its moments of inauguration and crisis."[4] In *Opera, Liberalism, and Antisemitism in Nineteenth-Century France: The Politics of Halévy's "La Juive,"* I interrogate the historical subject of the composer's first and most successful grand opera, viewing its political subtext as an exploration of the "Jewish question" concerning the place of Jews in the modern nation. Through *La Juive*'s portrayal of Inquisition-like actions of the Council of Constance (1414–18), the persecution of Jews by the council and Christian mobs, Rachel's ambiguous Christian-Jewish identity, and the dual-sided religious fanaticism of the cardinal and Eléazar, the opera resonated with renewed debates on social-religious intolerance and the fuller integration of Jews within Catholic France that circulated in the writings of liberal, Jewish and non-Jewish authors, as well as discussions of the 1831 law of the "culte israélite" in governmental houses.[5] In Mark Pottinger's study of four French grand operas, including *La reine de Chypre*, he draws comparisons between the historiography of Jules Michelet and grand opera narratives of historical figures who idealistically and anarchically transcend their former lives "to embrace a higher union with society"; Sarah Hibberd also examines the "striking" parallels between Michelet's "rhetorical strategies" and those of grand opera, while noting the genre's relationship to a "general awakening of historical consciousness" across Europe.[6] Hibberd acknowledges grand opera's multiplicity and ambiguity of meanings that emerge from its varied "conceptualisations of history: as an isolated, suspended moment in a particular relationship with the present; as a combination of faithful and fabricated 'authentic' memories; as a series of tableaux encouraging reflection; as reportage; as (variously) cathartic, reassuring or inspirational interpretations of events."[7]

In French grand opera, "authentic" and "fabricated" memories could be refracted through modifications of time, place, and character identity but at times directly evoked through real events of French history. During the first decade of the July Monarchy, Giacomo Meyerbeer and Eugène Scribe's *Les*

---

4. White, "Fictions and Librettos," 57.

5. Hallman, *Opera, Liberalism, and Antisemitism,* 9–12, 150–209, 254–56. See, e.g., Halévy, *Résumé de l'histoire des Juifs modernes.* Joseph Mérilhou, the *ministre de l'instruction publique et des cultes,* introduced the 1831 law in the Chambre des Députés, a clear turn from Charles X's "retrograde" clerical policies of the late 1820s; he appealed to his colleagues and the nation to "erase the last vestiges of an oppression that must never be reborn" and to accept Jews as "French citizens, rather than *réligionnaires* divided [from the rest of society] by their religion" (quoted in Hallman, *Opera, Liberalism, and Antisemitism,* 9). This and other translations are mine unless otherwise noted.

6. Pottinger, "Staging of History in France," 7–26, 48, 66–67; Hibberd, *French Grand Opera,* 12–16, 62–63.

7. Hibberd, *French Grand Opera,* 12.

Huguenots (1836) drew on the contested memories of the St. Bartholomew's Day Massacre of 1572, in resonance with Marie-Joseph Chénier's play *Charles IX ou la Saint-Barthélemy* of 1789 and several novels and dramas of the late 1820s.[8] By the early 1840s Halévy's and Casimir and Germain Delavigne's *Charles VI* (1843), set in the fifteenth century following the Battle of Agincourt, recalled France's historical battles as it reinterpreted the story of the "mad king" Charles VI in a veiled nationalistic reflection of current events in France. As Sarah Hibberd and I have explored, *Charles VI*'s anti-British plot elements, references to France's historical battles with England, belligerent words, and patriotic music tapped into national myths as they captured political *actualité* surrounding the eastern crisis of 1840: shortly after England's Lord Palmerston set up a coalition of European powers to oppose France's alliance with Egypt, foreign and prime minister Adolphe Thiers began to prepare for war. In the aftermath of the averted crisis, the opera's prominent public display of anti-British sentiments led François Guizot, Thiers's more peaceable and conservative replacement as foreign minister, to request changes to its libretto (particularly the phrase "Guerre aux anglais!"), as reported in the press and evidenced by Opéra documents.[9]

In this article my consideration of *La reine de Chypre*'s ties to the political moment of the early 1840s expands the study of French grand opera's role in confronting and transforming national memory, with a particular focus on the evocation of Napoleonic memory within the July Monarchy. As common to French operas of this and earlier periods, affected by both preventive and external censorship (as exhibited by Guizot's intrusion in *Charles VI*'s libretto), its mediation of past and present operates not only through historical displacement but also through largely symbolic, semiotic, and nonliteral complexes of visual, musical, and intertextual references. Although the opera's meanings also hinge on its use of the icons of Joan of Arc and the medieval crusader-chevalier, I contend that *La reine*'s Napoleonic allusions are equally (and perhaps more immediately) significant to its relevance to the political present. *La reine*'s portrayal of two exiled French heroes in an island setting—on the Mediterranean island of Cyprus (with plot links to the island of Rhodes)—invites remembrances of islands associated with the emperor: Corsica, the island of his birth; Elba, the island of his first exile in 1814, but especially Sainte-Hélène, the island of his

8. For a listing of dramas portraying the massacre, including Charles d'Outrepont's *La Saint-Barthélemi* (1826), Charles de Rémusat's play *La Saint-Barthélemy* (1828), and Louis-Ferdinand Hérold's *opéra comique Le pré aux clercs* (1832), see Thorel, "Romantics and the St Bartholomew's Day Massacre," 22–23.

9. In addition to my presentations on "l'affaire ministérielle de *Charles VI*" at the American Musicological Society (1999) and the International Conference on Nineteenth-Century Music (2000), see my brief examination of these political-operatic connections in Hallman, "Grand Operas of Fromental Halévy," 245–46. See also Hibberd's more expansive treatment on the work's historical-political significance in *French Grand Opera*, 114–22.

final days. Its story of triumph over tyranny, of the victory of French heroes and iconic French heroine over Venetian despotism, relates symbolically to Napoleonic ideology and efforts to free Venice from its oppressive councils in his Italian campaign of 1796–97, as well as to early texts linked to his anti-Venetian actions. While recognizing that the "outer drama" of La reine, with its adaptations of time, place, and personages, obscures the opera's contemporary meanings, I argue that its intermedial and intertextual links to Napoleonic heroism, exile, and death and its evocations of the "theater" of the retour des cendres in the prestigious theater of the Opéra—most pointedly with the onstage performance of grandes trompettes from Napoléon's cortege and funeral service—reveal an underlying engagement with what Maurice Samuels calls the "politics of Imperial nostalgia."[10]

Such nostalgia belongs to shifting forms in the nineteenth century, particularly the nostalgia of patriotic sentiment, or l'amour du pays, as described by Thomas Dodman: no longer the "deadly," melancholic emotion of homesick soldiers during the Napoleonic Wars, Napoleonic nostalgia during the July Monarchy represented a "new kind of benign longing for an idealized past."[11] Imperial nostalgia, long embraced by the Bonapartist cult, would become an important political tool in Louis-Philippe's juste-milieu memorializing of this politically divisive figure. His aim to find a balance and reconciliation between opposing republican, royalist, and Bonapartist ideologies aligned with his recognition that an adaptation of Napoléon's legacy, rather than a rejection of it, could offer renewed power and glory to the Monarchy.[12] As Michael Paul Driskel notes, the return of Napoléon's body to France "might be considered Louis-Philippe's assertion that he was strong or secure enough to bring a major ideological adversary into his synthetic embrace."[13] This embrace also extended to the reclamation of the "lost soldiers" of Napoléon's army who had been "denied any official recognition or public commemoration until the 1830s."[14] In the public ceremonies of the retour, as in La reine, remembrances of Napoléon as valiant warrior and revolutionary hero overshadowed those of Napoléon as emperor: though Driskel describes the structure of the commemoration as "liturgical ritual," Victor Hugo found the cortege "too exclusively military," apt for "Bonaparte, but not Napoléon."[15]

10. Samuels, Spectacular Past, 109.
11. Dodman, What Nostalgia Was, 118, 138–40. Dodman underpins his study with an examination of nostalgia as a clinical disease.
12. Hazareesingh, "Napoleonic Memory," 749.
13. Driskel, As Befits a Legend, 29.
14. Dodman, What Nostalgia Was, 118–20.
15. Driskel, As Befits a Legend, 32; Hugo, "Choses vues," 47: "Le cortege a été beau, mais trop exclusivement militaire, suffisant pour Bonaparte, non pour Napoléon."

The *Retour des Cendres* and the Politics of Imperial Memory

In historical assessments of the *retour des cendres*, scholars have focused attention on the extravagant military and religious ceremonies from embarkment to burial, the rich symbolism and visual design of the Invalides tomb, and the exalted eulogies to the emperor.[16] More fundamentally, they have evaluated the significance of the *retour*'s commemoration in light of fluctuating views and myths of Napoléon throughout the nineteenth century within varied political contexts, from the Restoration to the Second Empire. Sudhir Hazareesingh has explained that, in the years after the dissolution of the First Empire, the popular and institutional mythologizing of Napoléon as national hero vied with harsh portrayals of the imperial Napoléon as corrupt, despotic, and even criminal by liberal writers such as François Guizot, the young Benjamin Constant, Germaine de Staël, and Alexis de Tocqueville.[17] As Hazareesingh writes, the memory of Bonaparte as "warrior, ruler, and upholder of the values of the French Revolution" was reclaimed not only by Jacobin and Bonapartist republican groups during the Restoration but also by governmental institutions of the July Monarchy, and later the Second Empire, which would become primary restorers of the defeated emperor's image.[18] Hazareesingh notably positions France's rehabilitation of Napoléon more in "the realm of commemorations and symbols" than in "substantive texts" that have served as the main sources of historiography."[19]

The *retour des cendres*, although a central event within this commemorative, symbolic realm, joined with other institutional gestures of Napoleonic homage and restoration that proliferated during the two decades of the July Monarchy, as the government actively attempted to recover the imperial legacy as a legitimate part of France's national history. One manifestation of the government's Napoleonic reconciliation came in the form of historical battle paintings, commissioned by Louis-Philippe for his new Museum of the History of France, inaugurated in 1837 in the Versailles Palace and dedicated to "toutes les gloires de la France" (all the glories of France). Among images evoking the

---

16. Studies of Napoléon's commemoration and tomb include Humbert, *Napoléon aux Invalides*; Martineau, *Le retour des cendres*; and Driskel, *As Befits a Legend*. Driskel discusses the design of his ornate sarcophagus by Louis Visconti and, after a long delay, its completion in 1861 (8–10).

17. Hazareesingh, "Napoleonic Memory," 747.

18. Hazareesingh, "Napoleonic Memory," 747. Citing Jean Lucas-Dubreton's *Le culte de Napoléon*, Hazareesingh notes the importance of French Romantic authors Hugo, Balzac, and Stendhal in contributing to the restoration of Napoléon's image; see also Descotes, *La légende de Napoléon*.

19. Hazareesingh, "Napoleonic Memory," 748–49. Hazareesingh wrote further of "the evolving representation of the Napoleonic heritage in France" that "decisively determined the ideological structure and orientations of French liberalism" (*Legend of Napoléon*, 23–24). See also Mellon, "July Monarchy."

dynasties of France and juxtaposing revolutionary and imperial victories were paintings by Horace Vernet of Napoléon's triumphant battles, including those over the Prussians in the Battle of Jena (Iena) of 1806 and the Austrians in the Battle of Wagram of 1809. Bonapartist symbols also appeared in official and unofficial images of Louis-Philippe himself, merging with the revolutionary emblems of the tricolor and his National Guard uniform, which he had worn at the meeting seeking Lafayette's endorsement at the Hôtel de Ville on July 31, in the immediate aftermath of *les Trois Glorieuses* of 1830. In Eugène Lami's non-commissioned painting that commemorates this meeting, the artist places Napoléon's Vendôme Column, with a tricolor flag that had replaced the Restoration's fleur-de-lis, in the foggy background over the right shoulder of Louis-Philippe on horseback.[20] Images of a reglorified Napoléon also appeared in panoramas by the Napoleonic soldier turned artist Jean-Charles Langlois, as well as in histories such as Laure de Saint-Ouën's *Histoire de Napoléon* (1833), the reprint of Jacques de Norvin's *Histoire de Napoléon* (1839) illustrated by Denis-Auguste-Marie Raffet, and Paul-Mathieu Laurent de l'Ardèche's *Histoire de l'empereur Napoléon* (1842) illustrated by Horace Vernet.[21]

Three years after the inauguration of Louis-Philippe's history museum, the *retour des cendres* would intensify the monarchy's Napoleonic restoration. The extended, multistaged commemoration, which had been proposed by foreign and prime minister Adolphe Thiers,[22] began in November 1840 with the retrieval of Napoléon's remains from Sainte-Hélène, the South Atlantic island where the emperor had been exiled after his final defeat until his death. Louis-Philippe's third son, François d'Orléans, Prince de Joinville and admiral of the French Navy, escorted the remains on their journey to Cherbourg on the ship *Belle-Poule*, then to Val-de-la-Haye on the steamboat *La Normandie*, and finally to Courbevoie on the smaller vessel *La dorade*. After a delegation of government officials came aboard *La dorade*, docked at a quay on the left bank of the Seine a few miles from Paris on December 15, the public celebrations began.[23] Surrounded by cheering crowds lining the banks, a cortege of soldiers and clergy,

20. Marrinan, *Painting Politics*, 6, fig. 6. Napoléon's first ideas for the column at the Place Vendôme, modeled after Trajan's Roman column and commemorating French military victories, came in 1803; dedicated to Napoléon's Grande Armée, the column was inaugurated on August 15, 1810.

21. Samuels, *Spectacular Past*, 50–51, 69–77, 92–96. See also Hibberd, *French Grand Opera*, 122–23.

22. Mellon, "July Monarchy," 74. Notably, Thiers had already immersed himself in writing a multi-volume history of the consulate and empire, *Histoire du Consulat et de l'Empire*, published in Paris, Brussels, and London from 1845.

23. This scene was later depicted in the 1867 painting *L'arrivée de la Dorade à Courbevoie, 14 décembre 1840*, by Henri Félix Emmanuel Philippoteaux (1815–84), an artist who re-created scenes of Napoléon's war victories, such as the Battle of Rivoli in *Bataille gagnée par le Général Bonaparte le 14 janvier 1797* (1845).

FIGURE 1 *Débarquement des cendres de Napoléon à Courbevoie*, by Antoine Ferogio, 1841. Paris Musées.

led by Abbé Felix Coquereau and met by the Prince de Joinville, proceeded with the draped casket to a hundred-foot-high Grecian temple, where the body would remain for two hours (fig. 1). An imperial eagle, symbol of Napoléon's rule and Grande Armée, adorned the top of the temple, and tricolored banners decorated the back of the ornate funeral carriage that would then carry the emperor's body into Paris. Gilded wheels supported the gilded base of the massive carriage, with Grecian statues atop a pedestal that contained Napoléon's arms. The immense, largely military cortege organized by Marshal de Gérard would include, by stages, hundreds of sailors from the *Belle-Poule*, members of the National Guard, active troops, and veteran soldiers and aides-de-camp of the Napoleonic Wars, who accompanied the carriage drawn by sixteen festooned black horses. In the final stages of the commemoration in Paris, Napoléon's carriage and proces-sional would move past thousands of spectators (some singing "La Marseillaise"), alongside sites and monuments signifying the emperor's reign as well as the mutability of French memory—including the Luxor Obelisk installed in 1836 by Louis-Philippe at the center of the Place de la Concorde and the Arc de Triomphe, also completed in 1836, thirty years after Napoléon himself had begun planning the project. Temporary statues lined the route, including "an encyclopedic assemblage of figures from French history" placed on the Esplanade des Invalides; after the cortege arrived at the Invalides, the casket was shifted to the central cupola, and then to the chapel, where Louis-Philippe and institutional officials received the emperor's remains.[24]

During the long procession and in the Invalides funeral service, the intersecting musical worlds of Parisian lyric theaters and Conservatoire played important commemorative roles. Halévy, Opéra composer, Conservatoire professor, and Académie member, contributed a funeral march that was scored for a military band that included thirty-one distinctive ceremonial trumpets designed on "antique models" and expressly manufactured for the occasion.[25] A governmental committee also commissioned Daniel Auber, another leading composer of French grand opera, and Adolphe Adam, an adept creator of ballets, to write marches: *La revue et gazette musicale* announced that Halévy's march would be performed from Rouen to Neuilly, just west of Paris, and that Auber's would be heard as the funeral carriage passed the Arc de Triomphe.[26] Hector Berlioz, irritated that a request for him to write a march came only two weeks before the ceremony, refused, opting instead to schedule a December 13 performance at the Conservatoire featuring his cantata *Le cinq mai*, written in 1835 in honor of Napoléon's death.[27] Letters of Adam and Berlioz claim that the frigid weather or difficulties with coordinating music and movement prevented Halévy's march from being performed along the intended route;[28] however, it was featured at the Invalides service and in an open-to-the-press rehearsal at the Opéra the evening before. Critic Henri Blanchard admired the rhythms and orchestration of Halévy's march, noting the "picturesque and powerful effect" of the "new trumpets or tubas."[29] A reviewer for *Le ménestrel* also spoke of the "new effect" of the "antique trumpets" and "beautiful and noble things" in Halévy's march.[30] For the solemn musical tributes in the church of the Invalides,

24. Driskel, *As Befits a Legend*, 10, 30–32; Humbert, "Le parcours parisien et son décor," 52; Langlé, *Funérailles de l'empereur Napoléon*, 28–32.
25. Halévy, *Marche héroïque pour les funérailles de l'empereur Napoléon*, Bibliothèque Nationale de France (hereafter BNF), Département de la Musique, MS 8676. Florenc Gétreau gives the number of thirty-one trumpets in the cortege, some of them now housed in the Musée Instrumental du Conservatoire de Musique de Paris. Gétreau states emphatically that their construction was wrongly attributed to Adolphe Sax by Gustave Chouquet instead of to the true builder, M. Schiltz of Maison Darche ("Musique de circonstance," 73–76).
26. *La revue et gazette musicale*, Nov. 26, 1840, 573, also quoted in Gétreau, "Musique de circonstance," 73.
27. Robert, "De Berlioz aux compositions de circonstance," 79.
28. Prod'homme and Martens, "Napoléon, Music, and Musicians," 604; Robert, "De Berlioz aux compositions de circonstance," 79.
29. Henri Blanchard, *La revue et gazette musicale*, Dec. 13, 1840, quoted in Gétreau, "Musique de circonstance," 73: " D'un pittoresque et puissant effet"; "nouvelles trompettes ou tubas."
30. A.E., "Funérailles de Napoléon," 1: "Trompettes antiques"; "belles et nobles choses."

sixteen leading singers of the Opéra and Théâtre Italien—including Rosine Stoltz, Gilbert Duprez, and Eugène Massol, three future principals of *La reine de Chypre*—performed the solo parts of Mozart's Requiem (in quadrupled reinforcement), joining 134 more singers and 150 instrumentalists led by Opéra and Conservatoire conductor François Habeneck.[31]

Before and after the 1840 ceremonies, an increasing number of Napoléon-centered theatrical works appeared in the July Monarchy: in 1831 alone, at least twenty-nine plays on Napoléon had appeared at lyrical and nonlyrical theaters, including *Napoléon, ou Schoenbrunn et Sainte-Hélène* (Porte Saint-Martin), *Napoléon à Berlin* (Montparnasse), *Malmaison et Sainte-Hélène* (Gaité), and *Quatorze ans de la vie de Napoléon* (Luxembourg).[32] Samuels also notes that over 120 Napoleonic plays would be produced by 1848.[33] In the year between the *retour* and *La reine*'s premiere in December 1841, several Napoléon-focused plays overtly created plots that revolved around different stages of the emperor's commemoration. Clairville's *Le retour de Sainte-Hélène*, which appeared on December 17, 1840, at the Théâtre de la Porte-Saint-Martin shortly after the ceremony, centers its story on old soldiers of the Grande Armée who reunite in a café as they await the passing of Napoléon's remains.[34] On January 1, 1841, at the Théâtre Saint-Marcel, Auguste Jouhaud's *Les cendres de Napoléon, ou le retour en France* featured symbolic figures of the emperor's heroic past: Jérôme Hubert, the grenadier from Elba who faithfully guards Napoléon's tomb on Sainte-Hélène, returns to France on the *Belle-Poule* with his son and the emperor's remains to attend the funeral ceremony with reunited family members, surrounded by old soldiers of the Empire.[35] Similarly, at the Cirque Olympique the tableaux of *Le dernier voeu de l'empéreur* by Ferdinand Laloue and Fabrice Labrousse showcase a former soldier of the Imperial Guard who takes part in the retrieval from Sainte-Hélène and participates in the Invalides ceremony with his father and grandfather, both pensioned soldiers, to whom he has given a branch taken from the willow trees shading the emperor's tomb on Sainte-Hélène.[36] The Napoleonic origins of the Arc de Triomphe figure centrally in the five-act *pièce anecdotique*, *Un déjeuner de Napoléon*, put on at the Théâtre

31. *Le ménestrel*, "Nouvelles diverses"; *Le constitutionnel*, "Beaux-Arts," 2.

32. Samuels, *Spectacular Past*, 107–9.

33. Samuels, *Spectacular Past*, 108. Samuels cites Louis-Henri Lecomte's *Napoléon et l'Empire racontés*, which inventories Napoleonic plays in nineteenth-century France.

34. Lecomte, *Napoléon et l'Empire racontés*, 368–69.

35. Lecomte, *Napoléon et l'Empire racontés*, 372.

36. Lecomte, *Napoléon et l'Empire racontés*, 372–73. An engraving by Denis-Auguste-Marie Raffet for Adolphe Thiers's history depicts weeping willows shading Napoléon's island grave beneath a heavenly scene of soldiers awaiting their hero.

des Funambules on January 9, 1841: in this imaginary scenario, Napoléon comes into the present, interacting with French tradespeople as he inspects the completion of the monument.[37]

Napoleonic Evocation in *La Reine de Chypre*

Compared to these palpable renderings, the imperial nostalgia evoked in *La reine*'s appropriated story of the Venetian-born queen of Cyprus, Catarina Cornaro (1454–1510), operates subtextually and intertextually within and outside the drama of Saint-Georges's reimagined tale.[38] The librettist's history—or "fable," as tagged by *Le corsaire*[39]—of Cornaro's thwarted marriage, the rivalry of French chevaliers who claim her hand, and the exotic, festive ceremonies in both Venice and Cyprus fit the theatrical demands of grand opera and Halévy's musicodramatic strengths in juxtaposing scenes of affecting intimacy with those of magnificent pageantry. However, a crucial component of the plot that inspired Halévy—and one fundamental to this Napoleonic reading—was Saint-Georges's portrayal of the "sombre and mysterious terror" of Venice, as noted by the composer's brother, artistic partner, and biographer, Léon Halévy.[40] Léon's poetic reference to Venetian "terror" responds to the stereotyped portrayal of a corrupt, despotic Venetian republic that was common in the early nineteenth century, but one also strongly tied to Napoléon's ideological views and early military exploits, as suggested above. As James H. Johnson has noted, Napoléon played a large role in ratcheting up long-standing critiques of Venice's State Inquisition (Inquisitori di Stato) and Council of Ten (Consiglio dei Dieci) with revolutionary rhetoric as he fought to "liberate" the city during his Italian campaign of 1796–97.[41] As a commander of the French Revolutionary Army and Army of Italy, Napoléon equated Venetian patricians with the "corrupt *noblesse* of 1789" but aimed his fiercest denunciations at the State Inquisition, calling it a

37. Lecomte, *Napoléon et l'Empire racontés*, 373–74.

38. Cornaro operas related to Saint-Georges's libretto appeared throughout Europe but with some mitigation of political elements. Shortly before *La reine*'s premiere, Franz Lachner's adaptation, *Catarina Cornaro, Königin von Cypern*, premiered at the Munich Hofoper on December 3, 1841. Alfred Bunn then reworked the Parisian libretto for Michael William Balfe's *Daughter of St Mark*, which premiered in Drury Lane Theatre in London in 1844. Gaetano Donizetti and Giacomo Sacchèro's *Catarina Cornaro* premiered at the Teatro San Carlo in Naples, and Giovanni Pacini and Francesco Guidi's *La regina di Cipro*, at the Teatro Regio in Turin in 1846.

39. A., "Académie royale de musique, *La reine de Chypre*," *Le corsaire*, Dec. 24, 1841, in Métairie, *Fromental Halévy, La reine de Chypre*, 72.

40. Halévy, *F. Halévy*, 36. The liberal Halévys (sons of Elie Halévy, author of *Ha-Shalom*, a poem that praises Napoléon's peacemaking actions in the 1801 cease-fire with England) appear to have had Napoleonic leanings: Léon wrote that both were delighted when Ecole Polytechnique students defended Paris "on the hills of Saint-Chaumont" and were inspired to a "love of liberty" by the "painful" and "ill-fated" surrender of Paris in 1814 (12).

41. Johnson, "Myth of Venice," 535–36.

"barbarous institution of ancient times" and a repressive deliverer of "atrocities."[42] Following his conquest of Venice on May 12, 1797, Napoleonic rhetoric echoed in propagandistic banners, pamphlets, and engravings that flooded the city and demonized the Inquisition.[43]

Theatrical works in France, England, and Italy further solidified the Napoléon-endorsed "myth" of Venetian tyranny, particularly Antoine-Vincent Arnault's play *Blanche et Montcassin, ou les Vénitiens*, which premiered at the Théâtre Français on October 16, 1798,[44] a year and a half after the commander's victory over Venice. This five-act tragedy clearly reflects the revolutionary rhetoric of Napoléon's Italian campaign, as well as his theatrical oversight.[45] In Arnault's dedication of the play "to Bonaparte," whom he addresses as a "member of the Institute" and "friend of the arts," he reports that Napoléon suggested a more effective way to end the play with the death of Blanche's beloved, the French hero Montcassin: "For a long time I searched vainly for the means; your genius excited mine. Advice from Buonaparte led to victory."[46] Arnault's preface also includes the section "De quelques institutions politiques de la République de Venise," in which he speaks of the "effrayant pouvoir" (frightening power) of the Inquisition's Council of Three and refers to the law banning communication between nobles and foreign ambassadors, on penalty of death, that underpinned his tragedy. As evidence of the harshness of this law, he cites the nobleman Antonio Foscarini, accused of treason and executed by the council in 1622, as model for the character Montcassin and also refers to Marino Faliero, the fourteenth-century doge who was "arrested, judged and decapitated" for conspiring against the state.[47]

In the drama itself, Arnault effectively portrays the brutality of Venice's Council of Three, Council of Ten, and "Great Council" and characterizes Blanche's father, Contarini, as a heartless member of the Council of Three who threatens to curse her forever if she does not marry Capello, a powerful council member, rather than her true love, the Norman Montcassin.[48] In the final scene, Blanche dares

42. Johnson, "Myth of Venice," 535–36.
43. Johnson, "Myth of Venice," 536.
44. Arnault, *Blanche et Montcassin*.
45. Ruth Rosenberg notes that Arnault accompanied Napoléon on his Egyptian expedition of 1798 as one of a group of artists and writers assisting in plans for restructuring Egyptian society (*Music, Travel, and Imperial Encounter*, 26). Napoléon also nominated him as member of the Institut de France in 1799 and *chevalier de l'Empire* in 1809.
46. Arnault, *Blanche et Montcassin*, v: "Depuis long-tems j'en cherchais vainement le moyen; votre genie échauffa le mien. Un conseil de Buonaparte devait produire une victoire." Napoléon became a member of the Institut de France's Académie des Sciences in 1797.
47. Arnault, *Blanche et Montcassin*, vii–viii, xij.
48. Notably, the role of Montcassin was created by François-Joseph Talma (1763–1826), Napoléon's protégé and friend who would adopt his signature hairstyle in a performance of Etienne de Jouy's *Sylla* at the Théâtre-Français (Samuels, *Spectacular Past*, 119).

to come to the council chambers to try to save the condemned Montcassin, falsely accused of espionage, and claims that his only crime has been his love for her. After Capello removes a cloth to reveal Montcassin's strangled body, Blanche hurls herself atop her dead lover, sparking Capello to shout: "Father and murderous judge!" More just and humane than Contarini, Capello now regrets his alliance with the cruel council, as revealed in his closing words that offer a barely disguised tribute to Napoléon as liberator and avenger of those under the scourge of Venetian oppression:

> May one day this voice, perpetuating your crimes,
> Incite an avenger for so many other victims,
> For so many unfortunate people buried in the mud,
> Or devoured under our sun-scorched roofs!
> May the long crimes of arbitrary power
> Soon be annihilated with their sanctuary,
> With this tribunal surrounded by scaffolds,
> Where I myself sat among the executioners![49]

The author's ideological and personal connection to Napoléon, along with the emperor's presence as allusory reference, "collaborator," and dedicatee of *Blanche et Montcassin*, would contribute to the banning of Arnault's work after 1815, the dismissal of the dramatist from the Académie Française, and his exile from France until 1819.[50]

La reine de Chypre reverberates with similar images of Venetian tyranny in its retelling of Catarina Cornaro's history against the backdrop of Venetian-Cypriot alliances.[51] Its Napoleonic, or Arnaultian, ideology emerges in the opera's sinister portrayal of Pietro Mocenigo (or Mocénigo), a member of the Council of Ten who threatens the patrician Andrea with death if he does not prevent the marriage of his niece Catarina with the chevalier Gérard de Coucy and give her hand instead to the Cypriot king, Jacques de Lusignan, as a means of

---

49. Arnault, *Blanche et Montcassin*, 5.9.80: "Puisse un jour cette voix, éternisant vos crimes, / Susciter un vengeur à tant autres victimes, / A tant d'infortunés dans la fange enterrés, / Ou sous nos toîts brulans du soleil dévorés! / Puisse les longs forfaits du pouvoir arbitraire / Bientôt s'anéantir avec leur sanctuaire, / Avec ce tribunal entouré d'échafauds, / Où j'ai siégé moi-même au milieux des bourreaux!"

50. The dramatist and librettist Eugène Scribe wrote of the banning of Arnault's works and expulsion from the Académie in "Discours de réception à l'Académie française," 4–5. Scribe berates the Académie for declaring "by virtue of an ordinance countersigned by a minister" that *Les Vénitiens* and other great works by Arnault "had never existed" (5).

51. Before and after the premiere of *La reine de Chypre*, Venetian despotism resurfaced, though sometimes obscured, in other operas, including Gioachino Rossini's 1819 opera, *Bianca e Falliero, ossia Il consiglio dei tre*, loosely based on Arnault's play; Gaetano Donizetti's *Marino Faliero* of 1835; and Giuseppe Verdi's *I due Foscari*, a reworking of Lord Byron's play *The Two Foscari*, first performed in Rome in 1844. Byron's 1821 play *Marino Faliero*, about the fourteenth-century doge's beheading, used rhetoric sharply aligned with Arnault's messages.

securing Venetian power. The parallel to Arnault's plot choice of a broken engagement and politically forced marriage strongly implies a source connection to his 1798 play, a possibility that becomes more probable if one considers the close association between Arnault and the composer's brother Léon, as well as the dramatist's renewed prominence in the Académie during the July Monarchy.[52] Halévy and Saint-Georges's opera did not undergo strict censorship at the Opéra, and changes made to the libretto manuscript approved by the French *ministre de l'intérieur* Charles Marie Tanneguy, comte Duchâtel—the day before the first performance on December 22, 1841—do not alter the work's meaning in a substantial way, though modifications softened the directness of one phrase indicative of Venetian power ("Venise aujourd'hui le demande") and slightly affected localized meanings.[53] Although the *ministre* reported the day *after* the premiere that "spectators were shocked by the faithful reproduction of costumes and insignia of our clergy" in act 4, he mentioned nothing about representations of the Venetian council.[54]

The opera's intent to depict Venetian tyranny, with its veiled reminder of Napoléon's "liberation" of Italy, becomes more evident with the printing of a historical excerpt in the preface to the libretto's first edition. Included is a passage drawn from *Histoire de Venise* by Count Pierre Daru, a soldier and *homme d'Etat* who served as *commissaire* in Napoléon's Northern Italian campaign.[55] Although no mention of Napoléon appears, the excerpt based on Daru's account reflects interpretations similar to Arnault's: it describes Venice's oppression of the Cypriot people and the wresting of power over Cypriot finances, courts, and military from King Lusignan, shortly after Catarina's arrival on Cyprus.[56] As will be implied in the opera's plot, the Daru-based excerpt also refers to a possible Venetian conspiracy behind the king's likely poisoning, and Catarina's courageous refusal to submit to Venetian control, despite "the threats" of the Venetian admiral Pietro Mocenigo.[57] In other passages of his

52. Halévy, *F. Halévy*, 25. Léon Halévy, an artistic confidant who "silently" contributed to libretto revisions of the composer's *La Juive*, assisted and substituted for Arnault during his years (1831–34) as professor of literature at the Ecole Polytechnique; he also collaborated with Arnault in editing the liberal journal *L'opinion: Journal des moeurs, de la littérature, des arts, des théâtres et de l'industrie*.

53. Archives Nationales (hereafter AN), AJ13 204, *La reine de Chypre*, libretto manuscript, "Approuvé par Mr le ministre de l'intérieur le 21 Xbre [Dec.] 1841, pour l'Académie royale de musique . . . "

54. AN, AJ13 204, Draft letter from the *ministre de l'intérieur* to the *commandant du roi*, Dec. 23, 1841: "Les spectateurs ont été choqués de la reproduction fidèle des costumes et des Insignes de notre clergé."

55. In the multivolume work by Daru with the variant title *Histoire de la république de Venise*, the passage follows parts of the account in "Affaires de Chypre," vol. 2, bk. xvii, 482–95; in the third edition, vol. 3, bk. xvi, 144–47; and in a Brussels edition, vol. 1, bk. xvi, 249–50. The libretto description seems to be an adapted, condensed version, with interpolated ideas from the *Biographie universelle*, also cited in a footnote.

56. Saint-Georges, *La reine de Chypre*. This first edition of the libretto was published by Maurice Schlesinger, publisher of the first orchestral and piano-vocal scores.

57. Saint-Georges, *La reine de Chypre*.

Histoire, Daru emphasizes the malevolent authority of the Council of Ten, noting that this "monstrous" tribunal closely monitored the populace and authorized public and hidden deaths.[58]

Arnault's and Daru's interpretations of the council's absolute power and murderous conspiracies correspond with both implicit and explicit references in *La reine*'s staging, score, and libretto.[59] Mocenigo, for example, appears in a blood-red robe that resembles images of the Council of Ten in paintings from the fifteenth to nineteenth centuries (including those by Francesco Hayez and Eugène Delacroix) (fig. 2). Further conveying Mocenigo's menacing authority, Halévy creates a recurring motive built on an ominous, repeated-pitch ostinato in quarter notes, first sounding in C minor in the Mocenigo-Andrea duet of act 1 in the clarinet, and then in the horns (as shown in fig. 3). This motive underlies Mocenigo's threatening order to quash Catarina's betrothal to Gérard and permeates this tension-packed duet built on extended declamatory singing. Halévy will bring back this motive in full form, but he also varies and fragments it, to foreshadow, recall, or allude to the council's pervasive control. It returns overtly in act 2 (no. 8), immediately before Andrea conveys that "Venice has ordained" the breaking of Catarina's vows to Gérard and again when he informs her that the council would kill Gérard if she does not follow its command. In act 5 it appears in Catarina's poignant recitative, shortly before she questions Lusignan's succumbing to an unknown illness, thus musically confirming the council's guilt in poisoning the king. Halévy also subtly varies it to comment further on the council's control over the fate of the three principal characters. At times he highlights the motive's four repeated quarter notes: at act 1's end, as Gérard's friends and other attendees sing of vengeance after the disruption of the wedding; in act 2, in Mocenigo's threatening exchange with Catarina; and at the end of act 4.

In addition to the council's, or Mocenigo's, recurring motive, Halévy portrays Venice's menacing control with diminished harmonies and varied sequences of rising figures and dotted-rhythm bass motives, often in the low strings. Pottinger labels a series of recurring ascending figures against continuous tremolos, centered on diminished seventh harmonies, as the "Venetian Senate" motive, again dramatically associated with the senate's "sinister plans" and threats to the "destiny" of Catarina and Gérard.[60] At the end of act 2, repeated ascending

58. Daru, *Histoire*, vol. 1, bk. vii, 512–13.
59. *Score* in this article generally refers to primary music sources for the opera, including the autograph manuscript, the first edition of the orchestral score, and the first edition of the piano-vocal score: Fromental Halévy, *La reine de Chypre, Ms. autographe*, BNF, Département de la Musique, MS 7332; Halévy, *La reine de Chypre, opéra en cinq actes*, plate no. M.S. 3554; Halévy, *La reine de Chypre*, plate no. M.S. 3556 as well as Halévy, *La reine de Chypre*, plate no. B. et Cⁱᵉ 9223, the reprinted piano-vocal score that corresponds to the Schlesinger edition. Musical descriptions and libretto excerpts of the opera draw on all these sources.
60. Pottinger, "Wagner in Exile," 257–58.

FIGURE 2 Costume of Mocenigo, *La reine de Chypre*, Paris Opéra, 1841, design by Paul Lormier. Bibliothèque Nationale de France, Bibliothèque-Musée de l'Opéra.

FIGURE 3 "Council Motive," *La reine de Chypre*, act 1, no. 3, *Duo* (Mocenigo-Andrea),
mm. 1–9. Halévy, *La reine de Chypre*, piano-vocal score, plate no. B. et Cⁱᵉ 9223, Paris, n.d.

octaves include a tritone in C minor (an interval once known as the "devil's
interval," often signifying the demonic or macabre in Western music). Here,
Catarina falls to her knees at the anguish of rejecting Gérard, and as Mocenigo
gestures toward waiting assassins, he reminds her of the threat to her lover's life.
In act 3's casino gardens of Cyprus, Venetian seigneurs taunt Cypriot revelers
that Venice's enemies will face death or slavery and then sing, to the rising octave
motive of act 2: "The terrible voice of Venice dominates the world!" (De sa terrible
voix domine l'univers!). Later in act 5, after the reminiscence of the council
motive as Lusignan lies ill, Gérard directly accuses Mocenigo of poisoning the
king, and the Iago-like character admits, "Yes, Venice has broken this rebellious
instrument" (Oui, Venise a brisé cet instrument rebelle), but threatens to blame
Catarina and Gérard for the crime.

In other interpretations, the queen of Cyprus herself serves as the pivotal heroic figure in her resistance to the tyranny of Venetian power, as Pottinger
notes, and as one of many nineteenth-century operatic roles modeled after
Joan of Arc.[61] At the opera's culmination, she indeed functions as a nationalist
figure of French heroism, one who had begun to take on populist appeal by the

61. Pottinger relates Catarina's selfless "transcend[ence of] her own desires" to Michelet's portrayal
of Joan of Arc ("Staging of History in France," 66). Odette in *Charles VI* appears even more centrally as
Joan, as described by Hibberd (*French Grand Opera*, 123–27) and implied in the Parisian press.

1830s.[62] In this reading, as proposed above, the characters of Lusignan and Gérard, French warriors in exile, operate as conduits for the opera's oblique Napoleonic narrative (figs. 4 and 5). In broad terms, these chevaliers belong to the wave of medievalist nostalgia in postrevolutionary France and in Romantic literature and music, although the "cult of chivalry" held particular meaning for royalists or legitimists, who, as Chateaubriand, bemoaned the "ruins" left by the Revolution and yearned for the lost world of the ancien régime.[63] The original title of the opera, *Le chevalier de Malte*—which appears in original music manuscripts, costume sketches, and Opéra institutional documents—as well as the assigning of Gérard's role to the leading tenor Gilbert Duprez speak to the centrality of the chevalier in the conception of *La reine*. In the act 1 duet with Catarina, Gérard tells her that under the "laws of chivalry" he has "traveled the world in search of honor."[64] Yet in the context of 1840–41, both chevaliers, who find brotherhood on the island of Cyprus far from their beloved France, share in the allegorical evocation of the exiled Napoléon staring out to sea during his imprisonment on Sainte-Hélène, as depicted in illustrations that began to circulate during the Restoration.[65]

The nobler of the two warriors, Lusignan, who forgives Gérard for twice attempting to kill him after his loss of Catarina, takes on more evident correspondences to Napoléon. Though one might contend that this baritone role, first performed by Paul-Bernard Barroilhet, represents a secondary hero to Duprez's Gérard, Lusignan is depicted most empathetically as a monarch who is dying in act 5, having been poisoned by an insidious enemy, as many Frenchmen believed Napoléon to have been as well.[66] His portrayal resonates with images of the suffering emperor in published lamentations that appeared shortly after his death in 1821, such as an encomium by Emmanuel de Las Cases, as well as homages to a chained Prometheus, or a Christlike figure, by Romantic writers in the 1830s.[67] Edgar Quinet's 1835 poem "Napoléon," for example, depicts the "new Prometheus" whose blood is slowly being drunk by the "vulture of Albion" in a stark, rocky landscape—a prisoner guarded sleeplessly by the ocean. In a later verse,

62. Hibberd cites Michelet's influence in moving her from a royalist figure to an icon inspirational to varied political factions (*French Grand Opera*, 123–24, 127).

63. Amalvi, *Le goût du Moyen Age*, 24–25; Glencross, "Relic and Romance," 337, 342.

64. Halévy, *La reine de Chypre*, M.S. 3556, and Halévy, *La reine de Chypre*, B. et Cie 9223, 1.2: "Soumis aux lois de la chevalerie je parcourais le monde en y cherchant l'honneur."

65. Images of a contemplative, sometimes forlorn Napoléon gazing out to sea include François Joseph Sandmann's painting *Napoléon à Sainte-Hélène* (1820) and Pierre-Eugène Aubert's engraving *Napoléon sur le rocher de Sainte-Hélène* (1840).

66. Martineau, *Napoléon's St. Helena*, 222–26.

67. Driskel, *As Befits a Legend*, 22.

FIGURE 4 Costume of Lusignan, *La reine de Chypre*, Paris Opéra, 1841, design by Paul Lormier. Bibliothèque Nationale de France, Bibliothèque-Musée de l'Opéra.

FIGURE 5 Costume of Gérard, *La reine de Chypre*, Paris Opéra, 1841, design by Paul Lormier. Bibliothèque Nationale de France, Bibliothèque-Musée de l'Opéra.

Quinet wrote, "He is not dead! He is not dead! From his slumber / The giant will emerge even stronger at his awakening!"[68]

In the opera's extended *grand duo* that ends act 3, sung after Lusignan has saved his rival from assassins' swords and has discovered their common heritage, he and Gérard express their melancholia and torment "in a foreign land." In declamatory phrases, Gérard addresses his "liberator" as a chevalier who worthily follows laws and who risks his own life to defend the rights of the vulnerable.[69] They then sing a patriotic, martial salute to France (*Salut à cette noble France*), harmonizing in thirds to convey a shared bond to their beloved nation, before moving to the duet's ethereal *cantabile*, *Triste exilé*, set in a lulling 6/8 (see the opening measures in fig. 6). This melancholic andante had an "irresistible" and "electrifying" effect on the audience, according to *Le corsaire* and *Le moniteur des théâtres*; Berlioz admired its "penetrating" expression and designated the entire duet as the "principal piece" of the work.[70] Lusignan's beginning strophe (which Gérard soon echoes) expresses the anguish of being separated from his country:

> Sad exile in a foreign land,
> Ah, how many times have I sighed,
> How many torments, oh, dearest France,
> How many regrets, oh, beloved land!
> [*to Gérard*]
> Let my voice through you
> One day be heard,
> Tell France that in this place
> I cannot leave,
> There is an arm
> Prepared to defend it,
> There is an ardent heart to cherish it.[71]

No doubt Lusignan's mournful words and music touched the heart of many a French émigré, but they also align with sentimental images of Napoléon as a

68. Quinet, *Oeuvres complètes*, 7:308, as quoted in Driskel, *As Befits a Legend*, 20–21. See similar sentiments in Delavigne et al., "Poésies sur Napoléon."

69. Halévy, *La reine de Chypre*, M.S. 3556 [and Halévy, *La reine de Chypre*, B. et Cie 9223], 3.13: "Vous qui de la chevalerie / Suivez si dignement les lois, / Vous qui sans hésiter exposez votre vie, / Pour soutenir le faible et défendre ses droits" (You who follow the laws / Of knighthood so nobly, / You who risk your life without hesitation, / To support the weak and defend his rights).

70. A., *Le corsaire*, Dec. 24, 1841; unsigned, *Le moniteur des théâtres*, Dec. 25, 1841; Berlioz, *Le journal des débats*, Dec. 26, 1841. These three reviews appear in Métairie, *Fromental Halévy, La reine de Chypre*, 76, 95, 133.

71. Translation from Dratwicki, *Fromental Halévy*, 131–32: "Triste exilé sur la terre étrangère, / Ah, que de fois j'ai soupiré, / Que de tourments, ô ma France si chère, / Que de regrets, ô pays adoré! / (à Gérard) Que ma voix par la vôtre / un jour se fasse entendre, / Dites-lui qu'en ces lieux dont / je ne puis sortir, / Dites-lui qu'il est un bras / tout prêt à la défendre, / Il est un coeur ardent pour la chérir!"

FIGURE 6 *Triste exilé* from *La reine de Chypre*, act 3, no. 13, *Duo final* (Lusignan-Gérard), mm. 149–56. Halévy, *La reine de Chypre*, piano-vocal score, plate no. B. et Cie 9223, Paris, n.d.

banished hero who never forgot his country. His voice and memory speak through Gérard, who joins him in "sad exile" and who will outlive him, and metaphorically through present and future generations of France. At the beginning of act 5, after the dying Lusignan hears Catarina mention Gérard's name, he wakes to sing the first phrase of *Triste exilé*, recalling their fraternal bond in a faraway land and their reconciliation after rivalrous conflicts.

Perhaps the most strongly etched Napoleonic emblems come in the spectacle of act 4. Not only does this act allude to Courbevoie, with the disembarkment of a royal figure (the queen) from a ship, but it also creates a grand public ritual and processional that allegorically and literally elicit the Parisian commemoration of the *retour*. Though processional scenes factored in other French grand operas for the display of diverse social groups and local color, among multiple dramatic functions, they importantly offered contracted versions of "real" processions commonly experienced within Paris and throughout France.[72]

72. Smith, "Processions in French Grand Opera." In this 2012 paper for the American Musicological Society, Marian Smith underscored the linkage between real-life and operatic processionals and listed different types of processionals in both grand opera and ballet-pantomime, including the extravagant processions with royal figures, soldiers, clergy, and town residents in act 1 of *La Juive*, celebrating the Council of

The "real" and musically diegetic portions of *La reine*'s act 4 processional scene, set in the town square of Nicosia next to the sea in Cyprus, center on the sonic magnificence of two full-size, brass-laden orchestras, numbering close to the 150 to 200 musicians in the *retour*'s procession and led by Habeneck, the conductor of Napoléon's funeral music. One reviewer described three orchestras: one "on the ramparts," another "on the portico of the temple," and a third "in the usual place."[73] As essential links between the real and staged processions and sonic masses, twelve *grandes trompettes*, among those used in Napoléon's funeral cortege and Invalides service, also performed on the Opéra stage.[74] A week after the opera's premiere, Théophile Gautier and many other critics emphasized the trumpets' role in the *retour*; in *La presse*, Gautier offered a detailed account of the extravagant act, which he noted was "almost all about staging and spectacle."[75] After describing the queen's "heureux débarquement," the "majestic" trireme that brings her to shore, and her initial reception, he wrote:

> Batteries of *these long trumpets, called Roman trumpets, which you no doubt noticed in the emperor's convoy*, descend on the balustrade of the terrace and begin to sound brilliant fanfares to which the cannon, and the Cypriot music in another corner of the place, respond forcefully. Then a triumphal march begins. . . . The king, preceded by his pages, his heralds of arms, his grand officers, move toward the cathedral with the queen whom he holds by the end of his white glove. The clergy, pressed around the archbishop, then proceed; the banners of Venice and Cyprus are carried side by side as a sign of alliance and good union. The leaders of the army and navy, the deputies of the Venetian senate, the grand dignitaries of State, the high personages of the court follow at slight intervals. . . . The army of the king of Cyprus brings up the rear of the march: halbardiers, archers, pikemen, who advance beating drums, signs displayed; we don't believe we exaggerate in saying that there were at least five hundred people on the stage who cross, mingle and move in a picturesque disorder, but without confusion.[76]

Constance opening, and the act 5 procession preceding Rachel's execution. Théophile Gautier (*La presse*, Dec. 29, 1841, in Métairie, *Fromental Halévy, La reine de Chypre*, 191) noted that *La reine*'s processional had the same "goût" (taste) as *La Juive*'s, likely in reference to act 1 of the latter.

73. A., *Le corsaire*, Dec. 24, 1841, in Métairie, *Fromental Halévy, La reine de Chypre*, 73.

74. The number of *grandes trompettes* varies among reviews, as well as documents related to the production.

75. *La presse*, Dec. 29, 1841, in Métairie, *Fromental Halévy, La reine de Chypre*, 190.

76. Métairie, *Fromental Halévy, La reine de Chypre*, 191 (my emphasis): "Des batteries de *ces longues trompettes, dites trompettes romaines, que vous avez sans doute remarquées au convoi de l'empereur*, s'abbatent sur la balustrade de la terrasse et se mettent à sonner d'éclatantes fanfares auxquelles répond le canon des forts et la musique cypriote d'un autre coin de la place. Alors commence une marche triomphale. . . . Le roi précédé de ses pages, de ses héraults d'armes, de ses grands officiers se dirige vers la cathédrale avec la reine

A number of other reviewers also remarked on the use and sonic effect of the special trumpets, although offering fewer staging details. Hippolyte Prévost, before commenting on the trumpets' contribution to the scene's "splendor" in *Le commerce*, gave the composer sole credit for having requested their manufacture for Napoléon's cortege:

> Mr. Halévy had the fortunate idea of using the famous trumpets he had built expressly for the performance of the funeral march of the Emperor's convoy. The brilliance of the fanfares that a dozen tubas [*sic*], blended with powerful and harmonious chords of the orchestra, gives this triumphant music a character of splendor, magnificence, and pomp that is quite extraordinary. This is one of the most startling effects that you can imagine.[77]

The reviewer in *Revue des deux mondes* called them "gigantesques trompettes" from the emperor's funeral, and another described them as "the long trumpets used in the funeral of Napoléon."[78] Press descriptions correspond with specifications in Louis Palianti's staging manual, which adds that the trumpets were "decorated with banners in the national colors" and emphasizes the echoing volley of cannons, along with church bells, at the queen's arrival.[79] In a lithograph of Napoléon's cortege, Levilly shows banners hanging from the *grandes trompettes*, and in an account of the *retour*, Hugo describes the powerful effects of cannon heard simultaneously from "three different points of the horizon."[80] A photograph of these instruments, housed in the Conservatoire's Musée Instrumental,

---

qu'il tient par le bout de son gant blanc. Le clergé pressé autour de l'archevêque défile ensuite; les bannières de Venise et de Chypre sont portées côte à côte en signe d'alliance et de bonne union. Les chefs de l'armée de terre et de mer, la députation du sénat de Venise, les grands dignitaries de l'état, les hauts personnages de la cour suivent avec de légers intervalles. . . . La marche est fermée par l'armée du roi de Chypre : hallebardiers, archers, pertuisaniers qui s'avancent tambours battans, enseignes déployées; nous ne croyons pas exagérer en disant qu'il y a au moins cinq cents personnes sur la scène qui se croisent, se mêlent et se meuvent dans un désordre pittoresque, mais sans confusion pourtant." (The designation *Roman trumpets* suggests their "antique" appearance but may also allude to the emperor's attachment to Roman symbols.)

77. Hipp. P. [Hippolyte Prévost], *Le commerce*, Dec. 24, 1841, in Métairie, *Fromental Halévy, La reine de Chypre*, 61: "M. Halévy a eu l'heureuse idée de se servir des fameuses trompettes qu'il fit construire exprès pour l'exécution de la marche funèbre du convoi de l'Empereur. L'éclat des fanfares qu'une douzaine de tubas [*sic*] mêlé aux accords puissants et harmonieux de l'orchestre, donne à cette musique triomphale, un caractère de splendeur, de magnificence, de pompe tout à fait extraordinaires. C'est un des effets les plus saisissans qu'il soit possible d'imaginer." Prévost likely used *tubas* as a loose reference to the special trumpets; Halévy did not include the low brass instrument generally known as a tuba (and newly invented, ca. 1835) in the autograph or orchestral score of *La reine de Chypre*.

78. Unsigned, *Revue des deux mondes*, Dec. 31, 1841, in Métairie, *Fromental Halévy, La reine de Chypre*, 203; *Revue du progrès politique, social et littéraire*, "Révue des théâtres," 52: "Des longues trompettes employées aux funérailles de Napoléon."

79. Palianti, *Collections de mise en scène*, 98.

80. Levilly, *Les trompettes du cortège, place de la Concorde*, lithograph (1840), BNF; Hugo, "Choses vues," 42.

corresponds to Levilly's depiction of slender, valveless brass trumpets over two to three times as long as commonly used natural or valved trumpets.[81]

With the Opéra's staged military displays of soldiers, officers, and artillery in a ritual of political realignment, the "natural" movement of hundreds of people on stage, the soundscape of a double orchestra performing ceremonial music, and the emblematic use of *grandes trompettes* from Napoléon's funeral procession and Invalides service, this act could be viewed as a compressed "reprise" of the *retour des cendres*. Along with Gautier's and other reviewers' mnemonic references, Berlioz's comparison of the combined music of "the dozen Roman trumpets," the "military band in the theater," and the orchestra to "the solemn sound of grand national celebrations" reinforces the connection.[82] Even more explicitly, Eugène Guinot in *Le courrier français* noted that the composer "found the sublime harmonies which *le retour des cendres impériales* inspired in him not long ago."[83]

As mentioned above, Halévy, unlike Auber and Adam, scored for the *grandes trompettes* in his commissioned *Funeral March* (*Marche funèbre*) for the 1840 ceremony.[84] Not only does he include these long trumpets in his 1840 march and *La reine*'s *Triumphant March* (*Marche triomphale*), but he also makes a clear sonic link to Napoléon's funeral by his use of the very same fanfare in the key of A flat in both works (fig. 7).[85] In the opera's *Triumphant March*, as the royal cortege passes by, the repeated fanfare precedes the chorus's joyous cries of "Gloire!" to the queen and "our sovereigns." Even if Halévy's march with the *grandes trompettes* had only been heard in the 1840 Invalides service and not along the cortege route, it is possible that the marching musicians performed the fanfare itself; nonetheless, the long trumpets would certainly have been highly visible and memorable. With the many press references to Napoléon's *grandes trompettes* before and after the *retour*'s ceremonies, and again after

81. Gétreau, "Musique de circonstance," 74.

82. Berlioz, *Journal des débats*, Dec. 26, 1841, in Métairie, *Fromental Halévy, La reine de Chypre*, 134: "Ces douze trompettes romaines . . . , cette bande militaire sur le théâtre, unis à l'orchestre et aux voix . . . produisant en somme le bruit solennel des grandes fêtes nationales" (The dozen Roman trumpets . . . , the military band in the theater, combined with the orchestra and voices . . . all together generated the solemn sound of grand national celebrations).

83. E.G. [Eugène Guinot], *Le courrier français*, Dec. 24, 1841, in Métairie, *Fromental Halévy, La reine de Chypre*, 80: "a retrouvé là les sublimes accords que lui inspira naguère le retour des cendres impériales."

84. Halévy, *Marche héroïque pour les funérailles de l'Empereur Napoléon*, BNF, Département de la Musique, MS 8676; Halévy, *La reine de Chypre, opéra en cinq actes*. In comparison, Adolphe Adam's autograph manuscript, *Marche funèbre pour Napoléon*, BNF, Département de la Musique, MS 2696, and Adam's printed score *Marche funèbre* do not specify the *grandes trompettes*, nor do the autograph manuscript and sixty-three instrumental parts for Daniel Auber's *Marche funèbre exécutée en 184[0] (translation des cendres de Napoléon), 63 parties instruments à vent*, BNF, Département de la Musique, MS 1842, though his inclusion of twelve low-brass ophicleides would have created an impressive sound.

85. Perhaps signifying a dramatic association, Halévy also sets Lusignan's first strophe of *Triste exilé* in A flat major.

FIGURE 7 *Triumphant March* (*Marche triomphale*) for stage orchestra (*orchestre sur le théâtre*), with fanfare for the *grandes trompettes*. Halévy, *La reine de Chypre, opéra en cinq actes, paroles de Mr de Saint Georges, musique de F. Halévy*. Bibliothèque Nationale de France.

performances of the opera, audiences and readers no doubt had the connection secured for them. According to Florenc Gétreau, the *grandes trompettes* would come to represent the "heart of the ceremonies" as their association with Napoléon continued well into the century.[86]

The end of act 5 sharpens the Napoleonic allegory: in the final tableau in Cyprus, the weakened Lusignan calls for war on Venice; as he oversees the raging battle between Venetian forces and Cypriots, Gérard leads the Knights of Rhodes, with Catarina at the head of the Cypriot troops. As the knights and Cypriot fighters overcome the Venetian soldiers (symbolically echoing Napoléon's conquering of Venice), Lusignan exclaims before taking his final breath,

> My death is not lacking in glory
> I can die then
> On a day of victory![87]

The Cypriot people join Gérard and Catarina—who holds up her son, the future king—in singing a final pledge to the martyred Lusignan: "To win or die for his banner / His God, and his liberty!" After the last syllable of "liberté!," the *grandes trompettes* return in two punctuating fanfares, as Gérard points heavenward, then toward the ship that will transport not the body of the Napoleonic Lusignan but the chevalier who will carry forth his heroic deeds and honor his memory.

In the early reception of *La reine*, many writers briefly recounted Cornaro's history, with several complaining of Saint-Georges's distorted, imaginative, or "invented" interpretation of that history.[88] Several, in fact, did speak of Venetian despotism, the "terrible council," and the evil Mocenigo, with one critic referring to "the dreadful mysteries of Venetian politics"; Gustave Héquet insisted in *Le national* that "above all, there is too much politics" in the opera, explaining that music's role was to "depict passions" and not political arguments.[89] The rarity or vagueness of such comments by reviewers does not necessarily confirm that the opera was viewed apolitically or that the Napoleonic allusions were

86. Gétreau, "Musique de circonstance," 76–77.

87. Halévy, *La reine de Chypre*, M.S. 3554 [and B. et Cie 9223], 5.[no.] 23: "Ma mort n'est pas sans gloire, / Je pourrai donc mourir / En un jour de victoire."

88. A., *Le corsaire*, Dec. 24, 1841; Eugène Guinot, *Le courrier français*, Dec. 24, 1841; and Jean-Toussaint Merle, *La quotidienne*, Dec. 26, 1841; all in Métairie, *Fromental Halévy, La reine de Chypre*, 72, 77, 143.

89. *Revue du progrès politique, social et littéraire*, "Revue des théâtres," 52 ("cette impitoyable politique"); *Le commerce*, Dec. 24, 1841 ("du terrible conseil"); Guinot, *Le courrier français*, Dec. 24, 1841 ("aux terribles mystères de la politique vénitienne"); Gustave Héquet, *Le national*, Dec. 25, 1841: "Il y a surtout trop de politique. La politique est essentiellement raisonneuse, et il appartient à la musique de peindre des passions, mais non d'exprimer des raissonemens" (Above all, there is too much politics. Politics is essentially argumentative; it is up to music to depict passions, but not to voice arguments). The last three reviews are found in Métairie, *Fromental Halévy, La reine de Chypre*, 54, 77, 105.

entirely missed, however. Descriptions of the council's sinister dealings suggest a familiarity and affinity with Daru's and Arnault's imagery and an acceptance of Napoleonic ideology of a brutal Venice in need of liberation. Though the aura of chivalry and the figure and title of *Le chevalier de Malte* "remained enigmatically" throughout much of the opera, according to Prévost, the specter of Napoléon now joins in this once-royalist symbolism.[90] Both exiled warriors long for a France that has escaped them, centrally captured in the patriotic *Salut* and melancholic *Triste exilé* of their duet. With the appearance of the *grandes trompettes* and triumphant march that pierced the "sonic heart" of Napoléon's ceremonies, signifiers of chivalry merge with unforgettable links to the *retour* that offer codes to the opera's multivalent subtext. With the immediacy of the grand public ceremony of the *retour des cendres* and the prevalence of histories, encomiums, plays, paintings, and other imagery arousing memories of Napoléon, the portrayal of an exiled French warrior and dying king, the compressed cortege of act 4, and the recurring fanfare of the *grandes trompettes* framing the Triumphant March and final scene of liberation provided metaphorical triggers for recalling, and empathizing with, the defeated emperor and making him, once again, an inspirational hero of the French nation.

In visceral, ambiguous, obscure, and overt ways, *La reine de Chypre* reinforced the imperial nostalgia that flourished in the July Monarchy in its appeals to patriotic sentiments of *l'amour du pays* and longing for a heroic past. In the grand theater that featured performers and the composer who had participated in the musical tributes of the *retour*, the opera symbolically evoked the heroism and revolutionary spirit of Napoléon, echoing the monarchy's attempts to add the former glory of this controversial hero to "all the glories" of its national past. The opera's triumph-over-tyranny staging recuperates Napoléon as revolutionary "liberator" of Venice and offers an apt representation for a nation attempting to reconcile with the exiled hero imprisoned on Sainte-Hélène. Through a rich mix of musical, visual, literary, historical, and symbolic references embedded in its narrative, *La reine de Chypre* enacts symbols and commemoration in a theatrical "galérie" of "living" portraits—the illusory Napoléon (Lusignan) appears alongside Jeanne d'Arc (Catarina) and the crusading chevalier (Gérard), resonating with the eclectic mix of French icons in Louis-Philippe's Galérie des Batailles. With the return of the corporeal Napoléon to Paris and a figurative Napoléon to the Paris Opéra stage, *La reine de Chypre* effectively and powerfully engaged with the "politics of memory" and "politics of imperial nostalgia," as it joined in the dynamic reshaping of French history in the July Monarchy.

90. Prévost, *Le commerce*, Dec. 24, 1841, in Métairie, *Fromental Halévy, La reine de Chypre*, 58–59.

DIANA R. HALLMAN is associate professor of musicology at the University of Kentucky. She is author of *Opera, Liberalism, and Antisemitism in Nineteenth-Century France: The Politics of Halévy's "La Juive"* (2002) and editor of the forthcoming collection *America in the French Imaginary, c. 1789–1914: Music, Revolution, and Race.*

Acknowledgments

The author thanks Marian Smith for the gracious sharing of her American Musicological Society paper and the anonymous reviewers of *French Historical Studies* for their valuable insights.

References

Adam, Adolphe. *Marche funèbre pour harmonie militaire, composée pour les funérailles de l'empereur Napoléon.* Paris, n.d.

A.E. "Funérailles de Napoléon." *Le ménestrel,* Dec. 20, 1840, 1–2.

Amalvi, Christian. *Le goût du Moyen Age.* Paris, 1996.

Arnault, Antoine Vincent. *Blanche et Montcassin, ou les Vénitiens, tragédie en 5 actes.* Paris, 1798 [an VII].

Charlton, David, ed. *The Cambridge Companion to Grand Opera.* Cambridge, 2003.

Crosten, William. *French Grand Opera: An Art and a Business.* New York, 1948.

Daru, Pierre. *Histoire de la république de Venise.* 8 vols. Paris, 1819.

Daru, Pierre. *Histoire de la république de Venise.* 3rd ed. 8 vols. Paris, 1826.

Daru, Pierre. *Histoire de la république de Venise.* 8 vols. Brussels, 1838.

Delavigne, Casimir, et al. "Poésies sur Napoléon." *Le constitutionnel,* Dec. 16, 1840.

Descotes, Maurice. *La légende de Napoléon et les écrivains français du XIXe siècle.* Paris, 1967.

Dodman, Thomas. *What Nostalgia Was: War, Empire, and the Time of a Deadly Emotion.* Chicago, 2018.

Dratwicki, Alexandre, ed. *Fromental Halévy: La reine de Chypre.* Venice, 2018.

Driskel, Michael Paul. *As Befits a Legend: Building a Tomb for Napoléon, 1840–1861.* Kent, OH, 1993.

Fulcher, Jane. *The Nation's Image: French Grand Opera as Politics and Politicized Art.* Cambridge, 1987.

Gétreau, Florenc. "Musique de circonstance." In Humbert, *Napoléon aux Invalides,* 72–77.

Glencross, Michael. "Relic and Romance: Antiquarianism and Medievalism in French Literary Culture, 1780–1830." *Modern Language Review* 95, no. 2 (2000): 337–49.

Halévy, Fromental. *La reine de Chypre.* Piano-vocal score. Plate no. M.S. [Maurice Schlesinger] 3556. Arranged by Richard Wagner. Paris, 184[2].

Halévy, Fromental. *La reine de Chypre.* Piano-vocal score. Plate no. B. et Cie 9223. Paris, n.d.

Halévy, Fromental. *La reine de Chypre, opéra en cinq actes, paroles de Mr de Saint Georges, musique de F. Halévy.* Orchestral score. Plate no. M.S. [Maurice Schlesinger] 3554. Paris, 184[2].

Halévy, Léon. *F. Halévy: Sa vie et ses oeuvres.* 2nd ed. Paris, 1863.

Halévy, Léon. *Résumé de l'histoire des Juifs modernes.* Paris, 1828.

Hallman, Diana R. "The Grand Operas of Fromental Halévy." In Charlton, *Cambridge Companion to Grand Opera,* 233–57.

Hallman, Diana R. "L'affaire de *Charles VI,* ou la cause ministérielle." Paper presented at the Annual Meeting of the American Musicological Society, Kansas City, MO, November 4, 1999.

Hallman, Diana R. "Of French Patriotism and Franco-British Relations: 'L'affaire ministérielle de *Charles VI*,' 1843." Paper presented at the International Conference on Nineteenth-Century Music, Royal Holloway–University of London, July 1, 2000.

Hallman, Diana R. *Opera, Liberalism, and Antisemitism in Nineteenth-Century France: The Politics of Halévy's "La Juive."* Cambridge, 2002.

Hazareesingh, Sudhir. *The Legend of Napoléon.* London, 2004.

Hazareesingh, Sudhir. "Napoleonic Memory in Nineteenth-Century France: The Making of a Liberal Legend." *Modern Language Notes* 120, no. 4 (2005): 747–73.

Hibberd, Sarah. *French Grand Opera and the Historical Imagination.* Cambridge, 2009.

Hugo, Victor. "Choses vues—1840—Funérailles de Napoléon." In vol. 25 of *Oeuvres complètes*, 39–58. Paris, 1913.

Humbert, Jean-Marcel. "Le parcours parisien et son décor." In Humbert, *Napoléon aux Invalides*, 48–70.

Humbert, Jean-Marcel, ed. *Napoléon aux Invalides: 1840, Le retour des cendres.* Paris, 1990.

Johnson, James H. "The Myth of Venice in Nineteenth-Century Opera." *Journal of Interdisciplinary History* 36, no. 3 (2006): 533–54.

Langlé, Ferdinand, ed. *Funérailles de l'empereur Napoléon.* Paris, 1840.

Lecomte, Louis-Henri. *Napoléon et l'Empire racontés par le théâtre, 1797–1899.* Paris, 1900.

Le constitutionnel. "Beaux-Arts: Les funérailles de l'empereur." Dec. 17, 1840, 1–2.

Le ménestrel. "Nouvelles diverses." Dec. 13, 1840, 3.

Marrinan, Michael. *Painting Politics for Louis-Philippe: Art and Ideology in Orléanist France, 1830–1848.* New Haven, CT, 1988.

Martineau, Gilbert. *Le retour des cendres.* Paris, 1990.

Martineau, Gilbert. *Napoléon's St. Helena*, translated by Frances Partridge. Chicago, 1968.

Mellon, Stanley. "The July Monarchy and the Napoleonic Myth." *Yale French Studies*, no. 26 (1960): 70–78.

Métairie, Anne-Sophie, ed. *Fromental Halévy, La reine de Chypre: Dossier de presse parisienne (1841).* Weinsberg, 2005.

Palianti, L[ouis]. *Collections de mise en scène rédigées et publiées par M. L. Palianti, La reine de Chypre, opera en cinq actes.* Paris, 184[1].

Pottinger, Mark. "The Staging of History in France: Characterizations of Historical Figures in French Grand Opera during the July Monarchy." PhD diss., City University of New York, 2005.

Pottinger, Mark. "Wagner in Exile: Paris, Halévy, and the *Queen*." *Nineteenth-Century Music Review* 12, no. 2 (2015): 253–84.

Prod'homme, J. G., and Frederick H. Martens. "Napoléon, Music, and Musicians." *Musical Quarterly* 7, no. 4 (1921): 579–605.

Quinet, Edgar. *Oeuvres complètes de Edgar Quinet.* 11 vols. Paris, 1857–70.

Revue du progrès politique, social et littéraire. "Revue des théâtres." 3rd ser., 5 (1842): 52–53.

Robert, Frédéric. "De Berlioz aux compositions de circonstance." In Humbert, *Napoléon aux Invalides*, 79–83.

Rosenberg, Ruth. *Music, Travel, and Imperial Encounter in Nineteenth-Century France.* New York, 2014.

Saint-Georges, Henri de. *La reine de Chypre, opéra en cinq actes, paroles de M. de Saint-Georges, musique de F. Halévy. . . . Libretto.* Paris, 1841.

Samuels, Maurice. *The Spectacular Past: Popular History and the Novel in Nineteenth-Century France*. Ithaca, NY, 2004.

Scribe, Eugène. "Discours de réception à l'Académie française, prononcé dans la séance du 28 janvier 1836." In vol. 1 of *Oeuvres complètes de M. Eugène Scribe*, 1–14. Rev. ed. 5 vols. Paris, 1840–41.

Smith, Marian. "Processions in French Grand Opera." Paper presented at the Annual Meeting of the American Musicological Society, New Orleans, Nov. 2, 2012.

Thiers, Adolphe. *Histoire du Consulat et de l'Empire*. Paris, 1855.

Thorel, Sylvie. "The Romantics and the St Bartholomew's Day Massacre." In *Louis-Ferdinand Hérold: Le pré aux clercs*, edited by Alexandre Dratwicki, 21–27. Venice, 2016.

White, Nicholas. "Fictions and Librettos." In Charlton, *Cambridge Companion to Grand Opera*, 43–57.

"Zouk Is the Only Medicine We Need"
Kassav and the Cultural Politics of Music in the French Caribbean

PAUL COHEN

ABSTRACT   This article demonstrates how the history of Kassav, the French Caribbean music group founded in 1979, sheds light on the cultural politics of French Caribbean music and the history of "global France." It argues that Kassav's music represents an inventive cultural and commercial response to patterns of neocolonial and capitalist exclusion in the French Caribbean, one that drew on the islands' own cultural resources to fashion a new musical form, called zouk, that has had lasting influence. Kassav owes its commercial success in part to a global music industry hungry for new musics from postcolonial peripheries and to Paris's role as a world music capital. That Kassav was seen in metropolitan France as "Caribbean" or "world" music, rather than "French," speaks to the historical and racial fault lines that obscure the Frenchness of the French Caribbean to many in the Hexagon.

KEYWORDS   Caribbean, music, zouk, race, empire

In December 2013 the French-Caribbean ensemble Kassav played two dates at the Olympia, their first appearances at the venerable Paris music hall that has long served to consecrate popular music artists in France—as if one of the most important groups ever to come out of the Caribbean had any need for further consecration. Little known in the Anglophone world outside the Caribbean diaspora, Kassav boasts a formidable legacy as musical innovators who put their stamp on popular music around the world, transformed the music industry in the French Antilles, and projected French Creole culture onto the world stage. The Paris concerts capped the group's yearlong "Mawonaj Tour" and the release of its latest album, *Sonjé*. Thirty-four years after its creation in 1979, sixteen studio records, and countless concerts later, Kassav's Olympia shows offered joyous proof that the inventors of the musical style called zouk remained as important as ever.

In concert, Kassav comprises two lead singers, a guitarist and bass guitarist, two keyboardists, a brass section, three backup singers/dancers, and two

French Historical Studies • Vol. 45, No. 2 (April 2022) • DOI 10.1215/00161071-9532010
Copyright 2022 by Society for French Historical Studies

percussionists. Their sound is built on kinetic rhythms, strong grooves, rock-solid brass, and pure and powerful vocals, all in the service of a mesmerizing and infectiously danceable sound. The music is a seamless synthesis of diverse influences: a little hard rock, a touch of metal, a measure of funk, a taste of disco, lots of R&B and 1980s synthesizer pop, and healthy doses of a range of Caribbean styles, from salsa and merengue to reggae and ska. The group's musicians deliver constantly permutating arrangements, surefooted melodic, style, and rhythm changes, and intense energy. There are bands who, whatever their virtues on record, take on a luminous dimension in concert. The happy irony is that though Kassav was born in the studio, the brainchild of musicians experimenting with electronic music, the group delivers some of the most compelling live shows around.

To rehearse Kassav's history requires unraveling some of the intertwined strands that make up the rich tapestry of Caribbean music more broadly. This dense, variegated musical culture is itself the living legacy of the region's long history of cultural exchange, born of European colonialism, the slave trade, the sugar plantation complex, Atlantic revolution, abolition, and decolonization. Kassav forged their musical style in the Francophone Caribbean, made up of the islands that became part of the French Empire in the seventeenth and eighteenth centuries: Haiti, France's most important eighteenth-century colony before its slave population won their freedom and their country's independence during the Haitian Revolution; Dominica and Saint Lucia, both former French and British colonies where most inhabitants today speak French-influenced Creoles; and Kassav's home islands of Martinique and Guadeloupe, whose Black inhabitants continued to work under strict labor controls nearly a century after abolition in 1848 and which are today overseas departments of France.[1] Kassav's zouk isn't just great music—it is an important thread in an ongoing musical conversation within the Francophone islands, a considered response to the region's postcolonial situation, an attempt to reinvent Creole cultural identity, at once an artifact and an agent of transformation of the economic modes of musical production in the Caribbean.

Though historians have shown little interest in popular music as a subject for critical inquiry, over the past thirty years musicologists, ethnomusicologists, and cultural studies specialists have devoted considerable attention to Caribbean music. In this, they follow the lead of Caribbean intellectuals from C. L. R. James to Stuart Hall, who saw in local musical forms rich resources for helping

---

1. For historical perspectives, see Aldrich and Connell, *France's Overseas Frontier*; Butel, *Histoire des Antilles françaises*; Dumont, *L'amère patrie*; and Childers, *Seeking Imperialism's Embrace*. All translations are my own unless otherwise indicated.

Caribbean societies think through their own postindependence destinies.[2] Recent scholarship analyzes local musical styles as archetypes of a characteristically Caribbean cultural hybridity, sites for the negotiation and expression of cultural identities, media for the articulation of racial and class differences, weapons of resistance to colonial rule, crucibles for postcolonial national sentiment, and vehicles for political propaganda and contestation.[3] In the Dominican Republic, merengue's syncretism was celebrated as a symbol of a diverse nation's identity and a badge of resistance to the US military occupation early in the twentieth century before Rafael Trujillo harnessed it to his dictatorship. In Haiti, François Duvalier co-opted compas. In Trinidad, calypso lyrics habitually critiqued political and social themes.[4] In contrast, the music of the French-speaking islands has received less scholarly attention than that of the Anglophone and Hispanophone Caribbeans, in whose intellectual and cultural orbits the US-based scholars who have produced much of this literature tend to be situated.[5]

Located at the intersection of the histories of Atlantic empire, migration and transnational exchange, culture and language, economics and globalization, Kassav's story begs for historical investigation. The group's trajectory is ideally suited to tracing the cultural politics of music in the French Caribbean.[6] Its history has implications beyond the Caribbean as well. Their music, at once artistic invention, commercialized commodity, and popular music with global reach, offers a rich terrain on which to examine cultural exchange in a globalized age.[7]

2. James, "Mighty Sparrow"; Hall, "Negotiating Caribbean Identities."

3. Only a small sampling of this literature can be cited here. For surveys, see Bilby, "Caribbean as a Musical Region"; Manuel, Bilby, and Largey, *Caribbean Currents*; and Leymarie, *Musiques caraïbes*. On Barbados, see Best, *Barbadian Popular Music*. On Jamaican reggae, see Constant, *Aux sources du reggae*; Foster, *Roots, Rock, Reggae*; and Cooper, *Sound Clash*. On Trinidadian calypso, see Warner, *Kaiso!*; Quevedo, *Atilla's Kaiso*; Rohlehr, *Calypso and Society*; Rohlehr, *Scuffling of Islands*; Hill, *Calypso Calaloo*; and Guilbault, *Governing Sound*. On South Asian traditions, see Myers, *Music of Hindu Trinidad*; and Manuel, *East Indian Music*. On the Dominican Republic, see Hernandez, *Bachata*; and Austerlitz, *Merengue*.

4. Austerlitz, *Merengue*; Averill, *Day for the Hunter*, chap. 3; Guilbault, *Governing Sound*.

5. For a bibliographical guide to work on the Francophone Caribbean, see Gray, *From Vodou*. On Haiti, see Averill, *Day for the Hunter*; and Largey, *Vodou Nation*. On the French islands, see Desroches, "Les pratiques musicales"; Rosemain, *La musique*; *Les musiques guadeloupéennes*; Desroches, *Les instruments*; Benoit, *Musique populaire*; Desroches, "La musique aux Antilles"; Cally-Lézin, *Musiques*; Uri and Uri, *Musiques et musiciens*; Desroches, "Créolisation musicale"; Gerstin, "Traditional Music"; Mavounzy, *Cinquante ans*; and Hill, *Black Soundscapes*. For more impressionistic approaches, see Jallier and Lossen, *Musique aux Antilles*; Jallier and Jallier-Prudent, *Musique aux Antilles*, esp. 131–34; Bagoé, *Encyclopédie de la musique traditionnelle*; and *Tanbou-a*.

6. Jocelyne Guilbault's substantial body of scholarship on zouk and Kassav asks some of the same questions I do here, but from a musicological rather than a historical perspective. In addition to the works cited below, see Guilbault, "On Interpreting"; and Guilbault, *Zouk*. Brenda F. Berrian has also worked on Kassav; see, e.g., Berrian, "'An-Ba-Chen'n La'"; Berrian, "Sé Cho"; and Berrian, *Awakening Spaces*. See also Ledesma and Scaramuzzo, "Zouk."

7. Appadurai, "Disjuncture"; Appadurai, *Modernity at Large*.

The group's commercial fortunes allow us to interrogate the economic life of popular music on a postcolonial periphery.[8] Kassav's example also allows us to explore the dynamic of musicians' agency, market structures, and cultural imaginaries in "world music," a category whose historical formation, definition, and commercial vagaries are the object of a lively debate: praised by some as fruitful dialogue between locally rooted musical cultures, critiqued by others as a pure product of global capitalism, a commodity shaped by big record labels to appeal to a Western taste for the "exotic" that both reifies ethnicized music as "authentic" and nourishes cryptocolonial nostalgia.[9]

Such an investigation also speaks to efforts by a growing number of historians to integrate France's metropolitan, imperial, and transnational experiences into a broader "global French" history.[10] Like metropolitan French society in general, scholars have been particularly slow to consider the histories of Black people and blackness in France.[11] Kassav's musical and professional navigation between metropolitan France and its overseas Caribbean territories, their exploration of the history of African slavery in their songs, and their appeal to *Antillais* and metropolitan diaspora audiences throw into sharp relief aspects of the troubled relationship between metropole and DOM-TOMs, as well as the tortured negotiations over redefining national identity in the face of France's multicultural realities. The fact that one of the most commercially successful French musical formations does not enjoy a prominent place in histories of French popular music represents a telling absence that itself merits investigation.[12] Kassav's experience also points to Paris's role as a global capital for the production (and consumption) of world music. Situating zouk alongside musics like Algerian *raï* or Senegalese *mbalax* makes it possible to analyze the French encounter with world music in the context of France's ongoing relationship with its former colonies.[13]

This article sketches how Kassav's history sheds light on both the cultural politics of French Caribbean music and the history of global France between the

8. On the economics of music as industry, see Attali, *Bruits*; and Wallis and Malm, *Big Sounds*.

9. Nettl, "World Music"; Slobin, "Micromusics"; Erlmann, "Aesthetics"; Martin, "Who's Afraid"; Mitchell, *Popular Music*; Taylor, *Global Pop*; Bohlman, "World Music"; Feld, "Une si douce berceuse." On calypso, see Rohlehr, "We Getting the Kaiso." On zouk, see Guilbault, *Zouk*; Guilbault, "On Redefining the 'Local'"; Guilbault, "Interpreting World Music"; and Grenier and Guilbault, "*Créolité*."

10. Silverstein, *Algeria in France*; Lebovics, *Bringing the Empire Back Home*; Shepard, *Invention of Decolonization*; Boucheron, *Histoire mondiale*.

11. Notable exceptions include Dewitte, *Les mouvements nègres*; Peabody and Stovall, *Color of Liberty*; Chapman and Frader, *Race in France*; Thomas, *Black France*; Ndiaye, *La condition noire*; and Keaton, Sharpley-Whiting, and Stovall, *Black France*.

12. Dillaz, *La chanson française*; Dillaz, *La chanson sous la Troisième République*; Dillaz, *Vivre et chanter*; Rioux, *50 ans*, which contains a brief discussion of zouk on 408–10; Duneton, *Histoire de la chanson française*; Loosely, *Popular Music*, which briefly evokes Kassav and zouk (51, 53, 74) but does not integrate the DOM-TOMs into its narrative; Briggs, *Sounds French*.

13. Warne, "Impact of World Music," 138; Looseley, *Popular Music*, 50–58.

1970s and today. I argue that Kassav's music represents an inventive cultural and commercial response to structures of neocolonial and capitalist exclusion in the French Caribbean, one that drew on the islands' own cultural resources to fashion a new musical form that has had lasting influence. Kassav owes its global success in part to the emergence of multinational record companies hungry to market new musics from postcolonial peripheries, to the liberalization of France's audiovisual markets, and to Paris's triple role as a capital of world music, metropole of *Francophonie*'s soft-power empire, and home to a large Antillais diaspora. That the music industry, critics, and metropolitan audiences categorized Kassav's work as Antillais, Caribbean, and world music, rather than French, speaks to the historical and racial fault lines that traverse global France and obscure the Frenchness of the French Caribbean to many in the Hexagon.

Beginnings

Kassav took form during a period of intense musical ferment in the French Caribbean, under a broad range of regional and global influences, and amid a pointed debate over Francophone Antillais identity. Through the middle of the twentieth century, the dominant form of popular music in Guadeloupe and Martinique was *biguine*, a homegrown style with roots in the nineteenth century that bears striking similarities to New Orleans jazz.[14] Big bands like clarinetist Alexandre Stellio's Orchestre Antillais performed biguine in the dance halls that animated urban social life in the Antilles.[15] Beginning in the late 1950s, a new musical style from Haiti, invented by saxophonist and bandleader Nemours Jean-Baptiste, derived from merengue, and dubbed *compas direct* (*konpa dirèk* in Creole), began to displace biguine on bandstands. Haitian musicians who had honed their chops playing compas in Port-au-Prince's clubs looked beyond Haiti for new outlets for their music. Touring musicians like Jean-Baptiste's former bandmate and rival Webert Sicot (who called his version *cadence rampa*; *kadans ranpa* in Creole) popularized compas across the Caribbean. A decade later, a new generation of rock-influenced Haitian musicians transposed compas for smaller formations comprising electric guitars, drums, and saxophone and dubbed the new style mini-jazz (*mini-djaz* in Creole). More prosperous Guadeloupe and Martinique furnished the principal market for Haitian live music and records, and a steady flow of Haitian compas and mini-jazz musicians headed to the French islands to find work until the 1980s.[16]

14. Benoit, *Musique populaire*; Rosemain, *Jazz et biguine*.
15. Rosemain, *La danse aux Antilles*; Cyrille, "*Sa Ki Ta Nou*."
16. For a brief overview, see Leymarie, *Musiques caraïbes*, 115–25. See also Averill, *Day for the Hunter*, chaps. 3–4; and Averill, "'Toujou Sou Konpa.'"

By the 1970s, Haitian musicians had reshaped the French Antilles' musical landscape. Local groups like Les Vikings de la Guadeloupe—a talented ensemble who experimented with funk, jazz, and Latin sounds—still occasionally played hometown biguine, but mostly they offered audiences hungry for guitar-oriented compas what they wanted. Antillais musicians put their own touch on compas, creating an up-tempo form they called *cadence* (*kadans* in Creole). Musicians from other islands introduced still more influences into the cadence mix. In the same way that successive generations of Haitian musicians had sought employment in Martinique and Guadeloupe, Gordon Henderson left compas-crazy Dominica to join the Vikings as lead singer. He went on to found Exile One with other Dominican musicians. They mixed Trinidadian calypso with cadence, added horns and synthesizers, sang politically and socially trenchant lyrics more characteristic of calypso than compas, and named the new style *cadence-lypso*. Exile One won a broad following, became the first Creole-language group to sign a contract with a major recording label (Paris-based Barclay), and inspired a host of new groups in Dominica and the French Antilles, including La Perfecta, Selecta Martinique, Les Aiglons, and Expérience 7. Thanks to its reinvention of Haitian compas, Dominica supplanted Haiti as the primary purveyor of popular music in Martinique and Guadeloupe.[17]

Increasingly frustrated with the hegemony of styles and musicians from beyond the French islands, the Vikings' bassist, Pierre-Edouard Décimus, set out to fashion a new popular music specific to Guadeloupe and Martinique, at once modern and anchored in local musical traditions, technically accomplished and capable of winning broad popularity. Décimus brought his brother and fellow bassist Georges aboard and moved to Paris, where they teamed up with a Paris-born Guadeloupean, Jacob Desvarieux, an accomplished rock and R&B guitarist with the studio skills necessary to invent a new sound (and who died in July 2021). Recruiting some of the top musicians in the Guadeloupean expatriate community in Paris, they baptized themselves Kassav and in 1979 cut their first album, the deeply funk-inflected *Love and Ka Dance*. Building the group's sound around elements already present in cadence—modern percussions, brass, electric guitars, and electronic keyboards—Kassav took full advantage of the possibilities afforded by modern studio technology to weld their varied musical borrowings together into a novel form of dance music.[18] Moving away from the dense layering of rhythms, harmonies, and melodies that characterize biguine, compas, and cadence, they sought a cleaner, brighter, more easily danceable sound, one in which musical elements unfold in succession rather than superposition.

17. Leymarie, *Musiques caraïbes*, 120–30.
18. Negrit, *Musique*, 377–87.

Kassav were not the only Antillais musicians revisiting traditional musics in this period. The rise of nationalism, independence parties, and combative labor unions in the 1960s provided a supercharged context for musical experimentation on the islands, and many musicians set out to excavate local musical cultures as part of a broader quest to articulate a distinct Antillais national identity. But if it was one thing to call for a *retour aux sources*, it was another altogether to determine precisely which musical roots one wished to return to. In a society born from so violent a history and such diverse origins, the question of what constituted "authentic" Antillais music was inevitably a contested one. Should true Antillais music privilege musical forms drawn from the Black Caribbean's African past, or the hybridized musical cultures fashioned by enslaved peoples and their descendants? What place should a national music accord to traditions inherited from the white planter class or the imperial metropole?[19]

The musicians engaged in such revivals conceived them to be multidimensional projects, animated by a multitude of distinct (albeit interrelated) objectives. These were, first and foremost, musical projects whose participants worked to master traditional musics. But these projects were also were musicological in scope, aimed at deepening understanding of these musics in broader contexts and tracing their musical genealogies. More broadly still, these were historical projects, studied efforts to connect these musics to the Antillais past from which they came—and in particular to the African diaspora and slave plantation experiences. They were also performative projects, whose protagonists made it part of their mission to play these musics for audiences. These protagonists also understood their mission to be profoundly pedagogical and worked to transmit traditional musics to future generations. Taken together, all these objectives shared a common ideological program, insofar as they proposed drawing on these musics to redefine Antillais identity. And finally, these were explicitly political projects, proposing to mobilize this reinvigorated identity to strengthen national sentiment, demarcate the islands from France, and in some cases advance the cause of independence.

In Guadeloupe, many musicians privileged cultural forms associated with rural laborers, reifying them as authentic expressions of Guadeloupean nationhood precisely because they could be linked genealogically to slave and African cultures. They in turn discounted the orchestral biguines and quadrilles, disqualified as legacies of European colonialism and aspirational trappings of an

19. This was as much a scholarly as a musical and political debate. See discussions in Lafontaine, "Le carnaval de l'"autre""; and Gerstin, "Traditional Music", 190–94. For an example that treats the full range of local musics, whether derived from African, European, or homegrown sources, as equally valid components of Antillais musical tradition, see Rosemain, *La musique*.

urbanized middle class opposed to the people—that is, the Black rural laborers construed to represent the true repositories of an authentic Guadeloupean culture. In one important example, beginning in the 1960s local musicians sought to resurrect the *gwo ka* (Creole for "big drum"), the traditional medium for a form of folk music with deep roots in slave culture, articulated in a series of codified rhythms. Gwo ka revivalists like Vélo, Guy Konkèt (or Conquette), and jazz guitarist Gérard Lockel's Gwo Ka Modèn ensemble intended its rebirth to serve as a potent affirmation of Guadeloupe's identity and political aspirations.[20] The independence parties and trade unions that emerged in the 1960s embraced gwo ka, refigured as a musical symbol of marronage and slave revolt. Lockel is closely tied to the Union Populaire pour la Libération de la Guadeloupe, one of the island's separatist parties, and his song "Lendépendans" serves as the official anthem for the Union Générale des Travailleurs de la Guadeloupe trade union (whose logo features a gwo ka drum).[21] Informed by this Guadeloupean musical renaissance, Kassav incorporated the gwo ka drum into the group and laid down gwo ka rhythms on modern percussions.

Though the group's founders were all Guadeloupeans, they wanted their new style to be pan-Antillais—that is, to draw on Martinique's distinctive musical traditions as well. Like its sister island, Martinique experienced a revival of its own musical heritage in the same period. Formed in the late 1960s, the group Malavoi updated biguine and other traditional dancehall forms like mazurka (*mazouk* in Creole) and quadrille with string-heavy orchestrations and salsa, bossa nova, and Afro-Cuban borrowings. Other revival efforts focused on *chouval bwa* (Creole for wooden horse, because the music traditionally accompanied hand-operated merry-go-rounds), a carnival music with roots in slave dances and *bèlè* (or *ka*, a type of large drum). In traditional chouval bwa ensembles, a percussion section composed of a *bel-air, ka, ti bwa,* and rattle might play alongside an accordion, with accompanying vocalists singing songs poking fun at gender relations, local gossip, and politics. Dédé Saint-Prix, the drummer, flutist, music teacher, Malavoi veteran, inspired proponent of chouval bwa, and founder of the Pakatak ensemble, along with Bernard Pago, who performs as Marcé with his group Tumpak, put chouval bwa back on Martinique's musical map.[22] Kassav in turn incorporated chouval bwa rhythms into their own music.

Kassav also recruited a succession of new members from Martinique, most notably Jocelyne Beroard, who before joining Kassav had already built a resume

20. Lafontaine, "Le carnaval de l'"autre'"; Cyrille, "*Sa Ki Ta Nou*," 241–42; Schnepel, *In Search of a National Identity*, 84, 105–7, 146, 168, 213–14; Laumuno, *Gwoka et politique*; Laumuno, *Et le Gwoka s'est enraciné*.

21. Laumuno, *Gwoka et politique*; Laumuno, *Et le Gwoka s'est enraciné*, 120–23, 129–30.

22. On the bèlè, see Terrine, *La ronde*. On musical revivals in Martinique, see Gerstin, "Reputation"; Gerstin, "Musical Revivals"; and Pulvar, "Le bèlè en Martinique."

as backup vocalist for Cajun-Zydeco singer Zachary Richard, Cameroonian jazz fusion artist Manu Dibango, French pop singer Bernard Lavilliers, and Jamaican reggae star Lee "Scratch" Perry. Beroard provided backup vocals on Kassav's second album (released in 1980), before moving to lead vocals for the group's third album (1981). Two other Martiniquais musicians joined the group for that record: fellow lead singer and Pakatak veteran Jean-Philippe Marthély and keyboardist Jean-Claude Naimro. Guadeloupean Patrick Saint-Eloi signed on as the third lead vocalist the following year.[23]

Deeply influenced by the struggles for workers' rights, civil liberties, and political autonomy that shook Martinique and Guadeloupe in the 1960s and 1970s, Kassav's members envisioned their musical experiment as a contribution to a new, self-confident Antillais identity.[24] This was true of the revival movements, too. What set Kassav apart was the group's insistence on inventing a new, forward-looking popular music, built from an ecumenical borrowing of traditional musics from both islands, as well as musical sources drawn from across the Caribbean, Africa, the United States, and beyond. Desvarieux recalled, "In the context of independence and identity movements, this was a genuine intellectual and political project. The idea was to create an Antillais form of music, one accepted by Antillais, and to spread it everywhere."[25]

Language was an important part of their project. Kassav chose to sing not in French, but exclusively in the Creole language forged by slaves from French and African linguistic sources and still in everyday use in both Guadeloupe and (to a lesser extent) Martinique.[26] For Beroard, "We didn't just want to get every Antillais person dancing, we wanted to encourage them to think about their identity, at a time when one wasn't supposed to speak Creole. And I think we gave them a certain pride."[27] Most of the musical traditions from which Kassav borrowed were already sung in Creole. Kassav broke new linguistic ground in their commitment to sing a modern, commercially successful popular music, aimed at both Caribbean audiences and a broader global market, exclusively in the local tongue. Their music offered not only a pointed rejoinder to the powerful forces working against the use of Creole, like the French school system and broader attitudes that devalorized the idiom, but also a forward-looking model

---

23. Scaramuzzo, "Jocelyne Beroard"; Guilbault, Zouk, 25.
24. On Antillais political and labor movements in this period, see Guillerm, (In)dépendance créole; Placide, Les émeutes; and Gama and Sainton, Mé 67.
25. Le parisien, "Kassav a toujours."
26. On the linguistic situation in the Caribbean, see Alleyne, "Linguistic Perspective." On French Creoles, see Prudent, Des baragouins; Schnepel, In Search of a National Identity; Hazaël-Massieux, Les Créoles; and Hazaël-Massieux, "Les Créoles français." On Creole and Antillais music, see Lafontaine, "Terminologie"; and Chaudenson, Creolization, chap. 7.
27. Le parisien, "Kassav a toujours."

aimed at encouraging novel forms of Creole-language cultural activity.[28] To a certain extent, their move echoed the mobilization of Creoles as symbols of postindependence national identity in other Caribbean musics like Trinidadian calypso.[29] In an interesting exercise in linguistic engineering aimed at advancing their goal to use music to unite the two islands, Kassav's lyrics avoid Creole words specific to either Martinique or Guadeloupe.[30] This too had precedent: Dominican musicians habitually adapted their own Creole so as to be understood in the French islands, though their motivation was more commercial than cultural or political. Like Kassav's choice of language, the group's name was itself a powerful gesture, a good-humored nod to a familiar touchstone of everyday life in the islands: *kassav* is the Creole word for a traditional Caribbean staple, a cake made from manioc (or cassava) flour, coconut, and sugar.

Africa offered further inspiration. Shaped by musical cultures inherited from the islands' slave communities, Caribbean music already drank deeply from African sources. Contemporary West African popular music had also left its mark on the postwar Antillais musical scene. Groups like the Congo-Brazzaville formation Ry-Co Jazz set powerful dynamics of musical cross-fertilization in motion. Ry-Co Jazz put down stakes in Martinique in the late 1960s, introducing Cuban-inspired West African rumba to the islands, before appropriating biguine for themselves and blending it with their own Congolese sound.[31] Ry-Co Jazz's lush music, which Naimro knew firsthand from recording with them, offered Kassav a model for their own rich orchestration. Desvarieux, in turn, had played in the Marseille Afro-rock band Ozila before joining Kassav and was a regular in the Paris recording studios where many African musicians worked. Kassav's first African tour in 1985 sparked an intense engagement with West Africa, and the group worked African musical elements, languages, and historical references into their next album, *Gorée*. Desvarieux's Cameroonian bandmate from his Ozila days, Mbida Douglas, a member of Kassav between 1983 and the 1990s, played a prominent role in shaping *Gorée*.[32]

Kassav didn't just experiment with novel musical forms; they also tested new commercial strategies to promote their music. Their move to Paris coincided with tectonic shifts in the economics of popular music on the islands and beyond. Antillais musicians had traditionally made a living playing gigs in hotels

28. On broader efforts since the 1970s to revive Creole and secure it a place in the public sphere in Martinique and Guadeloupe, see Prudent, "La langue créole"; Prudent, "Ecrire le créole"; and Pulvar, "Créolité."
29. Guilbault, *Governing Sound*, 48–49.
30. Berrian, "'An-Ba-Chen'n La,'" 208–9.
31. Averill, "'Toujou Sou Konpa,'" 76–77.
32. Douglas, interview by Ebolé Bola et al.

and dance halls, but the advent of portable sound systems in the 1980s made it possible for people to organize private parties without live bands, ushering out the era of dance halls. As the doors closed on paid live performance, new ones opened in the recording studio. François Mitterrand's Socialist government deregulated the airwaves in the 1980s, opening the way for a multitude of *radios libres* (independent radio stations) that began broadcasting a broader range of musics and targeting new audiences across France. The left also promulgated a new copyright law in 1985, guaranteeing royalties to performers, composers, lyricists, and producers, and slapped a tax on blank audiocassettes to compensate the record industry for lost revenue. These two measures created new opportunities for artists willing to focus on records.[33] Kassav bridged the two worlds by bringing together musicians who had cut their teeth on the Antilles' bandstands and those who had perfected their craft in Parisian recording studios.

Taking on a grueling workload, Kassav each year put out one album under its own name and up to three additional albums under members' names. The group also followed the example of big European and American groups that toured to promote new albums. Beginning in 1981, Kassav regularly took to the road, putting on spectacular shows, replete with backup singers and dancers, elaborate choreographies, and infrastructure-heavy productions that quickly became the hallmark of their concerts. Their shows communicated loud and clear that zouk was not just dance music—Kassav insisted that they be watched and listened to.

It is a striking irony that a group whose music critiques France's colonial past owes its international success in part to the neo- and postcolonial networks that continue to bind France's overseas territories and former colonies to the metropole. It was precisely their decision to follow the connections that link the Caribbean to the Hexagon that led Kassav's founders to Paris, the global capital for Francophone music. There, they joined musicians from across the Francophone world, plugging themselves into lively Antillais and African music scenes.[34] In this, Kassav followed a long line of musicians who, beginning in the 1930s, had traveled to Paris to perform in the capital's Antillais cabarets and bars: Stellio and his Orchestre Antillais played at the 1931 Colonial Exposition; the Vikings de la Guadeloupe came to Paris in 1970; Haitian compas direct ensembles followed their example.[35] If *Francophonie*'s political, economic, and

33. Angelo, *Socio-économique de la musique*; Looseley, *Popular Music*, 50–51, 142–43, and chap. 8.

34. For many of Kassav's albums, the group's working practice is more transatlantic still: they record percussion and vocals in the Antilles and brass in Paris, and the songs are mixed in Paris. See Guilbault, "Interpreting World Music," 32.

35. On the Paris musical scene, see the exhaustive Negrit, *Musique*; on Kassav in particular, see 341–43, 351–56.

cultural infrastructures drew musicians from the postcolonial peripheries to the center, they also made it possible to broadcast their musics to novel points on the Francophone compass. With shows like Gilles Obringer's "Canal Tropical," Radio France International (RFI; the French state's world service) played a crucial role in bringing African musicians like Youssou N'Dour and Alpha Blondy to world attention in the 1980s. It was thanks to RFI and Obringer that listeners in West Africa first discovered Kassav.[36] When the group left for Africa in 1985 to play their first big stadium concerts on what was also their first tour outside the Caribbean, they were stunned to discover that they had already won a large and fervent fan base there.

Kassav now had an international following. Shortly after their African tour, they played a series of sold-out shows at the Zénith concert hall in Paris. The following year, Kassav's open-air concert capping Paris's annual Fête de la Musique drew nearly a quarter of a million people. Concerts across Europe, the Americas, and Asia followed. In 1989 Kassav became the first Black group to perform in the USSR. Eager to ride the rising world music tide, CBS (soon to be Sony) signed the group to its first big recording contract in 1987, and Kassav toured the United States for the first time in 1998. The deal provided financial breathing room, permitting the group to take more time on each studio album. It also cemented Kassav's international success and catapulted French Caribbean music onto the world stage.[37]

Reimagining Antillais Identity

Part of the pleasure of listening to Kassav's music is in picking out the myriad individual influences from the kinetic mix. They deploy a range of traditional Caribbean rhythms, including biguine, the gwo ka *mendé*, and carnival *mas a Sen Jan* beats from Guadeloupe, and chouval bwa from Martinique, as a readily danceable and—to Antillais audiences, at least—eminently familiar rhythmic vocabulary. Their instrumentation betrays the group's debts to compas and biguine, funk and R&B groups like Earth, Wind & Fire, and Desvarieux's taste for rock guitar. Consider their 1987 song "Soley" ("Sun"): gwo ka and ti bwa drums engage in syncopated dialogue with rhythms quoted from biguine and compas direct (complete with compas's characteristic cowbell), atop which big-band jazz, rock guitar, and salsa keyboards all rub shoulders. The group's borrowings are simply too varied and eclectic to allow for a precise accounting of musical debts, as Pierre-Edouard Décimus admits: "The music is so blended

---

36. Looseley, *Popular Music*, 54; Lee, "A Dakar."
37. Berrian, "'An-Ba-Chen'n La,'" 217–18; Bowermaster, "Zouk, Rattle, and Roll."

that it is impossible to 'dissect' it."[38] Kassav's Antillais fans dispensed with such musicological niceties altogether when, recognizing the birth of something new, they baptized the group's style *zouk*, the Creole word for dance party.

The accusation leveled by some critics that Kassav's songs are no more than festive, romantic fluff, however, does not stand up to an attentive reading of their Creole-language lyrics. In an otherwise sympathetic appraisal of zouk, one French critic reproached its frivolity, suggesting it constituted a blithe betrayal of artists' responsibilities to address hard Antillais realities: "Zouk presents itself as the friendly face of love and desire. Whereas the political and social situation in the islands is often tense, the zouk repertory ignores this context."[39] In fact, many of Kassav's songs engage thoughtfully with an array of themes beyond love and dance, including Antillais identity and history. "Péyi a bel" ("That Beautiful Country") sings of love of the islands. "Wonderful" narrates the metropolitan diaspora's longing for home. The songs on *Gorée*, the album inspired by their first visit to Africa, whose title is borrowed from an important site of memory for Atlantic slavery in Senegal, explore the African dimension of Caribbean history. The song "An-ba-chen'n la" ("Chained Below") remembers the transatlantic slave trade. "Doubout pikan" ("Standing Tall") exhorts Martiniquais and Guadeloupeans to take pride in their African roots. "Neg mawon / balata" (Black Maroon / Balata Tree) honors the memory of runaway slaves who joined with Amerindians to form highland communities free from colonial control. Their 1995 album *Difé* takes up youth unemployment, violence, and drug addiction in the islands (Stevie Wonder makes a guest appearance on harmonica). Far from a lightweight party band, Kassav creates music aimed at encouraging Antillais, as Beroard puts it, "to reflect on our future . . . to imagine that tomorrow, we could do beautiful things, . . . great things, and then to work hard to achieve them . . . to remind ourselves who we are . . . our history . . . our culture."[40]

The group's project rapidly found a sympathetic hearing among some of the most important intellectuals in the French Caribbean, who recognized in Kassav a powerful cultural and political voice. Among them were Patrick Chamoiseau and Jean Bernabé, two of the authors of the 1989 treatise *Eloge de la créolité* (*In Praise of Creoleness*), a cultural manifesto that stands as the most important statement of Antillais cultural identity today. Bernabé, a writer and professor of linguistics at the Université des Antilles et de la Guyane whose work

38. Quoted in Guilbault, *Zouk*, 147. Guilbault, "Interpretation out of Contradiction," develops a similar argument.

39. Rioux, *50 ans*, 408, 410.

40. Beroard, interview, *Outre-Mer 1ère*.

has done much to win legitimacy for the Creole language, celebrated zouk as a valuable expression of important elements of Antillais culture and society. Chamoiseau, a Martiniquais writer whose novels explore Martinique's relationship to Caribbean history and Creole culture, wrote the lyrics to Kassav's song "Pa ni pwoblem" ("No Problem").

Bernabé and Chamoiseau recognized in Kassav cultural fellow travelers, admiring in their music an instance of their own conception of Antillais identity put into practice. In *Eloge de la créolité*, they challenged the model for transatlantic Francophone black identity first articulated by the leaders of the Négritude movement during the 1930s: Léopold Senghor, the first president of postindependence Senegal; Léon Damas, deputy from Guyane to the French National Assembly; and Martiniquais deputy and mayor of Fort-de-France Aimé Césaire.[41] Senghor, Damas, and Césaire conceived Négritude as a poetic and political instrument whose purpose was in large part to convince Africans and Antillais to make common cause. Embracing the language and literary culture of the colonizer, they turned them against France to critique empire and racism. For Bernabé, Chamoiseau, and their coauthor Raphaël Confiant, Négritude sketched an overly monolithic vision of identity, defined primarily by race and leaving little room for thinking through the specificities of the French Caribbean. They critiqued the movement for its insufficiently critical use of French, arguing that the imposition of the language of Molière and the diglossic devalorization of vernacular Creoles had wrought lasting political, cultural, and social harm. They proposed to think in terms of *créolité* rather than "blackness." In search of new, historically and contextually rooted categories of identity, they imagined *Antillanité* as a hybrid composite of all the pieces that make up the Caribbean's rich cultural puzzle, including not only enslaved Africans but also the islands' Indigenous peoples, European settlers, and the Asian and South Asian laborers transported there early in the twentieth century. Bernabé, Chamoiseau, and Confiant emphatically proclaimed that "Our History is a braid of histories."[42]

By weaving together multiple musical influences from across Guadeloupe and Martinique, Kassav's music constitutes a creole "braid" writ small, a musical exemplar of this historicized and culturally composite vision of Antillanité.[43] It didn't hurt that its theorists assigned music a privileged place in their very conception of Antillais identity. For the creator of the Antillanité category,

41. Confiant, *Aimé Césaire*; Arnold, *Modernism*; Wilder, *French Imperial Nation-State*; Wilder, *Freedom Time*; Filostrat, *Negritude Agonistes*; Khalfa, "Naissance de la négritude."

42. Bernabé, Chamoiseau, and Confiant, *Eloge de la créolité*, 26. On *Antillanité*, see Glissant, *Le discours antillais*, esp. 422–25. See also Gallagher, "*Créolité* Movement."

43. For an analysis of how zouk embodies *créolité*, see Guilbault, "Créolité."

Martiniquais Edouard Glissant, "Music is so constitutive (via rhythm) of our historical and daily existence" that Antillais should be especially attentive to cultivating in it "a fruitful syncretism."[44] Musical renewal was also for Glissant a necessary means to preserve music from becoming a static, dust-covered vehicle of a fossilized, folklorized identity, empty of any substantive social or political critique.[45] Bernabé went furthest, recognizing in zouk a cultural form attuned to the specific character of creole social life, as well as an instrument for helping Antillais rid themselves of the cultural and psychic yoke of colonialism, "a practice integrating fundamental elements of creole conviviality. . . . Such therapy, moreover, would fit in with the belief that the salvation of our countries must first go through a cultural revolution, a decolonization of minds."[46]

Kassav's members were not the only musicians to seek inspiration from a plurality of sources, aiming in this way to recover and reproduce a hybridity they saw as characteristic of Antillais music and identity alike. Such approaches forcefully challenged competing efforts to identify a single local musical tradition, assign it a privileged status as an emblem of cultural identity, and devalorize other forms as inauthentic or tainted by association with colonial domination. It was for precisely these reasons that some criticized the proponents of gwo ka in 1970s Guadeloupe for insisting that the style's origins in the island's slave past lent it unrivaled legitimacy. To dismiss styles like biguine and quadrille for being too European, critics argued, belied the fact that these styles themselves encompass significant African elements and had long enjoyed genuine popularity in poor, predominantly Black, rural communities.[47] The prominent biguine musician Gérard Laviny looked with suspicion on "back to musical roots" movements in general, arguing that any attempt to parse the islands' varied musics in a quest for a single, true musical source would inevitably collapse under the weight of its own internal historical and musical contradictions: "What 'sources' do we mean precisely? In the beginning, the Antilles were inhabited by Caribs, then by whites, then Blacks. I am opposed to the move to focus any search on one single component of the Antillais population, because I feel myself to be a mix of Indian. white, and Black. I am Antillais and any research that can deepen *métissage* is of sincere interest to me."[48]

Kassav were arguably at their most lyrically inventive when singing about love. Some songs are straight-ahead celebrations of romance, like "Ou Lé," in which Desvarieux's deep, gravelly voice issues a happy invitation to erotic love.

---

44. Glissant, *Le discours antillais*, 225–26.
45. Glissant, *Le discours antillais*, 225–27.
46. Berrian, "'An-Ba-Chen'n La,'" 217.
47. Lafontaine, "Musique et société."
48. Laviny, interview, in Jallier and Lossen, *Musique aux Antilles*, 105.

More originally, in song after song Kassav turns its back on the male-centered, often sexually explicit lyrics that characterized much contemporary popular music in the Antilles.[49] The group prefers to describe new possibilities for gender roles and to challenge traditional arrangements. Their songs explore women's perspectives, celebrate mutually respectful relationships, and portray men confronted with heartbreak and self-doubt. In "Ki jan ké fè" ("What Am I to Do?"), Saint-Eloi's smooth, near falsetto cries a man's despair after his lover has left him. In Naimro's "Ou changé" ("You Have Changed"), a man in a dying marriage rehearses how he and his wife drifted apart. In "Bel kréati" ("Beautiful Creature"), Marthély wields his sensual voice to sing a man's declaration of love as he gazes at his life partner asleep beside him—Marthély's plaintive *ayayays* a tender expression of longing. Poking fun at men's reluctance to pull their weight in the domestic sphere, "Mari Mani Mélé" ("Mani's Husband Is in a Bind") relays the lament of a man at a loss with household tasks. The very fact that Beroard became a lead singer was in and of itself a significant break with the masculine world of Caribbean music, and she made certain to sing about strong women. In the heartrending "Ke sa leve" ("I Will Stand"), a woman holds herself with dignity as she responds to the man who has just announced he is leaving her—a perfect vehicle for Beroard's pure, powerful voice. In other songs, she scolds men allergic to fidelity. The tongue-in-cheek "Jilo Mayé" tells the story of a man who forgets to show at his own wedding. In "Pa kriyé mwen" ("Don't Call Me") Beroard blasts Antillais men for referring to their girlfriends as "cher la" (piece of flesh).[50]

Admittedly, many of their songs' lyrics are simple paeans to partying. Others revel in the pleasure of zouk itself, like their first international hit, the hypnotic "Zouk la sé sèl médikaman nou ni" ("Zouk Is the Only Medicine We Need"). For musicians seeking musical and thematic vocabularies with which to craft a new yet recognizably Caribbean musical idiom, few cultural sites could resonate more loudly with local audiences than carnival and dance. For Chamoiseau, "atop the fertile base of zouk's polyrhythms it is possible to sense and to live to its fullest that which we are: identities rooted yet open, opaque yet so very transparent to love, dance, friendship, the joy and the good things in life."[51]

In the face of commercial pressures to produce music in French for the metropolitan market or English for the world music market, Kassav's choice to

49. Mahabir, "Rise of Calypso Feminism"; Smith, "Performing Gender."
50. Kassav's treatment of gender has not always been entirely consistent; for a critique of the objectification of women on the group's early album covers, see Domiquin, "Faut-il brûler nos vieilles pochettes."
51. Delver and Chamoiseau, "Pour Patrick Saint-Eloi."

sing in Creole was also anything but self-evident. After all, not all Antillais musicians have displayed the same fidelity to the local vernacular, and by the 2000s other zouk ensembles were increasingly singing in French. To sing about dancing and carnival, courtship and love in Creole invested the language with relevance for new generations of listeners. Heeding the sociolinguistic truism that a language is headed for extinction when teenagers stop flirting in it, Kassav's songs fight language death by teaching a complete Creole grammar of seduction. Glissant preferred an economic metaphor to test an idiom's health: "A language in which a people can no longer produce things is a language in its death throes."[52] A mere decade after their founding, linguists were already calling Kassav and zouk the most dynamic motors for promoting Creole.[53]

Kassav's attachment to Creole is also in tune with Bernabé's, Chamoiseau's, and Confiant's ideas. As elsewhere in the Caribbean, Creole-language music offered an opportunity to fly the banner of Antillais identity. Moreover, the inherently composite linguistic character of Creole, born over a short period of time from contact between multiple languages, makes it a perfect instantiation of their ideal of *créolité*, a linguistic braid whose very grammar embodies the Caribbean's historical and cultural plurality. Kassav's international success in turn modified the very terms for Creole's use, creating new spaces for expression at a historical moment in which Antillais are under increasing pressure to adopt French or English, the languages of the postcolonial metropole, the national education system, labor markets, and transnational capitalism. For Kassav to take Creole-language popular music onto the global stage is, in some sense, to exercise what Glissant calls "the right to opacity."[54] Most listeners delight in Kassav's music without understanding the lyrics; it's up to outsiders interested in exploring further to take the next linguistic step.

Considered on purely musical terms, Kassav's integration of contemporary influences from across the Caribbean, North America, and Europe puts into practice a model for Antillais cultural creation and identity more open-ended still than the Antillanité framework. It is precisely this capacity for appropriation and renewal that Guadeloupean novelist Maryse Condé celebrates in zouk. For Condé, any search for purely local expressions of identity risks igniting vain debates over authenticity, setting islanders against a diaspora often accused of abandoning home and culture, and imposing an insoluble choice between

52. Glissant, *Le discours antillais*, 345.
53. Prudent, "La pub, le zouk, et l'album," 210, 213: "Creole and its culture are experiencing a clear period of popular awareness, thanks to the extraordinary success of zouk music. . . . Zouk has thus become the principal international vector of Antillais creole."
54. Glissant, *Le discours antillais*, 11, also 245.

Creole and French as idioms of cultural expression. "Are there not multiple versions of *Antillanité*?" she asks. Condé prefers identities and cultural forms that figure the Antilles as

> a space without defined boundaries, porous to distant sounds, traversed by even the most contradictory influences. Rap rubs shoulders with gwoka. . . . Cultural elements taken from everywhere collide, bleed one against the other, and give birth to new forms. We must valorize new cultural *métissages* which challenge the traditional *métissages* which have already become stratified by use. *Métissage* has always been a source of fear for constituted societies. . . . For all change provokes fear.[55]

Zouk for Condé offers precisely such a form: something akin to Paul Gilroy's call to embrace "mutation, hybridity, and intermixture" or James Clifford's notion of diasporic identity as "polythetic . . . a set of practices and dispositions"—a forward-looking, mutable counterpoint to what she sees as the still overly circumscribed character of Bernabé, Chamoiseau, and Confiant's ideal.[56] Hybridity for Condé is practice not essence, an ethic of openness rather than a badge of cultural distinctiveness, a method for building cultural bridges in the place of affirming difference. Born in the Paris metro region, zouk is the diaspora's gift to the Caribbean; ecumenical and unifying, "zouk is appreciated by everybody."[57] The group's multicultural personnel—having counted musicians from Martinique, Guadeloupe, metropolitan France, Trinidad, Cameroon, and Algeria—and its openness to musical styles from beyond the Antilles represent Condé's ideal of dynamic hybridity in cultural and social action.

Modes of Musical Production

Décimus founded Kassav in the hopes that it might stimulate the professionalization of the local music scene. By example and design, the group opened up new artistic and commercial opportunities in the Antilles. Their success inspired musicians to embrace zouk and drove the growth of the local music industry. An expanding network of recording studios and production companies made it possible for new ensembles to record on the islands, an option that Paris-based Kassav had not enjoyed, and by the late 1980s over a hundred locally produced zouk albums were hitting the market every year. Keeping faith with Décimus's original project, Kassav organized music competitions to promote young talents and regularly shared their stages with and offered their help to other zouk

55. Condé, "Chercher nos vérités," 309–10.
56. Gilroy, *Black Atlantic*, 223; Clifford, *Routes*, 44.
57. Condé, "Chercher nos vérités," 307, quoted in Pfaff, *Conversations*, 114.

formations. Zouk also opened doors to women artists, including the trio of female vocalists who fronted Zouk Machine (founded in 1986 by veterans from Expérience 7): Tanya Saint-Val (who had sung with the Vikings de la Guadeloupe), Joëlle Ursull, and former Kassav backup singer Edith Lefel.[58]

Once zouk became the dominant popular music on the French islands, it rapidly spawned a multitude of stylistic variants. Kassav themselves composed two distinct kinds of songs. The first, up-tempo, high-energy numbers like "Zouk la sé sèl médikaman nou ni" and "Syé bwa" ("Saw Wood"), draw on the *mizik vidé* traditionally played during carnival. Referred to as *zouk-béton* or *chiré*, this sound was ubiquitous in dance clubs in the Caribbean and Paris in the 1980s and 1990s. The second are slow love songs like "Bel kréati," a style known as *zouk-love*. Many of the biggest zouk stars gravitated to zouk-love, like Saint-Val and, less happily, Francky Vincent and his absurdist sexual bombast. Kassav pioneered reggae-inflected zouk with songs like "Lévé tèt' ou" ("Lift Your Head") and in the 1990s other zouk singers like Shango drew from Jamaican dancehall and raggamuffin. Some singers, including Thierry Cham, Jean-Michel Rotin, and Slaï, fused zouk with R&B. Still others, like the group Zouk Look, embraced rap. Signaling a return to zouk's Antillais sources, Marcé et Tumpak coined the term *zouk-chouval* for the title of their 1987 album composed of electrified versions of chouval bwa, gwo ka, and biguine.

Kassav's readiness to collaborate with musicians working in other styles reflects the same commitment to crossing musical borders that was a starting point for zouk itself. Committed to helping keep Martinique's and Guadeloupe's musical traditions alive, the group's members frequently work with musicians playing in more traditional modes. Beroard, for example, regularly sings from the biguine repertoire and performs with groups like Malavoi. Attentive to newer musics as well, Desvarieux and Beroard have sung with the Guadeloupean reggae-dancehall artist Admiral T, whom Desvarieux has all but appointed the next torchbearer of Antillais music. Haitian artists also represent natural collaborators: Wyclef Jean has invited Desvarieux and Beroard to perform on studio recordings, and Desvarieux produced a song for Michel Martelly, Haiti's former president as well as keyboardist and singer ("Pa Manyen Fanm Nan" on the compilation *Haitian Troubadours*). During Georges Décimus's 1991–2004 sabbatical from Kassav, he teamed up with Jeff Joseph, lead singer of the Dominican cadence-lypso band Gramacks, to form Volt-Face, playing a sharper, more

---

58. Guilbault, "Sociopolitical, Cultural, and Economic Development." On women in zouk, see Guilbault, "Sociopolitical, Cultural, and Economic Development," 31–32; Negrit, *Musique*, 364–73; and Beroard, interview by Sophie Vigroux.

cadence-lypso–oriented form of zouk. Further afield, Naimro toured with world music guru Peter Gabriel in 1993, and Desvarieux wrote a song melding raï with zouk for the Algerian singer Khaled (the 2004 "Zine Zina").[59]

Kassav's music has had enormous influence, as musicians far beyond Martinique and Guadeloupe adopted zouk and, by crossing it with local styles, made it their own. Zouk thus became not just a type of world music but also a manifold of musics articulated in various styles around the world. Across Latin America, musicians in search of sure hits churned out countless covers of Kassav's songs (frequently with a certain disregard for copyright law). Kassav returned the favor with its 1998 album *Un toque latino*, recorded in Cuba and mixed in Latin America's music capital, Miami, on which they sang salsa-inflected versions of their own songs in Spanish. In a similar musical-translation move, Kassav produced the album *Wonderful* in 1994, performing behind a trio composed of its three Trinidadian backup singers, Karla Gonzales, Natalie Yorke, and Juslyn Jones, dubbed Shades of Black for the occasion, who sang English-language versions of the group's songs. Across Africa, artists like Olivier N'Goma in Gabon and Awa Maïga and Monique Séka in Côte d'Ivoire have mixed zouk with local forms to create an Afro-zouk sound. In Angola, Eduardo Paim combined zouk with *semba*, the style invented by guitarist Liceu Vieira Dias and his ensemble Ngola Ritmos in the 1950s to affirm Angolan identity in the struggle against Portuguese colonialism, to create *kizomba*. Zouk also enjoys considerable popularity in Cape Verde, and musicians like Jorge Neto, Beto Dias, and Suzanna Lubrano have blended it with *coladeiro* to create *cola-zouk*. So blown away was Miles Davis upon hearing Kassav for the first time that he listened to one of their CDs for three days straight and then incorporated zouk into his 1989 album *Amandla*.[60] Less felicitously, Jimmy Buffett covered *Kolé séré* as "Love and Luck"—but we can't hold this against Kassav.

There is a certain irony that a musical genre created to free Guadeloupe and Martinique from compas's empire ultimately imposed a certain hegemony over Haiti itself. As Desvarieux recalled, "It's this Haitian imperialism that we were rising against when we began Kassav."[61] Although such remarks may exaggerate the extent to which Haitian musicians in fact enjoyed dominant positions outside Haiti in this period, they designated a musical other from which Antillais music needed to be defended, tracing a discursive limit on the group's explicit mappings of acceptable sources for their music's hybridity.[62] Zouk quickly

---

59. On Gabriel as archetype of a particular form of world music, see Taylor, *Global Pop*, 41–52.
60. Cole, *Last Miles*, 287.
61. Averill, "'Toujou Sou Konpa,'" 86.
62. Averill, *Day for the Hunter*, 27–29.

attracted audiences and imitators in Haiti, initiating a new cycle of musical influence and appropriation. In the late 1980s, Haitian compas ensembles like Top-Vice borrowed a page from Kassav's MIDI playbook, using synthesizers to invent *compas nouvelle génération*.[63]

Zouk in the Metropole

As we have seen, Kassav drew from—and helped reshape—musics situated in different cultural spaces and at different geographic scales: Martinique and Guadeloupe; the Caribbean, Latin America, and West Africa; and the world music genre broadly conceived. But Kassav's history is also intimately bound up with that of the French metropole. The social, commercial, and cultural geographies of the group's fortunes throw into sharp relief important features of metropolitan France's recent history: the emergence of a sizable Antillais diaspora in the Hexagon, rapid shifts in the commercial and broadcasting landscape for popular music, and the uneasy national conversation about race, diversity, and France's colonial past.

Indeed, Kassav's history is as much rooted in the metropole as it is in the Caribbean. By moving to Paris in the early 1980s, the group's musicians joined a significant Antillais diaspora several decades in the making. Beginning in the 1960s, the French state engineered the large-scale migration of Guadeloupeans and Martiniquais to the Hexagon, seeking to ease what it saw as unsustainably high demographic growth in the islands and to supply cheap labor to the civil service, police, hospitals, and postal and telecommunications services. Today one out of four Antillais lives in the metropole, of whom two-thirds are in the Paris region, making up a community that is sometimes playfully referred to as the "third island."[64] Antillais living in metropolitan France, those born in the Caribbean as well as the second generation born in Europe, continue to speak Creole widely.[65]

The diaspora in turn provided Kassav with one of its most important audiences. The group's cultural (and linguistic) project to create a pan-Antillais music made zouk well suited for a diaspora in which distinct Guadeloupean and Martiniquais identities, strongly felt in the islands, took second stage to a collective Antillais identity in the metropolitan context. A network of associations,

63. Averill, "'Toujou Sou Konpa,'" 83–88.

64. On Antillais migration to metropolitan France, see Anselin, *L'émigration antillaise en France: Du Bantoustan*; Anselin, *L'émigration antillaise en France: La troisième île*; Constant, "La politique française"; Domenach and Picouet, *La dimension migratoire*; Condon and Ogden, "Questions of Emigration"; and Condon, "Migrations antillaises." For recent statistics on the Antillais diaspora in metropolitan France, see Abdouni and Fabre, "365,000 Domiens."

65. See Condon, "Pratiques et transmission," esp. 297, 304; and Tessoneau, "Le Créole."

bars, clubs, and music groups provided a dense cultural infrastructure for Antillais sociability. In the 1970s, for example, Antillais musicians animated a small Parisian counterpart to the islands' gwo ka and bèlè revival movement.[66] With the deregulation of French airwaves in the 1980s came new radio stations targeted specifically to Antillais audiences that, along with Paris clubs catering to the same public, played important roles in popularizing zouk.

Its transatlantic appeal notwithstanding, Kassav's base in Paris touched the raw nerve of diaspora. For a group to claim to speak for Antillais identity from their home in the metropole was to pluck at the tense fault lines dividing Guadeloupeans and Martiniquais still on the islands from those who had left to find work in the Hexagon. During an interview with an Antilles-based newspaper following a series of sold-out concerts in Paris in 1987, Beroard found herself challenged to justify the group's decision to live in the capital: "You can reassure everyone, when we leave we are still Antillais, even in Paris we continue to eat Antillais food, we speak with each other—we sing—in Creole. Truly, there is really nothing to be worried about." In the same interview, Beroard protests the group's good Antillais faith, detailing a pragmatic variable-geometry approach to identity, in which Frenchness is an asset that can be mobilized when expedient to promote zouk: "I did an interview . . . and the journalist asked me if I felt French in Africa, I answered no. I told him that I only realize I am French when I show my passport at border controls. He asked me if I felt more American. I said no! I am Antillaise. . . . I labor on behalf of the Antilles. Now . . . if the fact of being French can . . . help me and the group be better known, why not?"[67] In their emphatic insistence on the authenticity and permanence of her Caribbean commitments, Beroard's answers adopt a defensive posture that acknowledges Antillais anxieties about emigration's threat to social and cultural life on the islands. As with the group's initial rejection of Haitian compas, Beroard refuses here to embrace the real diasporic dimensions to the group's music and history, fashioning a narrative about zouk that stops well short of the open-ended possibilities that Maryse Condé has discerned in their music.

Social and political change helped reshape metropolitan France's popular music scene in the 1980s, creating a context in which Kassav's music could find new audiences beyond the diaspora. Mitterrand's celebration of the "right to be different" signaled a substantial shift in official discourse and public policy, traditionally attached to rigid, assimilationist conceptions of French identity.[68] Exemplified by the 1983 "March for Equality and against Racism" and the

66. Negrit, *Musique*; Laumuno, *Et le Gwoka s'est enraciné*, 116–18.
67. Beroard, interview, *France-Antilles*.
68. Vichniac, "Socialists and *Droit*."

antiracism association SOS Racisme founded the following year, broad-based social movements campaigned for civil rights and recognition of France's ethnic and cultural diversity. Mitterrand's emblematic minister of culture, Jack Lang, embraced popular culture, putting substantial state support behind popular music, via copyright reform, funds, festivals, and the construction of a nation-wide network of concert halls. The deregulation of broadcasting witnessed the proliferation of *radios libres* like Radio Nova and Radio Beur in Paris or Radio Galère in Marseille, which introduced curious listeners to musical styles like raï that had occupied little place in the staid state-controlled radioscape of 1960s and 1970s France.[69]

Metropolitan musicians in this period increasingly borrowed from musical cultures outside France and fashioned lyrics that challenged traditional notions of French nationhood. The musical soundscape of many young people—the so-called *génération Mitterrand*—wore its internationalist, humanitarian good intentions on its sleeve. At Mitterrand's death, a record company put together a compilation of songs titled *Les Années Mitterrand* intended to evoke this shared musical experience. It included songs by Tunisian singer Amina, raï stars Khaled and Rachid Taha, and Cameroonian Manu Dibango as well as by mainstream white singers supportive of immigration and cultural diversity (such as Alain Bashung's "Tu touches pas à mon pote" ["Hands Off My Buddy"]—a song that borrowed SOS Racisme's slogan).[70] IAM took inspiration from American rap to affirm their own multicultural identities and challenge listeners to recognize how immigration had enriched French society. Other groups chose to sing in France's regional languages in defiance of a Jacobin tradition hostile to local idioms and cultures, from Alan Stivell in Breton and I Muvrini in Corsican to Massilia Sound System in Occitan.[71] After all, Mitterrand delivered his speech on the "right to be different" in 1981 with metropolitan France's regional cultures in mind, not its colonial past or postcolonial present. Such groups often made common cause with musicians tied to North and West Africa.[72]

While Kassav undoubtedly benefited from this favorable context, headlining the 1986 Fête de la Musique in Paris, performing in the new venues built on Lang's watch, and winning a broad following in the Hexagon, the group nonetheless bumped up against telling limits to this musical ecumenicism. Zouk

69. Angelo, *Socio-économique de la musique*, chap. 8, esp. 115–34; Looseley, *Popular Music*, 50–51 and chap. 7; Eling, *Politics of Cultural Policy*, esp. chap. 7.

70. Looseley, *Popular Music*, 3.

71. Rioux, *50 ans*, 244–50; Abjean and Dumontier, *Bretagne est musique*; Bensignor, "Alan Stivell"; Martel, *Massilia Sound System*.

72. Silverstein, *Algeria in France*, chap. 7; Lebovics, *Bringing the Empire Back Home*, chap. 1.

never received the same kind of state support, commercial backing, or media exposure as other genres.[73] In contrast, French rap won nothing less than official consecration.[74] The Socialist embrace of rap was an eminently political move, an emphatic declaration that the youth of France's disadvantaged banlieues (imagined in this reductive rhetoric all to be enthusiastic fans of hip-hop) represented full and legitimate members of the national community. Not only did the Socialist Party never fold French Caribbean music into its rhetoric in this way, but zouk is also tellingly absent from the *Années Mitterrand*'s cultural snapshot of the period: Tonton David, a reggae artist from Réunion, is the album's only representative from a DOM-TOM.

Following the 1989 controversy over Muslim girls wearing head scarves in schools and the rise of the far-right Front National as an electoral force, the public conversation on diversity grew considerably more contentious. The Socialists shelved Mitterrand's "droit à la différence" in favor of a narrower discourse on national identity. Media in the Hexagon paid less attention to Kassav. "There's no point in beating around the bush," insisted music journalist François Bensignor; "it must be said: there was a form of ambient racism in the mass media. In the 1980s, when Kassav was at its height, there was a genuine opening up of society. But it all changed in the 1990s."[75] Radio listeners in metropolitan France in this period were far likelier to hear a Guadeloupean rapper born in suburban Paris sing *about* zouk in a reggae-inflected song on the Antillais diaspora (Doc Gynéco's "Né ici") than they were actually to hear any zouk.

The music industry's commercial strategies threw these selective figurations of the French national community into even sharper relief. Record companies were perfectly happy to cash in on the commercial potential of new music, but they also lumped groups like Kassav or Massilia Sound System into the world music rubric—as if musics located on the peripheries of French history, sung in languages other than French, fell outside the boundaries of what constituted "French" music.[76] As Kassav's members ruefully remarked, "For us the only niche they have been able to find is world music. So as not to have to say the music of Third-World people!"[77] Though Kassav's record sales and worldwide concert attendance make it one of the most popular and commercially

73. The Angoulême festival, Musiques Métisses, represents a notable exception: originally a jazz festival, it headlined Caribbean and African musics in conjunction with government efforts to celebrate the cultures of the DOM-TOMs. See Angelo, *Socio-économique de la musique*, 93–94.

74. Béthune, *Le rap*, 205–33; Martínez; *Le rap français*; Hammou, *Une histoire du rap*, chap. 4.

75. Miclet, "Le zouk."

76. David L. Looseley remarks how Occitan groups like the Fabulous Trobadors and Massilia Sound System became categorized as world music groups (*Popular Music*, 56–58). On Corsican polyphony's repackaging as world music in the 1990s, see Bithell, *Transported*, chap. 7.

77. Quoted in Looseley, *Popular Music*, 53.

successful groups in the history of French music, its place in the public musical conversation remains modest. French media confidently proclaimed rock ensemble Indochine to be "the first French group to fill" the Stade de France even though Kassav had already performed there to sold-out crowds several years before.[78] "It's no big deal," Desvarieux mused, "but it makes you wonder. We all have French passports."[79] Kassav's lack of visibility in the metropole speaks to a broader amnesia with regard to France's colonial past in the Caribbean. The collective blind spot that obscures the realities of the DOM-TOMs and the presence of large numbers of French citizens of Caribbean origin in the Hexagon today manifests itself in the ways musicians, the music industry, journalists, and audiences—including those in metropolitan France with even the best of multicultural intentions—think about and categorize music. Music critic Lucien Rioux's affirmation that "Zouk enriches French *chanson*" makes his a rare metropolitan voice indeed.[80] Kassav's uneven metropolitan reception raises an important question: why, despite French popular music's self-conscious embrace of plurality since the 1980s, does zouk still not "sound French"?[81]

Kassav in Performance

At close to three high-energy hours with no intermissions—often with no gaps between songs—Kassav's 2013 show at the Olympia was true to form: tight, generous, and fun. The concert showed off their new album (notably the single "Sonjé PSE," a tribute to Saint-Eloi, who passed away in 2010). Perhaps it was the Olympia's high ticket prices, the venue's storied character, or the lack of room to dance, but the audience was uncharacteristically subdued.

Happily, several months earlier at the Zénith—the first of the venues built under Lang's cultural patronage and a bigger space with plenty of room to move that has hosted Kassav's most memorable concerts over the years (over forty to date)—the crowd had no trouble getting into the swing of things. Within thirty seconds of the group taking the stage, I and everyone else near me had already been showered with the ti' punch that a young man had excitedly hurled into the air. A none-too-happy rum-soaked elderly woman next to me collared him and sternly calmed his enthusiasm. The group's multigenerational appeal is at once a testament to the group's longevity and an ingredient of happy concerts. At the Zénith, three generations of fans, from young children with their parents and smartly dressed teenagers to gray-haired grandparents, sang and danced

78. Rodineau and Rivet, "Indochine."
79. *Le parisien*, "Kassav a toujours."
80. Rioux, *50 ans*, 410.
81. Briggs, *Sounds French*.

their way through three and a half hours of high-cadence musical communion. At times, the six-thousand-strong audience drowned out the group's vocalists altogether; almost everyone at a Kassav concert knows the lyrics, and most can shout their parts in the numerous call-and-response sequences borrowed from carnival *mizik vidé*. The sheer fun Kassav's members are having onstage is palpable and contagious, and the energy of their playing finds its inexorable echo in an audience in constant, ebullient movement.

Kassav's concerts exemplify an important feature of music as a cultural form. Music doesn't simply articulate, repeat, or reflect a preexisting cultural identity. As Simon Frith has argued, music is performative, a form that is experienced in action, an instrument for eliciting assent and conjuring community into being that itself helps create identity.[82] In this, Kassav's zouk shares much with Trinidadian *soca*: musicians work hard to inspire audience participation through call-and-response, dancing, and communal singing in what one musicologist has dubbed a "politics of pleasure."[83] For Gilroy, such dialogic relationships between performer and audience are a characteristic feature of Black musical cultures more broadly and set in motion "collective processes . . . which may symbolize or even create community."[84] Like Creole-language soca and calypso, Kassav's zouk also engages different segments of its audiences in different ways, speaking to "insiders" (Creole speakers, Antillais, and those steeped in zouk's constituent rhythmic vocabularies) and "outsiders" (those unversed in the linguistic, cultural, and musical codes wielded by the musicians) at distinct degrees of comprehension.[85] Though most of the audience at the Zénith were from Paris's Antillais diaspora, Kassav's music and ethos also operate to resolutely inclusive ends. This is precisely the vibe they succeed in creating in concert, eliciting a strong sentiment of identification and belonging from Guadeloupeans and Martiniquais, on the one hand, and binding insiders and outsiders together in an intense, shared experience akin to Durkheimian "collective effervescence," on the other.[86]

Conclusion

When, just over three decades after their first concerts at the Zénith, Kassav returned there to play three dates in June 2016 amid rumors that these would be

---

82. Frith, "Music and Identity."
83. Guilbault, "Music, Politics, and Pleasure."
84. Gilroy, *There Ain't No Black in the Union Jack*, 290.
85. See also Gordon Rohlehr, quoted in Birth, *Bacchanalian Sentiments*, 25.
86. For an example of Emile Durkheim's sociology applied to popular music, see Partridge, *Lyre of Orpheus*.

their last shows in the Paris venue, French media published a wave of retrospectives.[87] That the group invited their Vikings de la Guadeloupe progenitors to open for them suggested that they, too, were looking back, a closing of the musicological circle that all but called for critical assessment of Kassav's history and legacy.

Over the years, some have discounted Kassav's music as too pop, too polished, too commercial, too electronic. The accomplished Guadeloupean percussionist Charlie Chomereau-Malotte dismissed zouk as "an assemblage of bits and pieces of traditional music. It's not music played with real drums; it's only the product of a drum machine. Zouk is a degenerate music."[88] Kassav's story also points to the paradoxes and pressures of the globalized popular music industry that took shape in the 1980s and the challenges faced by musicians balancing artistic and commercial imperatives, particularly those hailing from postcolonial peripheries.[89] Witness the fact that a group committed to developing the French Antilles' music industry needed to move to Paris to make it or that CBS/Sony imposed musical choices on Kassav to ensure that the two albums they recorded under contract in the late 1980s hewed to the company's vision of what "world music" should sound like. Zouk's commercial success could elicit exasperation from Antillais musicians worried by the shadow it cast over their own work—those like pianist Roland Malmin, who feel obliged to remind audiences that "Zouk constitutes only a small part of Antillais music."[90] Still others reproach zouk for the place it has come to occupy in reductive stereotypes of the Antilles, epitomized by the caricatural zouk-rum-Antillais food triptych.[91] And the sad fact of the matter is that most of the zouk cranked out by Kassav's legion of imitators is derivative junk.

Such considerations don't do justice to Kassav's musical, cultural, and political legacy. The group invented a new form of music embraced and appropriated by Antillais society. They put into practice an open-ended creative process that builds on local musical traditions yet refuses the trap of reifying

87. Berthod, "'Le zouk est passé de mode'?"; Denis, "Au départ"; Commeillas, "Kassav', Vikings, Kalash."

88. Quoted in Guilbault, "Créolité," 174. See also Beriss, *Black Skins*, chap. 4; and Beriss, "High Folklore," esp. 117–20.

89. In many ways, Kassav's trajectory resembles that of the Senegalese musician Youssou N'Dour: both hail from the French colonial periphery, both have worked to reenergize local musical scenes, both have crafted sounds all their own by mixing their own traditions with European and North American influences, both sing in local idioms, both shuttle between home and Western capitals, and both have been accused of betraying "authentic" traditional musics in pursuit of popular success. See Taylor, *Global Pop*, chap. 5.

90. Leymarie, *Musiques caraïbes*, 128.

91. Beriss, *Black Skins*, 84–86. Kassav pointedly reject such caricatures. See Beroard, interview, *France-Antilles*.

"authentic" cultural forms. They built their success in spite of an industry reluctant to promote or broadcast their music in metropolitan France beyond specialized outlets aimed at the expatriate Antillais community. They played a crucial part in building a viable music industry in the Antilles, in reviving interest in local musical traditions, in fashioning a vibrant contemporary Creole identity, and in challenging traditional gender conventions.[92] Guadeloupe and Martinique boast lively music scenes today thanks in part to Kassav. Far from stifling musical diversity, zouk's reign helped advance the cause of the Antilles' other musics. Consider the remarkable renaissance of traditional forms, like the biguine revival led by a number of exciting musicians: Kali, the stage name for the Martiniquais Jean-Marc Monnerville, a veteran of both the zouk reggae group 6th Continent and Pakatak, who has also worked with Desvarieux and Naimro; clarinetist and La Perfecta alumnus Michel Godzom; and Martiniquais jazz pianist Mario Canonge, who after forming his own zouk group Sakiyo and accompanying Desvarieux on tour, returned to Martinique's biguine and mazurka sources, marrying traditional dancehall music with jazz.

Kassav's project isn't political in any strict sense. While its members occasionally speak out on behalf of the French Caribbean in contemporary France's fierce debates about national identity—Beroard, for example, publicly supported the much-contested 2001 law put forward by Guyane deputy Christiane Taubira declaring slavery a crime against humanity—the group does not explicitly attach its music to specific political or social movements in the way that Guadeloupean musicians harnessed gwo ka to the cause of independence.[93] Kassav's significance lies, rather, in the group's very engagement with the market—that is, in their success at creating a new form of commodified pop culture on their own musical, linguistic, and productive terms. Many of its critics reproach the group for precisely this, as if artistic authenticity can take shape only at a distance from capitalism. Kassav's invention of an innovative musical style rooted in the Francophone Caribbean and shaped by political and cultural debates in Martinique and Guadeloupe, and their insistence on performing it in Creole, helped rewrite the terms of Antillais identity and remind an unmindful metropole of important imperial histories and legacies. In the words of one Guadeloupean musician, "Zouk's own musical crossover has in a way helped us to legitimate who we are."[94]

92. Women in recent years have won broader space in other Caribbean musics, as well (Smith, "Performing Gender").

93. Beroard, interview by Sophie Vigroux; Labesse, "Jocelyne Béroard." On recent debates over the commemoration of slavery and abolition in France, see Cahiers de l'histoire, "Les enjeux de la mémoire"; Weil and Dufoix, L'esclavage; Chivallon, "L'émergence récente"; and Weil, Liberté, égalité, discriminations, pt. 3.

94. Michel Rupaire, quoted in Guilbault, "Créolité," 174.

PAUL COHEN is associate professor of history at the University of Toronto. His book *Kingdom of Babel: The Making of a National Language in France, 1450–1815* is forthcoming.

Acknowledgments

The author thanks the journal's editors, Kay Edwards and Carol Harrison, the editors of this special issue, Jonathyne Briggs and William Weber, and the anonymous readers for their careful readings and helpful suggestions.

References

Abdouni, Sarah, and Edouard Fabre. "365,000 Domiens vivent en métropole." *INSEE première*, Feb. 2012. www.insee.fr/fr/themes/document.asp?ref_id=ip1389#inter5.

Abjean, René, and Louis Dumontier. *Bretagne est musique: Le point sur 50 ans de renouveau.* Vannes, 2006.

Aldrich, Robert, and John Connell. *France's Overseas Frontier: Départements et Territoires d'Outre-mer.* Cambridge, 1992.

Alleyne, Mervyn C. "A Linguistic Perspective on the Caribbean." In *Caribbean Contours*, edited by Sidney Mintz and Sally Price, 155–79. Baltimore, 1989.

Angelo, Mario d'. *Socio-économique de la musique en France: Diagnostic d'un système vulnérable.* Paris, 1997.

Anselin, Alain. *L'émigration antillaise en France: Du Bantoustan au ghetto.* Paris, 1979.

Anselin, Alain. *L'émigration antillaise en France: La troisième île.* Paris, 1990.

Appadurai, Arjun. "Disjuncture and Difference in the Global Cultural Economy." *Public Culture* 2, no. 2 (1990): 1–24.

Appadurai, Arjun. *Modernity at Large: Cultural Dimensions of Globalization.* Minneapolis, 1996.

Arnold, A. James. *Modernism and Negritude: The Poetry and Poetics of Aimé Césaire.* Cambridge, MA, 1981.

Attali, Jacques. *Bruits: Essai sur l'économie politique de la musique.* 2nd ed. Paris, 2001.

Austerlitz, Paul. *Merengue: Dominican Music and Dominican Identity.* Philadelphia, 1997.

Averill, Gage. *A Day for the Hunter, a Day for the Prey: Popular Music and Power in Haiti.* Chicago, 1997.

Averill, Gage. "'Toujou Sou Konpa': Issues of Change and Interchange in Haitian Popular Dance Music." In Guilbault, *Zouk*, 68–89.

Bagoé, Aude-Anderson. *Encyclopédie de la musique traditionnelle aux Antilles-Guyane: Musiciennes et musiciens ayant évolué en France métropolitaine.* Case Pilote, Martinique, 2005.

Benoit, Edouard. *Musique populaire de la Guadeloupe: De la biguine au zouk, 1940–1980.* Pointe-à-Pitre, 1990.

Bensignor, François. "Alan Stivell." *Hommes et migrations*, no. 1293 (2011): 148–53.

Beriss, David. *Black Skins, French Voices: Caribbean Ethnicity and Activism in Urban France.* New York, 2004.

Beriss, David. "High Folklore: Challenges to the French Cultural World Order." *Social Analysis*, no. 33 (1993): 104–29.

Bernabé, Jean, Patrick Chamoiseau, and Raphaël Confiant. *Eloge de la créolité.* Paris, 1989.

Beroard, Jocelyne. Interview. *France-Antilles*, May 30, 1987, 15–16.

Beroard, Jocelyne. Interview. *Outre-Mer 1ère*, May 13, 2013. www.la1ere.fr/2013/05/13/sonje-le-dernier-album-de-kassav-sort-ce-lundi-34781.html.

Beroard, Jocelyne. Interview by Sophie Vigroux. "Jocelyne Beroard, chanteuse de Kassav: 'Le zouk a permis aux femmes de danser seules.'" *La dépêche*, June 9, 2013. www.ladepeche.fr/article /2013/06/09/1646015-jocelyne-beroard-chanteuse-kassav-zouk-permis-femmes-danser-seules .html.

Berrian, Brenda F. "'An-Ba-Chen'n La' (Chained Together): The Landscape of Kassav's *Zouk*." In *Language, Rhythm, and Sound: Black Popular Cultures into the Twenty-First Century*, edited by Joseph K. Adjaye and Adrianne R. Andrew, 203–20. Pittsburgh, 1997.

Berrian, Brenda F. *Awakening Spaces: French Caribbean Popular Song, Music, and Culture.* Chicago, 2000.

Berrian, Brenda F. "Sé Cho (It's Hot): French Antillean Musicians and Audience Reception." In *Caribe 2000: Definiciones, identidades, y culturalas regionales y/o nacionales: Simposio III: Un convite de poetas y teatreros: Voz y performance en la(s) cultura(s) caribeña(s)*, edited by Lowell Fiet and Janette Becerra, 117–26. San Juan, PR, 1999.

Berthod, Anne. "'Le zouk est passé de mode'? Qu'importe, Kassav continue de remplir les stades." *Télérama*, May 22, 2016. www.telerama.fr/sortir/le-zouk-est-passe-de-mode-qu-importe -kassav-continue-de-remplir-des-stades,142762.php.

Best, Curwen. *Barbadian Popular Music and the Politics of Caribbean Culture.* Rochester, VT, 1999.

Béthune, Christiane. *Le rap: Une esthétique hors la loi.* Paris, 2003.

Bilby, Kenneth M. "The Caribbean as a Musical Region." In *Caribbean Contours*, edited by Sidney Mintz and Sally Price, 181–218. Baltimore, 1989.

Birth, Kevin K. *Bacchanalian Sentiments: Musical Experiences and Political Counterpoints in Trinidad.* Durham, NC, 2008.

Bithell, Caroline. *Transported by Song: Corsican Voices from Oral Tradition to World Stage.* Lanham, MD, 2007.

Bohlman, Philip V. "World Music at the 'End of History.'" *Ethnomusicology* 46, no. 1 (2002): 1–32.

Boucheron, Patrick, ed. *Histoire mondiale de la France.* Paris, 2017.

Bowermaster, Jon. "Zouk, Rattle, and Roll: The Hip-Shaking Music of the French Antilles Is Now Going Global." *Elle*, Oct. 1988, 120, 122.

Briggs, Jonathyne. *Sounds French: Globalization, Cultural Communities, and Pop Music, 1958–1980.* Oxford, 2015.

Butel, Paul. *Histoire des Antilles françaises.* Paris, 2007.

Cahiers de l'histoire. "Les enjeux de la mémoire: Esclavage, marronage, commémorations." Special issue, no. 89 (2002).

Cally-Lézin, Sully. *Musiques et danses afro-caraïbes: Martinique.* Paris, 1990.

Chapman, Herrick, and Laura L. Frader, eds. *Race in France: Interdisciplinary Perspectives on the Politics of Difference.* New York, 2004.

Chaudenson, Robert. *Creolization of Languages and Culture*, translated by Salikoko S. Mufwene, Sabrina Billings, and Michelle AuCoin. New York, 2001.

Childers, Kristen Stromberg. *Seeking Imperialism's Embrace: National Identity, Decolonization, and Assimilation in the French Caribbean.* Oxford, 2016.

Chivallon, Christine. "L'émergence récente de la mémoire de l'esclavage dans l'espace public: Enjeux et significations." *Revue d'histoire moderne et contemporaine* 52, no. 4bis (2005): 64–81.

Clifford, James. *Routes: Travel and Translation in the Late Twentieth Century.* Cambridge, MA, 1997.

Cole, George. *The Last Miles: The Music of Miles Davis, 1980–1991.* Ann Arbor, MI, 2007.

Commeillas, David. "Kassav', Vikings, Kalash: Pourquoi la métropole n'a jamais rien compris à la musique antillaise." *Les Inrocks*, May 30, 2016. abonnes.lesinrocks.com/2016/05/30/musique /kassav-vikings-kalash-pourquoi-la-metropole-na-jamais-rien-compris-a-la-musique-antillaise -11829521.

Condé, Maryse. "Chercher nos vérités." In *Penser la créolité*, edited by Maryse Condé and Madeleine Cottenet-Hage, 305–10. Paris, 1995.

Condon, Stéphanie A. "Migrations antillaises en métropole: Politique migratoire, emploi et place spécifique des femmes." *Les cahiers du CEDREF*, nos. 8–9 (2000): 169–200. cedref.revues.org /196.

Condon, Stéphanie A. "Pratiques et transmission des créoles antillais dans la "troisième île." *Espace, populations, sociétés*, no. 2 (2004): 293–305.

Condon, Stéphanie A., and Philip E. Ogden. "Questions of Emigration, Circulation, and Return: Mobility between the French Caribbean and France." *International Journal of Population Geography* 2, no. 1 (1996): 35–50.

Confiant, Raphaël. *Aimé Césaire: Une traversée paradoxale du siècle*. 2nd ed. Montreal, 2006.

Constant, Denis. *Aux sources du reggae: Musique, société et politique en Jamaïque*. Roquevaire, 1982.

Constant, Fred. "La politique française de l'immigration antillaise de 1946 à 1987." *Revue européenne des migrations internationales* 3, no. 3 (1987): 9–30.

Cooper, Carolyn. *Sound Clash: Jamaican Dancehall Culture at Large*. New York, 2004.

Cyrille, Dominique. "*Sa Ki Ta Nou (This Belongs to Us)*: Creole Dances of the French Caribbean." In *Caribbean Dance from Abakuá to Zouk: How Movement Shapes Identity*, edited by Susanna Sloat, 221–44. Gainesville, FL, 2002.

Delver, Gérard, and Patrick Chamoiseau. "Pour Patrick Saint-Eloi." *Madínín'Art*, Sept. 19, 2010. papalagi.blog.lemonde.fr/2010/09/22/patrick-saint-eloi-un-hommage-de-g-delver-et-p -chamoiseau.

Denis, Jacques. "Au départ, Kassav' était un laboratoire." *Libération*, May 23, 2016. next.liberation.fr /musique/2016/05/23/au-depart-kassav-etait-un-laboratoire_1454622.

Desroches, Monique. "Créolisation musicale et identité culturelle aux Antilles françaises." *Canadian Journal of Latin American and Caribbean Studies*, no. 34 (1992): 41–51.

Desroches, Monique. "La musique aux Antilles." In *Arts et traditions*, edited by Danielle Begot, 178–93. Vol. 10 of *La grande encyclopédie de la Caraïbe*, edited by Bruno Caredda. N.p., 1990.

Desroches, Monique. *Les instruments de musique traditionnelle*. Fort-de-France, Martinique, 1989.

Desroches, Monique. "Les pratiques musicales aux Antilles françaises: Image de l'histoire, reflet d'un contexte." In *Guadeloupe et Martinique: Des îles aux hommes*, edited by Jean-Luc Bonniol, 491–500. Vol. 1 of *Historial antillaise*, edited by Jacques Sabatier. Pointe-à-Pitre, 1981.

Dewitte, Philippe. *Les mouvements nègres en France, 1919–1939*. Paris, 1985.

Dillaz, Serge. *La chanson française de contestation: Des barricades de la Commune à celles de mai 68*. Paris, 1973.

Dillaz, Serge. *La chanson sous la Troisième République, 1870–1940*. Paris, 1991.

Dillaz, Serge. *Vivre et chanter en France*. 2 vols. Paris, 2005–7.

Domenach, Hervé, and Michel Picouet. *La dimension migratoire des Antilles*. Paris, 1992.

Domiquin, Dominique. "Faut-il brûler nos vieilles pochettes d'albums de Kassav?" *Creolways*, Aug. 16, 2014. creoleways.com/2014/08/16/kassav-faut-il-bruler-nos-vieilles-pochettes-dalbums.

Douglas, Mbida. Interview by F. C. Ebolé Bola, J. B. Akono, and N. Vounsia. *Mboa.info*. www .mbidadouglas.com/index.php/blog-categories/blog-vivamus-luctus-lectus-sit/39-il-ya-eu -des-incompatibilites-chez-les-kassav.

Dumont, Jacques. *L'amère patrie: Histoire des Antilles françaises au XXe siècle*. Paris, 2010.

Duneton, Claude. *Histoire de la chanson française*. 2 vols. Paris, 1998.

Eling, Kim. *The Politics of Cultural Policy in France*. New York, 1999.

Erlmann, Veit. "The Aesthetics of the Global Imagination: Reflections on World Music in the 1990s." *Public Culture* 8, no. 3 (1996): 467–87.

Feld, Steven. "Une si douce berceuse pour la 'World Music,'" translated by Giancarlo Siciliano. *L'homme*, nos. 171–72 (2004): 389–408.

Filostrat, Christian. *Negritude Agonistes: Assimilation against Nationalism in the French-Speaking Caribbean and Guyane*. Cherry Hill, NJ, 2008.

Foster, Chuck. *Roots, Rock, Reggae: An Oral History of Reggae Music from Ska to Dancehall*. New York, 1999.

Frith, Simon. "Music and Identity." In *Questions of Cultural Identity*, edited by Stuart Hall and Paul du Gay, 108–27. London, 2005.

Gallagher, Mary. "The *Créolité* Movement: Paradoxes of a French Caribbean Orthodoxy." In *Creolization: History, Ethnography, Theory*, edited by Charles Stewart, 220–36. London, 2007.

Gama, Raymond, and Jean-Pierre Sainton. *Mé 67: Mémoire d'un événement*. 2nd ed. Port-Louis, Guadeloupe, 2011.

Gerstin, Julian. "Musical Revivals and Social Movements in Contemporary Martinique: Ideology, Identity, Ambivalence." In *The African Diaspora: A Musical Perspective*, edited by Ingrid Monson, 295–327. New York, 2003.

Gerstin, Julian. "Reputation in a Musical Scene: The Everyday Context of Connections between Music, Identity, and Politics." *Ethnomusicology* 42, no. 3 (1998): 385–414.

Gerstin, Julian. "Traditional Music in a New Social Movement: The Renewal of *Bèlè* in Martinique (French West Indies)." PhD diss., University of California, Berkeley, 1996.

Gilroy, Paul. *The Black Atlantic: Modernity and Double Consciousness*. New York, 1993.

Gilroy, Paul. *There Ain't No Black in the Union Jack: The Cultural Politics of Race and Nation*. New York, 2002.

Glissant, Edouard. *Le discours antillais*. Paris, 1981.

Gray, John. *From Vodou to Zouk: A Bibliographic Guide to Music of the French-Speaking Caribbean and Its Diaspora*. Nyack, NY, 2010.

Grenier, Line, and Jocelyne Guilbault. "*Créolité* and *Francophonie* in Music: Socio-musical Repositioning Where It Matters." *Cultural Studies* 11, no. 2 (1997): 207–34.

Guilbault, Jocelyne. "Créolité and the New Cultural Politics of Difference in Popular Music of the French West Indies." *Black Music Research Journal* 14, no. 2 (1994): 161–78.

Guilbault, Jocelyne. *Governing Sound: The Cultural Politics of Trinidad's Carnival Musics*. Chicago, 2007.

Guilbault, Jocelyne. "Interpretation out of Contradiction: A World Music in the West Indies." *Canadian University Music Review*, no. 14 (1994): 1–16.

Guilbault, Jocelyne. "Interpreting World Music: A Challenge in Theory and Practice." *Popular Music* 16, no. 1 (1997): 31–44.

Guilbault, Jocelyne. "Music, Politics, and Pleasure: Live Soca in Trinidad." *Small Axe* 14, no. 1 (2010): 16–29.

Guilbault, Jocelyne. "On Interpreting Popular Music: Zouk in the West Indies." In *Caribbean Popular Culture*, edited by John A. Lent, 79–97. Bowling Green, OH, 1990.

Guilbault, Jocelyne. "On Redefining the 'Local' through World Music." *World of Music* 35, no. 2 (1993): 33–47.

Guilbault, Jocelyne. "Sociopolitical, Cultural, and Economic Development through Music: Zouk in the French Antilles." *Canadian Journal of Latin American and Caribbean Studies*, no. 34 (1992): 27–40.

Guilbault, Jocelyne. *Zouk: World Music in the West Indies*, with Gage Averill, Edouart Benoit, and Gregory Rabess. Chicago, 1993.

Guillerm, François-Xavier. *(In)dépendance créole: Brève histoire récente du nationalisme antillais.* Pointe-à-Pitre, 2007.

Hall, Stuart. "Negotiating Caribbean Identities." *New Left Review*, no. 209 (1995): 3–14.

Hammou, Karim. *Une histoire du rap en France.* Paris, 2014.

Hazaël-Massieux, Guy. *Les Créoles: Problèmes de genèse et de description.* Aix-en-Provence, 1996.

Hazaël-Massieux, Marie-Christine. "Les Créoles français." In *Histoire sociale des langues de France*, edited by Georg Kremnitz, 639–70. Rennes, 2013.

Hernandez, Deborah Pacini. *Bachata: A Social History of a Dominican Popular Music.* Philadelphia, 1995.

Hill, Donald R. *Calypso Calaloo: Early Carnival Music in Trinidad.* Gainesville, FL, 1993.

Hill, Edwin C., Jr. *Black Soundscapes, White Stages: The Meaning of Francophone Sound in the Black Atlantic.* Baltimore, 2013.

Jallier, Maurice, and Vivette Jallier-Prudent. *Musique aux Antilles: Zouk à la Mazouk.* Paris, 1999.

Jallier, Maurice, and Yollen Lossen. *Musique aux Antilles: Mizik bô kay.* Paris, 1985.

James, C. L. R. "The Mighty Sparrow." In *The Future in the Present: Selected Writings*, 191–201. Westport, CT, 1977.

Keaton, Trica Danielle, T. Denean Sharpley-Whiting, and Tyler Stovall, eds. *Black France/France Noire: The History and Politics of Blackness.* Durham, NC, 2012.

Khalfa, Jean. "Naissance de la négritude." *Les temps modernes*, no. 656 (2009): 38–63.

Labesse, Patrick. "Jocelyne Béroard, échappée provisoire." *RFI Musique*, May 20, 2011. www.rfimusique.com/actu-musique/20110520-jocelyne-beroard-echappee-provisoire.

Lafontaine, Marie-Céline. "Le carnaval de l''autre': A propos de l''authenticité' en matière de musique guadeloupéenne; Théories et réalités." *Les temps modernes*, nos. 441–42 (1983): 2126–73.

Lafontaine, Marie-Céline. "Musique et société aux Antilles: 'Balakadri' ou le bal de quadrille au commandement de la Guadeloupe; Un sens, une esthétique, une mémoire." *Présence africaine*, nos. 121–22 (1982): 72–108.

Lafontaine, Marie-Céline. "Terminologie musicale en Guadeloupe: Ce que le créole nous dit de la musique." *Langage et société*, no. 32 (1985): 7–24.

Largey, Michael. *Vodou Nation: Haitian Art Music and Cultural Nationalism.* Chicago, 2006.

Laumuno, Marie-Héléna. *Et le Gwoka s'est enraciné en Guadeloupe . . . Chronologie d'un patrimoine culturel immatériel sensible.* Paris, 2012.

Laumuno, Marie-Héléna. *Gwoka et politique en Guadeloupe, 1960–2003: 40 ans de construction du "pays."* Paris, 2011.

Lebovics, Herman. *Bringing the Empire Back Home: France in the Global Age.* Durham, NC, 2004.

Ledesma, Charles de, and Gene Scaramuzzo. "Zouk." In vol. 2 of *World Music: The Rough Guide*, edited by Simon Broughton, Mark Ellingham, and Richard Trillo, 289–303. 2nd ed. New York, 2000.

Lee, Hélène. "A Dakar, en souvenir de Gilles Obringer." *RFI Musique*, Feb. 4, 2005. www.rfimusique.com/musiquefr/articles/062/article_15353.asp.

Le parisien. "Kassav a toujours du punch." June 6, 2013. www.leparisien.fr/espace-premium/culture-loisirs/kassav-a-toujours-du-punch-06-06-2013-2870951.php.

Les musiques guadeloupéennes dans le champ culturel afro-américain au sein des musiques du monde, Nov. 1986. Pointe-à-Pitre, 1988.

Leymarie, Isabelle. *Musiques caraïbes.* Paris, 1996.

Looseley, David L. *Popular Music in Contemporary France: Authenticity, Politics, Debate.* New York, 2003.

Mahabir, Cynthia. "The Rise of Calypso Feminism: Gender and Musical Politics in the Calypso." *Popular Music* 20, no. 3 (2001): 409–30.

Manuel, Peter. *East Indian Music in the West Indies: Tan-Singing, Chutney, and the Making of Indo-Caribbean Culture*. Philadelphia, 2000.

Manuel, Peter, Kenneth Bilby, and Michael Largey. *Caribbean Currents: Caribbean Music from Rumba to Reggae*. 2nd ed. Philadelphia, 2006.

Martel, Camille. *Massilia Sound System: La Façon de Marseille*. Marseille, 2014.

Martin, Denis-Constant. "Who's Afraid of the Big Bad World Music? [Qui a peur des grandes méchantes musiques du monde?]: Désir de l'autre, processus hégémoniques et flux transnationaux mis en musique dans le monde contemporain." *Cahiers de musiques traditionnelles*, no. 9 (1996): 3–21.

Martinez, Isabelle Marc. *Le rap français: Esthétique et poétique des textes (1990–1995)*. Bern, 2008.

Mavounzy, Marcel Susan. *Cinquante ans de musique et de culture en Guadeloupe: Mémoires, 1928–1978*. Paris, 2002.

Miclet, Brice. "Le zouk, victime des préjugés de la métropole." *L'Obs*, Oct. 25, 2014. rue89 .nouvelobs.com/rue89-culture/2014/10/25/zouk-victime-prejuges-metropole-255688.

Mitchell, Tony. *Popular Music and Local Identity: Rock, Pop, and Rap in Europe and Oceania*. London, 1996.

Myers, Helen. *Music of Hindu Trinidad: Songs from the India Diaspora*. Chicago, 1998.

Ndiaye, Pap. *La condition noire: Essai sur une minorité française*. Paris, 2008.

Negrit, Frédéric. *Musique et immigration dans la société antillaise*. Paris, 2004.

Nettl, Bruno. "World Music in the Twentieth Century: A Survey of Research on Western Influence." *Acta Musicologica* 58, no. 2 (1986): 360–73.

Partridge, Christopher. *The Lyre of Orpheus: Popular Music, the Sacred, and the Profane*. Oxford, 2014.

Peabody, Sue, and Tyler Stovall, eds. *The Color of Liberty: Histories of Race in France*. Durham, NC, 2003.

Pfaff, Françoise. *Conversations with Maryse Condé*. Lincoln, NE, 1996.

Placide, Louis-Georges. *Les émeutes de décembre 1959 en Martinique: Un repère historique*. Paris, 2009.

Prudent, Lambert-Félix. *Des baragouins à la langue antillaise: Analyse historique et sociolinguistique du discours sur le créole*. Paris, 1999.

Prudent, Lambert-Félix. "Ecrire le créole à la Martinique: Norme et conflit sociolinguistique." In *Les Créoles français entre l'oral et l'écrit*, edited by Ralph Ludwig, 65–80. Tübingen, 1989.

Prudent, Lambert-Félix. "La langue créole aux Antilles et en Guyane (Enjeux pédagogiques, espaces artistiques et littéraires, intérêts scientifiques)." *Les temps modernes*, nos. 441–42 (1983): 2072–89.

Prudent, Lambert-Félix. "La pub, le zouk, et l'album." In "Antilles: Espoirs et déchirement de l'âme créole." Special issue, *Autrement*, no. 41 (1989): 209–16.

Pulvar, Olivier. "Créolité: Affirmation identitaire et dialogue interculturel." *Hermès* 40, no. 3 (2004): 71–74.

Pulvar, Olivier. "Le bèlè en Martinique, défense du patrimoine et promotion de produits culturels." In *Communication et dynamique de globalisation culturelle*, edited by Alain Kiyindou, Jean-Chrétien Ekambo, and Ludovic-Robert Miyouna, 39–48. Paris, 2009.

Quevedo, Raymond [Attila the Hun]. *Atilla's Kaiso: A Short History of Trinidad Calypso*. St. Augustine, Trinidad and Tobago, 1983.

Rioux, Lucien. *50 ans de chanson française: De Trenet à Bruel.* 2nd ed. Paris, 1994.

Rodineau, Claire, and Louise Rivet. "Indochine triomphe au Stade de France." *Le Figaro,* June 30, 2014. www.lefigaro.fr/musique/2014/06/30/03006–20140630ARTFIG00157-indochine-triomphe-au-stade-de-france.php.

Rohlehr, Gordon. *Calypso and Society in Pre-independence Trinidad.* Port of Spain, 1990.

Rohlehr, Gordon. *A Scuffling of Islands: Essays on Calypso.* San Juan, PR, 2004.

Rohlehr, Gordon. "'We Getting the Kaiso That We Deserve': Calypso and the World Music Market." *Drama Review* 42, no. 3 (1998): 82–95.

Rosemain, Jacqueline. *Jazz et biguine: Les musiques noires du Nouveau-Monde.* Paris, 1993.

Rosemain, Jacqueline. *La danse aux Antilles: Des rythmes sacrés au zouk.* Paris, 1990.

Rosemain, Jacqueline. *La musique dans la société antillaise, 1635–1902: Martinique, Guadeloupe.* Paris, 1986.

Scaramuzzo, Gene. "Jocelyne Beroard." In vol. 2 of *World Music: The Rough Guide,* edited by Simon Broughton, Mark Ellingham, and Richard Trillo, 296. 2nd ed. New York, 2000.

Schnepel, Ellen M. *In Search of a National Identity: Creole and Politics in Guadeloupe.* Hamburg, 2004.

Shepard, Todd. *The Invention of Decolonization: The Algerian War and the Remaking of France.* Ithaca, NY, 2006.

Silverstein, Paul A. *Algeria in France: Transpolitics, Race, and Nation.* Bloomington, IN, 2004.

Slobin, Mark. "Micromusics of the West: A Comparative Approach." *Ethnomusicology* 36, no. 1 (1992): 1–87.

Smith, Hope Munro. "Performing Gender in the Trinidad Calypso." *Latin American Music Review / Revista de música latinoamericana* 25, no. 1 (2004): 32–56.

Tanbou-a sé vwa pèp nèg: Le ka, écho de l'identité antillaise. Nouméa, 2011.

Taylor, Timothy D. *Global Pop: World Music, World Markets.* New York, 1997.

Terrine, Jean-Marc. *La ronde des derniers maîtres du bèlè: La musique traditionnelle dans le nord de la Martinique.* Paris, 2004.

Tessoneau, Alex-Louise. "Le Créole en métropole." In vol. 2 of *Vingt-cinq communautés linguistiques de la France,* edited by Geneviève Vermes, 165–93. Paris, 1988.

Thomas, Dominic. *Black France: Colonialism, Immigration, and Transnationalism.* Bloomington, IN, 2007.

Uri, Alex, and Françoise Uri. *Musiques et musiciens de la Guadeloupe: Le chant de Karukéra.* Paris, 1991.

Vichniac, Judith E. "Socialists and *Droit à la Différence*: A Changing Dynamic." *French Politics and Society* 9, no. 1 (1991): 40–56.

Wallis, Roger, and Krister Malm. *Big Sounds from Small Peoples: The Music Industry in Small Countries.* London, 1984.

Warne, Chris. "The Impact of World Music in France." In *Post-colonial Cultures in France,* edited by Alec G. Hargreaves and Mark McKinney, 133–49. New York, 1997.

Warner, Keith Q. *Kaiso! The Trinidad Calypso.* Washington, DC, 1982.

Weil, Patrick. *Liberté, égalité, discriminations: L'identité nationale au regard de l'histoire.* Paris, 2009.

Weil, Patrick, and Stéphane Dufoix, eds. *L'esclavage, la colonisation, et après. . . .* Paris, 2005.

Wilder, Gary. *Freedom Time: Negritude, Decolonization, and the Future of the World.* Durham, NC, 2015.

Wilder, Gary. *The French Imperial Nation-State: Negritude and Colonial Humanism between the Two World Wars.* Chicago, 2005.

News

Call for Papers: Global Labor History in France and the French Colonial and Postcolonial Worlds

The editors of *French Historical Studies* seek articles for a special issue on labor in France and the Francophone world in global perspective, to appear in 2024.

Since the turn of the new millennium, a new global history of labor has emerged that focuses on the relationship between structures and practices of labor from at least medieval times to the present day. However, most French historians of labor continue to focus on the Hexagon and to underestimate wider European and global connections and comparisons. Similarly, specialists of slavery and postslavery in the French colonies rarely extend their analyses to other empires or to labor history in France. This special issue seeks to bridge these gaps by inviting submissions relating labor in mainland France to labor in its colonies and/or other areas, from the early modern to the present day.

Potential themes that lend themselves to comparative or global approaches include

Economic and social structures of labor and bondage
Labor structures and practices in imperial metropoles and colonies
Gender, race and age profiles in labor structures and practices
Labor protest and revolt
Worker migration and mobility

Queries about submission and other matters should be addressed to the guest editors, Alessandro Stanziani (alessandro.stanziani@ehess.fr) and Gwyn Campbell (gwyn.campbell@mcgill.ca).

To submit an article, visit www.editorialmanager.com/fhs/default.aspx. After registering, follow the submission instructions under "Instructions for Authors." Articles may be either in English or in French but must in either case conform to *FHS* style and must be accompanied by 150-word abstracts in both French and English. Manuscripts may be between 8,000 words and 12,000 words. For illustrations, stills, or film clips, authors must obtain written permission for both print and online publication from the relevant persons or institutions.

The deadline for submission of papers to *FHS* is August 20, 2022.

French Historical Studies • Vol. 45, No. 2 (April 2022) • DOI 10.1215/00161071-9532024

Appel à contributions : Histoires croisées du travail dans le monde francophone

Les éditrices de *French Historical Studies* lancent un appel à articles pour un numéro spécial de la revue sur le travail en France et dans le monde francophone à la lumière de l'histoire globale, à paraître en 2024.

Depuis le tournant du nouveau millénaire, l'histoire globale du travail a donné vie à une énorme quantité de travaux reliant les formes et les pratiques du travail de régions différentes, depuis le Moyen Age jusqu'à nos jours. Cependant, dans les mondes francophones, cette tendance est encore incertaine ; les historiens du travail en France se limitent le plus souvent à l'Hexagone et négligent les connexions et les comparaisons avec d'autres régions d'Europe et du monde. Pour leur part, les spécialistes de l'esclavage et du post-esclavage dans les colonies françaises relient difficilement leurs investigations aux dynamiques dans d'autres empires ou même à l'évolution du travail en France. Cet appel vise à dépasser ces barrières et invite des soumissions reliant le travail en France à celui d'autres pays et/ou de ses colonies. La période couverte s'étale de l'époque moderne jusqu'à nos jours.

Thématiques envisagées (liste non exclusive), toutes dans une perspective d'histoire connectée, globale ou comparée :

> Les structures économiques et sociales du travail et de la coercition
> Les structures et pratiques du travail dans les métropoles impériales et dans les colonies
> Le genre, la race et l'âge dans les structures et les pratiques du travail
> La résistance au travail
> Les migrations et la mobilité

Adressez vos questions aux directeurs du numéro spécial : Alessandro Stanziani (alessandro .stanziani@ehess.fr) et Gwyn Campbell (gwyn.campbell@mcgill.ca).

Pour soumettre un article, veuillez consulter www.editorialmanager.com/fhs /default.aspx. Après vous être enregistré.e, suivez les instructions de la section « Instructions for Authors ». Les articles peuvent être soumis en anglais ou en français, mais, dans les deux cas, ils doivent être conformes au style de *FHS*, et doivent être accompagnés d'un résumé ou abstract de 150 mots, dans les deux langues. Les manuscrits doivent comporter entre 8 000 et 12 000 mots. Concernant les illustrations, prises de vue, ou extraits de film, les auteurs doivent obtenir la permission écrite de les publier sous forme papier et digitale de la part des personnes dépositaires des droits sur ces images ou extraits audiovisuels, ou de la part des responsables des institutions d'où les images sont originaires.

La date limite pour soumettre les articles est fixée au 20 août 2022.

Recent Books and Dissertations on French History

Compiled by SARAH SUSSMAN

This bibliography is designed to introduce readers to recent publications on French history, broadly defined. It is organized according to commonly recognized periods, with works that bridge multiple categories listed under "General and Miscellaneous."

General and Miscellaneous

Ajavon, Lawoetey-Pierre. *Traites négrières et esclavage: Comment réparer les irréparables crimes contre l'humanité?* Paris: Anibwé, 2020. 344p. €23.00.

Allorant, Pierre, Walter Badier, Alexandre Borrell, and Jean Garrigues, eds. *Lieux de mémoire en Centre-Val de Loire*. Rennes: Presses Universitaires de Rennes, 2021. 324p. €25.00.

Artières, Philippe. *Le peuple du Larzac: Une histoire de crânes, sorcières, croisés, paysans, prisonniers, soldats, ouvrières, militants, touristes et brebis*. Paris: Découverte, 2021. 303p. €21.00.

Astaing, Antoine, ed. *250 ans: De la Lorraine ducale à la Lorraine française*. Nancy: Presses Universitaires de Nancy, 2021. 239p. €20.00.

Azzoug-Montané, Jade. *D'Havas à l'AFP: Histoire d'une agence de presse unique*. Paris: Harmattan, 2020. 266p. €27.50.

Balayre, Amélie, Nathan Rousselot, Marie-Cécile Pineau, and Claire Le Bras, eds. *Le diplomate en représentation (XVIe–XXe)*. Rennes: Presses Universitaires de Rennes, 2021. 259p. €25.00.

Barbot, Michela, Jean-François Chauvard, and Stefano Levanti, eds. *L'expérience du déclassement social: France-Italie, XVIe–premier XIXe siècle*. Rome: Publications de l'Ecole Française de Rome, 2021. 446p. €35.00.

Bard, Christine. *Mon genre d'histoire*. Paris: Presses Universitaires de France, 2021. 199p. €15.00.

Beauvalet, Scarlett, Annie Duprat, and Armelle Le Bras-Chopard. *Femmes et République*. Paris: Documentation Française, 2021. 262p. €32.00.

Becker, Roland. *Carnac=Karnag: Des pierres racontées par les voyageurs des 18e et 19e siècles*. Spézet: Coop Breizh, 2021. 205p. €39.00.

Berthereau, Estelle. *La fabrique politique du journal, Pierre-Sébastien Laurentie (1793–1876), un antimoderne au temps de Balzac*. Paris: Champion, 2021. 476p. €69.00.

Bertrand, Gilles. *Le grand tour revisité: Le voyage des Français en Italie (milieu XVIIIe siècle–début XIXe siècle)*. Roma: Ecole Française de Rome, 2021. 620p. €20.00.

Bigorgne, Didier. *Non à la guerre! Les combattants de la paix dans les Ardennes*. Charleville-Mézières: Société d'Histoire des Ardennes, 2020. 153p. €18.00.

Black, Jeremy. *France: A Short History*. London: Thames and Hudson, 2021. 256p. $24.95.

Blier, Gérard. *France-Angleterre: Un millénaire de lutte armée; Deux siècles d'alliance*. Paris: Economica, 2021. 219p. €23.00.

Bodinier, Bernard, and François Neveux, eds. *La Normandie en mouvement: Entre terres et mers; Actes du 54e congrès organisé par la Fédération des sociétés historiques et archéologiques de Normandie (Dieppe, 9–12 octobre 2019)*. Louviers: Fédération des Sociétés Historiques et Archéologiques de Normandie, 2020. 495p.

Bonhomme, Eric. *D'une monarchie à l'autre histoire: Politique des institutions françaises, 1814–2020*. Malakoff: Colin, 2021. 383p. €24.90.

Boutier, Jean, and Stéphanie Mourlane, eds. *Marseille l'Italienne: Histoires d'une passion séculaire*. Marseille: Bizalion, 2021. 207p. €25.00.

Brizay, François, and Thierry Sauzeau, eds. *Les étrangers sur les littoraux européens et méditerranéens: A l'époque moderne (fin XVe–début XIXe siècle)*. Rennes: Presses Universitaires de Rennes, 2021. 240p. €22.00.

Cathelineau, Philippe de. *Du don jusqu'au pardon: La saga des trois Cathelineau*. Maulévrier: Hérault, 2020. 263p. €20.00.

Condette, Jean-François, Jean-Noël Luc, and Yves Verneuil, eds. *Histoire de l'enseignement en France, XIXe–XXIe siècle*. Paris: Colin, 2020. 412p. €24.90.

Crook, Malcolm. *How the French Learned to Vote: A History of Electoral Practice in France*. Oxford: Oxford University Press, 2021. 288p. $100.00.

Crouzet, Denis. *Un historien dans ses lendemains: Pierre Chaunu*. Caen: Presses Universitaires de Caen, 2021. 330p. €21.90.

Cubero, José-Ramon. *Histoire sociale et industrielle des Hautes-Pyrénées: Les entrelacs du local et du national*. Morlaàs: Cairn, 2021. 368p. €25.00.

Danvers, Christophe. *Le corps souverain: Une histoire des représentations du pouvoir en France*. Paris: Harmattan, 2021. 175p. €19.00.

Delacotte, Sabrina. *La famille Liais: Dynastie-phare de Cherbourg, 1780–1907*. Bayeux: Orep, 2021. 453p. €27.00.

Delouis, Anne Friederike. *Voyages au centre de la France: L'identité d'une région au regard de ses visiteurs (XVIe–XXe siècle)*. Rennes: Presses Universitaires de Rennes, 2021. 313p. €25.00.

Delouis, Anne Friederike, Aude Déruelle, Philippe Haugeard, and Gaël Rideau, eds. *Rituels de la vie publique et privée: Du Moyen Age à nos jours*. Paris: Classiques Garnier, 2021. 370p. €34.00.

Descendre, Romain, and Jean-Claude Zancarini, eds. *La France d'Antonio Gramsci*. Lyon: Ecole Normale Supérieure, 2021. 278p. €34.00.

De Weerdt-Pilorge, Marie-Paule, and Malina Stefanovska, eds. *Récits de vie et pratiques de sociabilité, 1680–1850*. Paris: Classiques Garnier, 2021. 170p. €22.00.

Dosse, François. *Pierre Vidal-Naquet, une vie*. Paris: Découverte, 2020. 672p. €25.00.

Figeac, Michel. *Echanges et métissage des cultures matérielles entre la Nouvelle-Aquitaine et les outre-mers (XVIIIe–XIXe siècles)*. Pessac: Maison des Sciences de l'Homme d'Aquitaine, 2021. 280p. €29.00.

Figuères, Léo. *Histoire des communistes français: Essai (textes inédits, 1996–2011)*. Paris: Temps des Cerises, 2020. 288p. €14.00.

Fossier, Arnaud, Dominique Le Page, and Bruno Lemesle, eds. *La représentation politique et ses instruments avant la démocratie: Moyen Age–temps modernes.* Dijon: Editions Universitaires de Dijon, 2020. 282p. €18.96.

Fournié, Alain, and Jean-Paul Riffard. *Mémoire de Lisle-sur-Tarn du XIXe au XXe siècle: La vie commerciale, artisanale, fêtes et traditions.* Lisle-sur-Tarn: Association Editions du Rabisteau, 2020. 368p. €23.00.

Frenkiel, Stanislas. *Le football des immigrés: France-Algérie, l'histoire en partage.* Arras: Artois Presses Université, 2021. 311p. €24.00.

Gaulmyn, Constance de, and Olivier Rozenberg. *Nous vous aimons, Madame: Simone Veil, 1927–2017.* Paris: Flammarion, 2021. 208p. €23.00.

Gaveau, Fabien. *Propriété, cadastre et usages locaux dans les campagnes françaises (1789–1960): Histoire d'une tension légale.* Besançon: Presses Universitaires de Franche-Comté, 2021. 480p. €40.00.

Gili, Eric. *Comté de Nice: 40 ans de recherches; Actes du colloque de Saint-Martin-Vésubie, 6, 7 et 8 novembre 2020.* Saint Martin Vésubie: Association Amont, 2020. 613p. €50.00.

Granger, Christophe. *Voter au village: Les formes locales de la vie politique, XXe–XXIe siècles.* Villeneuve-d'Ascq: Presses Universitaires du Septentrion, 2021. 310p. €26.00.

Haynin, Eric de. *La crosse et l'épée: Histoire des princes et évêques de Strasbourg.* Bernardswiller: I.D. l'Edition, 2020. 192p. €20.00.

Houte, Arnaud-Dominique. *Propriété défendue: La société française à l'épreuve du vol, XIXe–XXe siècle.* Paris: Gallimard, 2021. 400p. €24.00.

Lachaise, Bernard. *Alcide Dusolier, 1836–1918, et la République.* Beaumontois-en-Périgord: Secrets de Pays, 2021. 222p. €24.00.

Lagoueyte, Patrick. *Les coups d'Etat, une histoire française.* Paris: Centre National de la Recherche Scientifique, 2021. 230p. €24.00.

Lançon, Bertrand. *Quand la France commence-t-elle? Essai de francoscopie.* Paris: Perrin, 2021. 250p. €18.00.

Lapasset, Michel. *Joinville: Une ville seigneuriale en Champagne.* Vol. 1. Danmarie-les-Lys: Auditoire, 2020. 512p. €39.00.

Le Bouëdec, Gérard. *La Presqu'île de Quiberon, au pays des deux mers: Du XVIIIe siècle à la Seconde Guerre mondiale.* Spézet: Coop Breizh, 2020. 199p. €29.00.

Le Brun, Dominique. *Charcot.* Paris: Tallandier, 2021. 141p. €17.00.

Le Brun, Dominique. *Les pôles: Une aventure française.* Paris: Tallandier, 2020. 333p. €20.90.

Ledbury, Mark, and Robert Wellington. *The Versailles Effect: Objects, Lives, and Afterlives of the Domaine.* London: Bloomsbury, 2021. 320p. $120.00.

Lemagnent, Cédric. *De Clodion le Chevelu au Roi Soleil: Révisez l'histoire de France à partir des surnoms des rois et des reines.* Paris: Colin, 2020. 256p. €16.90.

Le Mao, Caroline. *Les arsenaux de la Marine: Du XVIe siècle à nos jours.* Paris: Presses de l'Université Paris–Sorbonne, 2021. 558p. €32.00.

Maillet, Fanny. *Le médiévisme érudit en France: De la Révolution au Second Empire.* Geneva: Droz, 2021. 206p. €35.00.

Malon, Claude. *Le promeneur des non-lieux (récit).* Rouen: Falaises, 2020. 319p. €17.10.

Marquié, Claude, and Claude Martinez. *Petite histoire de Carcassonne.* Morlaàs: Cairn, 2020. 149p. €11.00.

Mary, Luc. *La France en colère: 500 ans de rébellions qui ont fait notre histoire.* Paris: Buchet-Castel, 2021. 343p. €28.90.

Maudhuy, Roger. *S'aimer autrefois: Amours et épousailles dans les pays de France*. Chamalières: Bonneton, 2021. 175p. €18.00.

McIlvanney, Siobhan. *Figurations of the Feminine in the Early French Women's Press, 1758–1848*. Liverpool: Liverpool University Press, 2019. 270p. £90.00.

McLaughlin, Mairi. *La presse française historique: Histoire d'un genre et histoire de la langue*. Paris: Classiques Garnier, 2021. 407p. €48.00.

Miller, Lynn H., and Therese Dolan. *Salut!: France Meets Philadelphia: The French Presence in Philadelphia's History, Culture, and Art*. Philadelphia: Temple University Press, 2021. 416p. $40.00.

Missoffe, Alain, and Philippe Franchini. *Femmes de fer: Elles ont incarné la saga Wendel*. Paris: Tallandier, 2020. 327p. €21.50.

Mossuz-Lavau, Janine. *Le clivage droite gauche: Toute une histoire*. Paris: Sciences Po, 2020. 176p. €12.00.

Nowak, Agnès. *Les Bonamy: Une famille de libraires, éditeurs d'images pieuses à Poitiers*. Poitiers: Nowak, 2020. 144p. €20.00.

Patin, Nicolas, and Dominique Pinsolle, eds. *Déstabiliser l'Etat en s'attaquant aux flux: Des révoltes antifiscales au sabotage, XVIIe–XXe siècles*. Nancy: Arbre Bleu, 2020. 228p. €19.00.

Phalip, Bruno. *Pour une histoire de la restauration monumentale (XIXe–début XXe siècles): Un manifeste pour le temps présent*. Clermont-Ferrand: Presses Universitaires Blaise-Pascal, 2021. 552p. €30.00.

Pouillard, Véronique. *Paris to New York: The Transatlantic Fashion Industry in the Twentieth Century*. Cambridge, MA: Harvard University Press, 2021. 336p. $39.95.

Roussel, Vincent. *Naissance d'une station: Une histoire du Cap-Ferret*. La Crèche: Geste, 2021. 350p. €35.00.

Schneider, Robert. *Maîtresses et femmes d'influence: Le coeur du pouvoir depuis 1789*. Paris: Perrin, 2021. 313p. €21.00.

Sirinelli, Jean-François. *Ce monde que nous avons perdu: Une histoire du vivre-ensemble*. Paris: Tallandier, 2021. 400p. €21.90.

Tauzin-Castellanos, Isabelle. *De l'émigration en Amérique latine à la crise migratoire: Histoire oubliée de la Nouvelle-Aquitaine, XIXe–XXIe siècle*. Morlaàs: Cairn, 2021. 348p. €18.96.

Tropeau, Christophe. "La sociabilité associative dans les communes rurales du département de la Mayenne des années 1830 aux années 1930." PhD diss., Université de Bretagne Sud, 2020.

Zarch, Frédéric. *Une histoire des étrangers à Saint-Etienne: Les indésirables, XIXe–XXe siècle*. Paris: Harmattan, 2020. 602p. €45.00.

Medieval and Renaissance

Audéon, Gaëlle. *A la cour de Philippe le Bel, 1305–1313*. Paris: Harmattan, 2021. 287p. €30.00.

Bainton, Henry. *History and the Written Word: Documents, Literacy, and Language in the Age of the Angevins*. Philadelphia: University of Pennsylvania Press, 2020. 272p. $69.95.

Balossino, Simone. *Le pont d'Avignon: Une société de bâtisseurs (XIIe–XVe siècle)*. Avignon: Editions Universitaires d'Avignon, 2021. 243p. €20.00.

Bonzon, Anne. *Justices croisées: Histoire et enjeux de l'appel comme d'abus, XIVe–XVIIIe siècle*. Rennes: Presses Universitaires de Rennes, 2021. 357p. €30.00.

Borello, Céline. *Cathérine de Médicis*. Paris: Presses Universitaires de France, 2021. 224p. €14.00.

Broomhall, Susan. *The Identities of Catherine de' Medici*. Leiden: Brill, 2021. 394p. $189.00.

Cancellieri, Jean-André, and Vannina Marchi Van Cauwelaert. *Les lieux de mémoire de la Corse médiévale: Bonifacio, un territoire d'exception; Exposition, Bonifacio, Espace Saint-Jacques, 5–30 septembre 2020*. Bonifacio: Ville de Bonifacio, 2020. 150p. €20.00.

Carrier, Nicolas, ed. *Alleux et alleutiers: Propriété foncière, seigneurie et féodalité (France, Catalogne, Italie, Xe–XIIe siècle)*. Lyon: CIHAM, 2021. 338p. €40.00.

Cassagnes-Brouquet, Sophie. *Capétiennes: Les reines de France au Moyen Age (Xe–XIVe siècles)*. Paris: Ellipses, 2020. 288p. €24.50.

Chevalier-Royet, Caroline. *Les livres des Rois dans l'empire carolingien: Exégèse et actualité*. Paris: Classiques Garnier, 2021. 602p. €59.00.

Claustre, Julie. *Faire ses comptes au Moyen Age: Les mémoires de besogne de Colin de Lormoye*. Paris: Belles Lettres, 2021. 320p. €25.00.

Corbiau, Marie-Hélène, Baudouin Van den Abeele, and Jean-Marie Yante, eds. *La route au Moyen Age: Réalités et représentations*. Turnhout: Brepols, 2021. 346p. €55.00.

Dehayes, Thierry. *La fabrique de Jeanne d'Arc*. Neuilly-sur-Seine: Atlande, 2021. 397p. €15.00.

Devaux, Jean. *Les premiers imprimés français et la littérature de Bourgogne (1470–1550): Actes du colloque international organisé à l'université Littoral-Côte d'Opale, Dunkerque*. Paris: Champion, 2021. 371p. €50.00.

Dieltiens, Dominique. *Un blanc manteau de châteaux: L'implantation des Capétiens en Languedoc et en Provence, 1209–1328*. Brignon: Fenestrelle, 2020. 299p. €25.00.

Duteil, Jean-Pierre. *Marguerite de Navarre*. Paris: Ellipses, 2021. 218p. €24.50.

Edmundson, William G. "The Participation of Women Believers and the Family in Later Languedocian Catharism, 1300–1308." PhD diss., University of Wisconsin–Milwaukee, 2020.

Eygun, Jean. *Le cartulaire d'Oloron*. Toulouse: Letràs d'Oc, 2019. 387p. €30.00.

Giard, Elodie. *Une terre convoitée: Le Poitou et les pays de l'Ouest entre la France et l'Angleterre entre 1337 et 1416*. Paris: Indes Savantes, 2021. 416p. €29.00.

Grévin, Benoît. *La Première Loi du royaume: L'acte de fixation de la majorité des rois de France (1374)*. Paris: Classiques Garnier, 2021. 651p. €29.00.

Hélary, Xavier. *L'ascension et la chute de Pierre de La Broce, chambellan du roi (1278): Etude sur le pouvoir royal au temps de Saint Louis et de Philippe III (v. 1250–v. 1280)*. Paris: Champion, 2021. 518p. €78.00.

Juchs, Jean-Philippe. *"Des guerres que aucuns nobles font entre eulx": La faide à la fin du Moyen Age*. Paris: Classiques Garnier, 2021. 765p. €58.00.

Keipo, Lekpaï Yves. "La détention des Templiers dans le royaume de France, 1307–1314: Le cas des frères de l'Ordre du Temple dans les prisons du bailliage de Senlis." PhD diss., Université de Nantes, 2020.

Lake-Giguère, Danny. "Administrer les forêts du roi au Moyen Age: Le negotium forestarum en Normandie capétienne (1204–1328)." PhD diss., Université de Rouen, 2020.

La Popelinière, Lancelot Voisin de. *L'histoire de France*, edited by Thierry Rentet, Pierre-Jean Souriac, Odette Turias, and Denise Turrel. Vol. 4. Geneva: Droz, 2021. 314p. €86.00.

Lemesle, Bruno. *Procès en récit: Formes et perception de procès avant l'an mil (IXe–Xe siècles)*. Paris: Classiques Garnier, 2021. 294p. €31.00.

Le Nézet-Célestin, Monique. *Roanne au Moyen Age: Une histoire renouvelée par l'archéologie récente (Ve siècle–milieu XVe siècle)*. Lyon: Association de Liaison pour le Patrimoine et l'Archéologie en Rhône, 2020. 236p. €45.00.

Lorette, Jacky. *Le Camp du Drap d'or, juin 1520*. Paris: Dacres, 2021. 414p. €20.00.

Marchandin, Pierre. "Moulins et énergie à Paris du XIIIe au XVIe siècle." PhD diss., Université Paris/Ecole Nationale des Chartes, 2021.

Pécout, Thierry. *Les officiers et la chose publique dans les territoires angevins (XIIIe–XVe siècle): Vers une culture politique? / Gli ufficiali e la cosa pubblica nei terrorori angioini (XIII–XV secolo): Verso una cultura politica?* Rome: Ecole Française de Rome, 2020. 669p. €62.00.

Prétou, Pierre. *L'invention de la piraterie en France au Moyen Age*. Paris: Presses Universitaires de France, 2021. 228p. €23.00.

Rabot, Brice. *Jeanne d'Arc*. Paris: Ellipses, 2021. 287p. €24.50.

Ripart, Laurent, Christian Guilleré, and Pascal Vuillemin. *La naissance du duché de Savoie (1416): Actes du colloque international de Chambéry (18, 19 et 20 février 2016)*. Chambéry: Presses Universitaires, Université Savoie Mont Blanc, 2020. 396p. €25.00.

Seabolt, A. P. "A Knight and His Horse: The Social Impact of Horses in Medieval France, 1150–1300." PhD diss., Trent University, 2020.

Shopkow, Leah. *Saint and the Count: A Case Study for Reading Like a Historian*. Toronto: University of Toronto Press, 2021. 216p. $65.00 cloth, $24.95 paper.

Soukupová, Vera. *La construction de la réalité historique chez Jean Froissart: L'historien et sa matière*. Paris: Champion, 2021. 553p. €75.00.

Ancien Régime

Andries, Lise. *Bandits, pirates et hors-la-loi au temps des Lumières*. Paris: Classiques Garnier, 2021. 248p. €29.00.

Athimon, Emmanuelle. *Tempêtes et submersions marines sur les territoires de la côte atlantique (XIVe–XVIIIe siècle)*. Paris: Indes Savantes, 2021. 450p. €33.00.

Barry, Stéphane, Marie Fauré, and Anne-Marie Cocula. *Préservez-nous du Mal! Les Bordelais face à la peste, XIVe–XVIIIe siècles*. Saint-Macaire: Memoring, 2021. 440p. €28.00.

Beaufils, Oriane. *L'art de la fête à la cour des Valois*. Paris: In Fine, 2021. 318p. €42.00.

Bonn, Gérard. *Deux magistrats dans la lumière du XVIIIe siècle: Le président Hénault et les salons parisiens; Le président de Brosses et ses "Lettres italiennes."* Paris: Glyphe, 2020. 238p. €22.00.

Bonnet, Marie-Rose. *Arles: Une cité rhodanienne sous l'Ancien Régime; Aristocratie, culture et violence (XVIe–XVIIe siècles)*. Paris: Harmattan, 2021. 169p. €18.00.

Bonzon, Anne, and Caroline Galland, eds. *Justices croisées: Histoire et enjeux de l'appel comme d'abus, XIVe–XVIIIe siècle*. Rennes: Presses Universitaires de Rennes, 2021. 360p. €30.00.

Bost, Hubert. *Bayle: Calviniste libertin*. Paris: Champion, 2021. 456p. €75.00.

Boudon, Jacques-Olivier. *Les quatre sergents de La Rochelle: Le dernier crime de la monarchie*. Paris: Passés Composés, 2021. 283p. €22.00.

Boyer, Anne. *Les d'Houry: Une dynastie de libraires-imprimeurs parisiens, éditeurs de l'"Almanach royal" et d'ouvrages médicaux (1649–1790)*. Geneva: Droz, 2021. 534p. €85.00.

Burson, Jeffrey D. *The Culture of Enlightening: Abbé Claude Yvon and the Entangled Emergence of the Enlightenment*. Notre Dame, IN: University of Notre Dame Press, 2019. 600p. $75.00.

Burson, Jeffrey D., and Anton M. Matytsin, eds. *The Skeptical Enlightenment: Doubt and Certainty in the Age of Reason*. Liverpool: Liverpool University Press, 2019. 248p. $99.99.

Callemein, Gwenaëlle. *Un crime atroce et secret: L'empoisonnement devant la justice royale (1682–1789)*. Rennes: Presses Universitaires de Rennes, 2021. 434p. €30.00.

Carretero Zamora, Juan Manuel. *La Bourgogne et la monarchie hispanique: Etudes d'histoire politique et financière*. Paris: Editions Hispaniques, 2020. 272p. €22.00.

Charpentier, Emmanuelle. *Les campagnes françaises à l'époque moderne*. Malakoff: Colin, 2021. 361p. €32.00.

Coleman, Charly. *The Spirit of French Capitalism: Economic Theology in the Age of Enlightenment*. Stanford, CA: Stanford University Press, 2021. 392p. $28.00.

Conroy, Derval, ed. *Towards an Equality of the Sexes in Early Modern France*. New York: Routledge, 2021. 296p. $160.00.

Cossic-Péricarpin, Annick, and Emrys Jones, eds. *La sociabilité en France et en Grande-Bretagne au siècle des Lumières*. Vol. 7, *La représentation et la réinvention des espaces de sociabilité au cours du long XVIIIe siècle*. Paris: Manuscrit, 2021. 431p. €37.00.

Crelier, Damien. *Passions de Saint-Simon: Ecriture de l'histoire et affectivité*. Paris: Hermann, 2021. 540p. €42.00.

Cuillé, Tili Boon. *Divining Nature: Aesthetics of Enchantment in Enlightenment France*. Stanford, CA: Stanford University Press, 2020. 350p. $65.00.

Darnton, Robert. *Pirating and Publishing: The Book Trade in the Age of Enlightenment*. New York: Oxford University Press, 2021. 391p. $34.95.

Dauge-Roth, Katherine. *Signing the Body: Marks on Skin in Early Modern France*. New York: Routledge, 2020. 334p. $128.00.

Delorme, Philippe. *Fêtes et cérémonies à Versailles*. Saint-Cloud: SOTECA, 2021. 98p. €14.90.

Delsalle, Paul. *Les tibériades du comté de Bourgogne, XVIe–XVIIe siècles: Publication des cartes frontalières de la Franche-Comté, et des textes s'y rapportent; Lorraine, Barrois, landgraviat de Haute-Alsace, comté de Montbéliard, principauté épiscopale de Bâle, comté de Neuchâtel, Pays de Vaud, Savoie (Pays de Gex, Bugey, Bresse), Bourgogne, Champagne et Bassigny*. Vol. 5. Vy-lès-Filain: Franche-Bourgogne, 2020. 273p. €55.00.

Demouy, Patrick. *Les sacres des rois à Reims: Etat des lieux et perspectives; Reims, le 4 novembre 2017*. Reims: Académie Nationale de Reims, 2020. 192p. €44.00.

Ducharlet, Emile. *Brouage au temps des prisons: La persécution des protestants au XVIIe s. et l'internement des suspects et la déportation des prêtres pendant la Révolution de 1789*. La Rochelle: Comité du Mémorial des Origines de la Nouvelle-France, 2020. 103p. €10.00.

Duvauferrier, Régis. *De l'âme éternelle au cerveau des plaisirs biographie de Julien Offray de La Mettrie, médecin-philosophe des Lumières*. Saint-Suliac: Yellow Concept, 2021. 324p. €17.00.

Elster, Jon. *France before 1789: The Unraveling of an Absolutist Regime*. Princeton, NJ: Princeton University Press, 2020. 280p. $39.95.

Faivre d'Arcier, Louis, Bruno Galland, and Pierre-Jean Souriac. *Lyon et la charte sapaudine, XIVe–XVIIIe siècle: Traduction [du latin] et analyse*. Lyon: Archives Municipales de Lyon, 2020. 110p. €13.00.

Gabard, Louis. *Voyage de M. et Mme Cradock: Deux Anglais à Paris et dans le Midi de la France (1783–1786)*. Saint Laurent-le-Minier: Massanne, 2020. 191p. €15.00.

Gelbart, Nina Rattner. *Minerva's French Sisters: Women of Science in Enlightenment France*. New Haven, CT: Yale University Press, 2021, 352p. $40.00.

Gras, Aurélien. *Les faiseurs de notes: Etre musicien en Provence au siècle des Lumières.* Avignon: Editions Universitaires d'Avignon, 2021. 380p. €28.00.

Grimmer, Claude. *Le duc de Nevers: Prince européen sous Louis XIII.* Paris: Fayard, 2021. 364p. €24.00.

Guillon-Metz, Françoise, and Mélanie Guérin-Boyer. *Louis XIV, un souverain diabétique, ou De regis gallicorum re medica.* Paris: Harmattan, 2021. 215p. €22.50.

Hammond, Nicholas. *The Powers of Sound and Song in Early Modern Paris.* University Park: Pennsylvania State University Press, 2021. 216p. $89.95.

Kang, Sukhwan. "Between Peaceful Coexistence and Ongoing Conflict: Religious Tolerance and the Protestant Minority in Seventeenth-Century France." PhD diss., Georgetown University, 2021.

Lagardère, Vincent. *Le commerce fluvial, maritime, la batellerie et la pêche sur l'Adour aux XVIIe et XVIIIe siècles: Peyrehorade et Bourg-Saint-Esprit-lès-Bayonne.* Paris: Harmattan, 2021. 499p. €42.00.

Legay, Marie-Laure. *Finance et calomnie: L'abbé Terray, ministre de Louis XV.* Paris: Centre National de la Recherche Scientifique, 2021. 310p. €25.00.

Leonhard, Jörn, and Hans-Jürgen Lüsebrink. *Handbuch politisch-sozialer Grundbegriffe in Frankreich 1680–1820: Opinion publique, Révolution, Contre-révolution.* Berlin: De Gruyter Oldenbourg, 2021. 233p. $45.99.

Loskoutoff, Yvan. *Mazarin, Rome et l'Italie.* Mont-Saint-Aignan: Presses Universitaires de Rouen, 2021. 391p. €19.00.

Lukas, Benjamin. "From Knights to Captains: Nobility, Masculinity, and Martial Violence in Sixteenth-Century France." PhD diss., University of Toronto, 2020.

Lurgo, Elisabetta G. *Marie-Louise d'Orléans: La princesse oubliée, nièce de Louis XIV.* Paris: Perrin, 2021. 377p. €23.00.

Marchini, Anna Maria. *Dalla femme savante alla madre di famiglia: La donna nell'Illuminismo francese.* Canterano: Aracne, 2020. 212p. €12.00.

Marraud, Mathieu. *Le pouvoir marchand corps et corporatisme à Paris sous l'Ancien Régime.* Ceyzérieu: Champ Vallon, 2021. 512p. €30.00.

Mironneau, Paul. *Réconciliations Henri IV et Rome (1589–1610).* Paris: Réunion des Museés Nationaux, 2020. 167p. €30.00.

Montpensier, Anne-Marie-Louise-Henriette d'Orléans. *Mémoires,* edited by Jean Garapon. Vols. 1–2. Paris: Champion, 2020. 1,462p. €95.00.

Nelson, William Max. *The Time of Enlightenment: Constructing the Future in France, 1750 to Year One.* Toronto: University of Toronto Press, 2021. 224p. $75.00.

O'Byrne, Henry. *Un conseiller au parlement de Toulouse: Clément de Rey de Saint Géry, 1731–1794; D'après les archives du château de Saint Géry.* Val-des-Prés: Transhumances, 2020. 256p. €16.00.

Parrott, David. *1652: The Cardinal, the Prince, and the Crisis of the "Fronde."* New York: Oxford University Press, 2020. 336p. $85.00.

Patterson, Jonathan. *Villainy in France (1463–1610): A Transcultural Study of Law and Literature.* Oxford: Oxford University Press, 2021. 352p. $90.00.

Poulet, Olivier. "Les orangers du Soleil: Culture et représentation de l'oranger sous le règne de Louis XIV (1643–1715)." PhD diss., Université de Rennes 2, 2021.

Rovere, Ange. *L'Eglise de Corse en révolutions (XVIIe–XVIIIe siècles).* Ajaccio: Albiana, 2021. 331p. €22.00.

Schoenaers, Christian. *Trois hommes des Lumières à l'île de Gorée: Michel Adanson, Stanislas-Jean de Boufflers, Sylvain Meinrad Xavier de Golbery*. Paris: Harmattan, 2020. 344p. €35.00.

Sewell, William H. *Capitalism and the Emergence of Civic Equality in Eighteenth-Century France*. Chicago: University of Chicago Press, 2021. 416p. $105.00 cloth, $35.00 paper.

Sturla, Roberto. *Nello specchio dei lumi: La Russia di Caterina 2. nel dibattito politico francese (1762–1783)*. Scandicci: Centro Editoriale Toscano, 2020. 238p. €20.00.

Villars, Marie Gigault de Bellefonds. *Letters from Spain: A Seventeenth-Century French Noblewoman at the Spanish Royal Court*, edited and translated by Nathalie Hester. New York: Iter, 2020. 100p. $41.95.

Zhou, Nan. "From the Physical Body to the Body Social: The Development of Enlightenment French Materialism." PhD diss., Queen's University (Canada), 2020.

Zum Kolk, Caroline, ed. *Grandeur et déclin d'un hôtel parisien: L'hôtel de Lauzun et ses propriétaires au XVIIe siècle*. Paris: Maison des Sciences de l'Homme, 2021. 250p. €23.00.

French Revolution and Napoleonic Era

Alpaugh, Micah. *The French Revolution: A History in Documents*. New York: Bloomsbury Academic, 2021. 290p. $100.00.

Ancely, Jean-Luc. *Valmy: La fin de la Vieille France, 1774–1792*. Wavre: Mols, 2020. 316p. €23.90.

Arisi Rota, Arianna. *Il cappello dell'imperatore: Storia, memoria e mito di Napoleone Bonaparte attraverso due secoli di culto dei suoi oggetti*. Rome: Donzelli, 2021. 160p. €28.00.

Bamford, Andrew. *Glory Is Fleeting: New Scholarship on the Napoleonic Wars*. Warwick: Helion, 2021. 227p. $37.95.

Bernot, Jacques. *Edouard Walckiers (1758–1837): Banquier et révolutionnaire*. Monfaucon: Wuillaume, 2020. 230p. €34.90.

Bianchi, Paola, and Andrea Merlotti. *Andare per l'Italia di Napoleone*. Bologna: Mulino, 2021. 176p. €12.00.

Biard, Michel. *En finir avec Robespierre et ses amis, juillet 1794–octobre 1795*. Chamalières: Lemme, 2021. 115p. €15.90.

Bond, Elizabeth Andrews. *The Writing Public: Participatory Knowledge Production in Enlightenment and Revolutionary France*. Ithaca, NY: Cornell University Press, 2021. 272p. €19.95.

Bonnet, Jean-Claude. *Les aléas de la parole publique (1789–1815)*. Saint-Etienne: Publications de l'Université de Saint-Etienne, 2021. 192p. €22.00.

Bornet, Philippe. *Napoléon et Dieu*. Le Chesnay: Via Romana, 2021. 179p. €19.00.

Boudon, Jacques-Olivier. *Le maréchal Marmont, d'un empire à l'autre, 1774–1852*. Paris: SPM, 2021. 214p. €19.00.

Boudon, Jacques-Olivier. *Napoléon: Le dernier Romain*. Paris: Belles Lettres, 2021. 168p. €19.00.

Bouget, Boris. *Napoléon n'est plus*. Paris: Gallimard, 2021. 307p. €35.00.

Boulant, Antoine. *La journée révolutionnaire: Le peuple à l'assaut du pouvoir, 1789–1795*. Paris: Passés Composés, 2021. 221p. €18.00.

Branda, Pierre. *Napoléon à Sainte-Hélène*. Paris: Perrin, 2021. 652p. €27.00.

Brücker, Axel. *Le maréchal Moncey*. Paris: Michalon, 2021. 349p. €25.00.

Bruyère-Ostells, Walter. *Les maréchaux d'Empire: Les paladins de Napoléon*. Paris: Perrin, 2021. 379p. €23.00.

Burg, Martijn van der. *Napoleonic Governance in the Netherlands and Northwest Germany: Conquest, Incorporation, and Integration.* Basingstoke: Palgrave Macmillan, 2021. 165p. $59.99.

Caiani, Ambrogio A. *To Kidnap a Pope: Napoleon and Pius VII.* New Haven, CT: Yale University Press, 2021. 376p. $32.50.

Cercle de Généalogie et d'Histoire Locale de Coutances et du Cotentin. *La Révolution à Coutances et dans le département de la Manche, 1789–1799: Acte du colloque de Coutances, 21 et 22 mai 2016.* Coutances: Cercle de Généalogie et d'Histoire Locale de Coutances et du Cotentin, 2019. 199p. Gratis.

Chabert, Hélène de. *Un coeur hardi dans la tourmente: De la Terreur à la Restauration; Mémoires inédits, 1777–1837,* edited by Béatrice de Kergorlay. Paris: Lacurne, 2020. 445p. €26.00.

Chevallier, Bernard, and Arthur Chevallier. *Napoléon: Exposition, Paris, grande halle de La Villette, du 14 avril au 19 septembre 2021.* Paris: Réunion des Musées Nationaux, 2021. 260p. €25.00.

Colonna d'Istria, Robert. *Le secret de Napoléon.* Paris: Equateurs, 2021. 326p. €21.00.

Costamagna, Philippe. *Les goûts de Napoléon.* Paris: Grasset, 2021. 287p. €20.90.

Courroye, Philippe. *Accusé Napoléon, levez-vous! L'empereur à la barre de l'histoire.* Paris: Laffont, 2021. 309p. €21.50.

Couvet, Tom-Hugo. *L'Alligator: L'odyssée d'un navire négrier havrais; Au temps de la révolution de Saint-Domingue (1789–1792).* Paris: Hémisphères, 2021. 224p. €24.00.

Craplet, Michel. *L'ivresse de la Révolution: Histoire secrète de l'alcool, 1789–1794.* Paris: Grasset, 2021. 289p. €22.00.

Damaggio, Jean-Paul. *Daniel Ligou face à Jeanbon Saint-André.* Angeville: Brochure, 2020. 130p. €10.00.

De Francesco, Antonino. *Il naufrago e il dominatore: Vita politica di Napoleone Bonaparte.* Vicenza: Neri Pozza, 2021. 236p. €18.00.

Delenne, Laurent. *Sur les routes d'Europe avec Napoléon: Histoires de grognards.* La Roche-sur-Yon: Centre Vendéen de Recherches Historiques, 2021. 420p. €27.00.

Demory, Jean-Claude. *Claude-François de Malet, ou L'obsession du complot.* Paris: Félin, 2021. 224p. €20.00.

Duperray, Eve. *Mémoires républicaines en Vaucluse: La mémoire "douloureuse" de la réunion d'Avignon et du Comtat Venaissin à la France jusqu'à la chute de Robespierre (1791–1794).* Paris: Mare et Martin Arts, 2021. 240p. €35.00.

Fiechter, Jean-Jacques, and Alain-Jacques Tornare. *Révolution française et christianisme: L'exemple du réseau Chaffoy en Franche-Comté (1794–1797).* Gollion: Infolio, 2021. 487p. €29.00.

Field, Andrew W. *The French at Waterloo: Eyewitness Accounts; Napoleon Imperial Headquarters and 1st Corps.* Barnsley: Pen and Sword Military, 2020. 154p. $34.95.

Flichy de La Neuville, Thomas. *L'empire de Bonaparte: Laboratoire de la domination absolue.* Poitiers: Morin, 2021. 116p. €11.50.

Frerejean, Alain. *Napoléon face à la mort.* Paris: Archipel, 2021. 300p. €20.00.

Goupil-Travert, Maria. *Braves combattantes, humbles héroïnes trajectoires et mémoires des engagées volontaires de la Révolution et de l'Empire.* Rennes: Presses Universitaires de Rennes, 2021. 212p. €25.00.

Griffon de Pleineville, Natalia. *1812, la campagne de Russie.* Saint-Cloud: SOTECA, 2021. 98p. €14.90.

Guillon, Claude. *Robespierre, les femmes et la Révolution*. Paris: Imho, 2021. 360p. €18.00.

Guillou, Yannick. *Napoléon et l'Empire ottoman*. Senones: Edhisto, 2021. 429p. €21.00.

Harris, Jeffrey Ryan. "The Struggle for the General Will and the Making of the French and Haitian Revolutions." PhD diss., University of North Carolina at Chapel Hill, 2020.

Le Bozec, Christine. *Révolution et religion*. Paris: Passés Composés, 2021. 172p. €16.00.

Lentz, Thierry. *Le plus puissant souffle de vie . . . : La mort de Napoléon (1821–2021)*. Paris: Centre National de la Recherche Scientifique, 2021. 301p. €25.00.

Leterrier, Sophie-Anne. *Rhétorique et politisation: De la fin des Lumières au printemps des peuples*. Arras: Artois Presses Université, 2021. 260p. €21.00.

Mandon, Guy. *La Révolution française en Dordogne, 1789–1794: Le cas de Pierre-Eléonor Pipaud des Granges*. Neuvic-sur-l'Isle: Livres de l'Ilot, 2020. 222p. €15.00.

Martin, Jean-Clément. *L'exécution du roi, 21 janvier 1793: La France entre République et Révolution*. Paris: Perrin, 2021. 411p. €21.00.

Necci, Alessandra. *Al cuore dell'Impero: Napoleone e le sue donne fra sentimento e potere*. Venice: Marsilio, 2020. 405p. €18.00.

Nester, William. *Napoleon and the Art of Leadership: How a Flawed Genius Changed the History of Europe and the World*. Barnsley: Frontline, 2021. 532p. $49.95.

Petit, Vincent. *Napoléon saint: L'empereur au paradis*. Besançon: Cêtre, 2021. 150p. €19.00.

Rey, Jean-Philippe. *Les hommes de Bonaparte: La conquête du pouvoir, 1793–1800*. Paris: Perrin, 2021. 315p. €22.00.

Roelly, Aude. *Dessiner pour Napoléon: Trésors de la secrétairerie d'Etat impériale*. Neuilly-sur-Seine: Lafon, 2021. 213p. €29.00.

Roucaud, Michel. *Dans les rangs de la Grande Armée de Napoléon*. Vanves: EPA, 2021. 287p. €39.95.

Sabourdin-Perrin, Dominique. *Marie-Clothilde de France: La soeur oubliée de Louis XVI*. Paris: Salvator, 2020. 357p. €22.00.

Samoyault, Jean-Pierre. *Registre du dépôt de Nesle: Oeuvres d'art saisies pendant la Révolution chez les émigrés et condamnés parisiens en vue de l'instruction publique*. 2 vols. Paris: De Boccard, 2021. 1,069p. €95.00.

Sandoni, Luca. *Addomesticare la Rivoluzione: I "principî del 1789" nella cultura cattolica francese del Secondo Impero*. Pisa: Normale, 2020. 371p. €30.00.

Scurr, Ruth. *Napoleon: A Life in Gardens and Shadows*. New York: Liveright, 2021. 416p. $28.95.

Tarente, Louise-Emmanuelle de, and Grace Dalrymple Elliott. *Captives sous la Terreur: Souvenirs de la princesse de Tarente, 1789–1792. Suivi de Mémoires de Madame Elliott sur la Révolution française*, edited by Sandrine Fillipetti. Paris: Mercure de France, 2021. 353p. €11.50.

Tulard, Jean. *Marengo, ou L'étrange victoire de Bonaparte*. Paris: Buchet-Chastel, 2021. 202p. €19.50.

Vial, Charles-Eloi. *Histoire des Cent-Jours, mars–novembre 1815*. Paris: Perrin, 2021. 672p. €27.00.

Vincent, Johan. *Le périple en Espagne d'un curé en exil: Journal de l'abbé Paillaud (1792–1797)*. La Roche-sur-Yon: Centre Vendéen de Recherches Historiques, 2020. 264p. €23.00.

1815–1871

Aali, Heta. *French Royal Women during the Restoration and July Monarchy: Redefining Women and Power*. Cham: Palgrave Macmillan, 2021. 261p. $109.99.

Amalie, Auguste, and Antoine Darnay. *Lettres au baron Antoine Darnay (1824–1837): Corre-spondances*, edited by Christophe Pincemaille. Rouen: Falaises, 2020. 272p. €24.00.

Anceau, Eric. *L'empire libéral: Essai d'histoire globale*. Paris: SPM, 2021. 371p. €33.00.

Audin, Michèle. *La semaine sanglante: Mai 1871, légendes et comptes*. Paris: Libertalia, 2021. 258p. €10.00.

Bantigny, Ludivine. *La Commune au présent: Une correspondance par-delà le temps*. Paris: Découverte, 2021. 397p. €22.00.

Baquiast, Paul, and Bertrand Sabot. *Emmanuel Arago, ou Le roman de la République*. Paris: Félin, 2021. 332p. €25.00.

Berthereau, Estelle. *La fabrique politique du journal: Pierre-Sébastien Laurentie (1793–1876), un antimoderne au temps de Balzac*. Paris: Champion, 2021. 476p. €69.00.

Bodart, Benoit, and Gabriel Garrote, eds. *Un autre regard sur la guerre de 1870–1871: Pour une approche pluridisciplinaire*. Avon-les-Roches: Amarque Histoire, 2021. 203p. €19.00.

Boudon, Jacques-Olivier. *Les quatre sergents de La Rochelle: Le dernier crime de la monarchie*. Paris: Passés Composés, 2021. 283p. €22.00.

Bourguinat, Nicolas, and Gilles Vogt. *La guerre franco-allemande de 1870: Une histoire globale*. Paris: Flammarion, 2020. 521p. €15.00.

Brulant, Claude. *L'empereur et le photographe: Essai sur l'usage de la photographie au Second Empire*. Paris: Lettrage, 2021. 363p. €37.00.

Chuzeville, Julien. *Léo Frankel: Communard sans frontières*. Montreuil: Libertalia, 2021. 276p. €15.00.

Contes, Julien. *Ce que publier signifie: Une révolution par l'encre et le papier, Nice (1847–1850)*. Paris: Champion, 2021. 738p. €35.00.

Cordillot, Michel. *La Commune de Paris 1871: Les acteurs, l'événement, les lieux*. Ivry-sur-Seine: Atelier/Editions Ouvrières, 2021. 1,348p. €34.50.

Danvier, G. *Blanqui: Una vita per la rivoluzione*. 2 vols. Naples: Città del Sole, 2021. €70.00.

Decraene, Jean-François. *Lieux de mémoire des deux sièges, 1870+1871: Guide des Hauts-de-Seine*. Trouville-sur-Mer: Librairie des Musées, 2020. 159p. €18.00.

Déruelle, Aude, and Corinne Legoy, eds. *Les mots du politique, 1815–1848*. Paris: Classiques Garnier, 2021. 196p. €16.00.

Dittmar, Gérald. *Figures normandes de la Commune de Paris de 1871*. Ouistreham: Dittmar, 2021. 217p. €20.00.

Dupeyron, Jean-François. *A l'école de la Commune de Paris: L'histoire d'une autre école*. Dijon: Raison et Passions, 2020. 306p. €20.00.

Dupeyron, Jean-François. *Commun-Commune: Penser la Commune de Paris (1871)*. Paris: Kimé, 2021. 420p. €29.00.

Effros, Bonnie. *Incidental Archaeologists: French Officers and the Rediscovery of Roman North Africa*. Ithaca, NY: Cornell University Press, 2021. 392p. $34.95 paper.

Ferreira, Oscar. *Le pouvoir royal (1814–1848): A la recherche du quatrième pouvoir?* Paris: Librairie Générale de Droit et de Jurisprudence, 2021. 570p. €72.00.

Franconie, Grégoire. *Le Lys et la Cocarde: Royauté et nation à l'âge romantique (1830–1848)*. Paris: Presses Universitaires de France, 2021. 491p. €26.00.

Frigerio, Vittorio. *Nous nous reverrons aux barricades: Les feuilletons des journaux de Proudhon (1848–1850)*. Grenoble: Université Grenoble Alpes, 2021. 227p. €22.00.

Frobert, Ludovic. *Vers l'égalité ou au-delà: Essai sur l'aube du socialisme*. Lyon: Ecole Normale Supérieure, 2021. 200p. €18.00.

Godineau, Laure. *La Commune de 1871 expliquée en images*. Paris: Seuil, 2021. 151p. €29.00.

Graaf, Beatrice de. *Fighting Terror after Napoleon: How Europe Became Secure after 1815*. New York: Cambridge University Press, 2020. 518p. $39.99.

Landgraf, Eric. "Louis-Philippe, roi bâtisseur: Le rêve d'une nation unifiée; Le chantier du château de Versailles de 1830 à 1848." PhD diss., Université de Paris–Saclay, 2021.

Lecaillon, Jean-François. *Les femmes et la guerre de 1870–1871: Histoire d'un engagement occulté*. Paris: Taillac, 2021. 371p. €26.90.

Lecat, Marie-France. *Napoléon III: Bâtisseur du Sud-Ouest; Le développement de l'Aquitaine sous le Second Empire*. Morlaàs: Cairn, 2021. 157p. €20.00.

Le Tréhonda, Patrick, ed. *La Commune au jour le jour: Le "Journal officiel" de la Commune de Paris, 20 mars–24 mai 1871*. Paris: Syllepse, 2021. 133p. €10.00.

Mancini, Mirella, and Emilio Gianni. *1871–2021, la Commune de Paris: 150 ans, les militants du Conseil de la Commune*. Montreuil-sous-Bois: Science Marxiste, 2021. 390p. €10.00.

McAuliffe, Mary Sperling. *Paris, City of Dreams: Napoleon III, Baron Haussmann, and the Creation of Paris*. Lanham, MD: Rowman and Littlefield, 2020. 329p. $26.95.

Norguez, Marc. *Les ouvriers du livre au XIXe siècle: Luttes sociales et révolutions, 1848–1871*. Paris: Indes Savantes, 2021. 191p. €21.00.

Popiel, Jennifer J. *Heroic Hearts: Sentiment, Saints, and Authority in Modern France*. Lincoln: University of Nebraska Press, 2021. 366p. $65.00.

Quinlan, Sean M. *Morbid Undercurrents: Medical Subcultures in Postrevolutionary France*. Ithaca, NY: Cornell University Press, 2021. 336p. $45.00.

Riviale, Philippe. *1849, une République mise à mort*. Paris: Harmattan, 2021. 195p. €21.50.

Roy-Reverzy, Eléonore. *Témoigner pour Paris: Récits du siège et de la Commune (1870–1871); Anthologie*. Paris: Kimé, 2020. 588p. €30.00.

Sancton, Tom. *Sweet Land of Liberty: America in the Mind of the French Left, 1848–1871*. Baton Rouge: Louisiana State University Press, 2021. 336p. $50.00.

Schiffer, Liesel. *Olympe: Etre femme et féministe au temps de Napoléon III*. Paris: Vendémiaire, 2021. 550p. €26.00.

Sircana, Giuseppe. *A Parigi! A Parigi! Italiani alla Comune*. Milan: Biblion Edizioni, 2021. 124p. €15.00.

Sureau, Dominique. *Gustave Lefrançais: Histoire d'une rencontre avec un Angevin; Président du conseil de la Commune de Paris (1871)*. Brissac: Petit Pavé, 2021. 215p. €20.00.

Verhaeghe, Sidonie. *Vive Louise Michel! Célébrité et postérité d'une figure anarchiste*. Vulaines-sur-Seine: Croquant, 2021. 374p. €20.00.

Viard, Bruno, ed. *Pierre Leroux: Le socialisme républicain et l'Orient (Mahomet, les Védas, Bouddha, Confucius, le tao), 1832*. Lormont: Bord de l'Eau, 2020. 87p. €12.00.

Third Republic

Bantman, Constance. *Jean Grave and the Networks of French Anarchism, 1854–1939*. Basingstoke: Palgrave Macmillan, 2021. 243p. $109.99.

Baquiast, Paul, and Bertrand Sabot. *Emmanuel Arago (1812–1896), ou Le roman de la République*. Paris: Félin, 2021. 332p. €25.00.

Bouchet, Julien, and Pierre Triomphe. *Emile Combes: Cent ans après; Exposition, Paris, Palais du Luxembourg, 1er mai–1er juin 2021 puis Pons, Donjon de Pons, 9 juin–9 juillet 2021*. Bordeaux: Festin, 2021. 95p. €10.00.

Bouglé Moalic, Anne-Sarah. *La marche des citoyennes: Le droit de vote des femmes en France, 1870–1944*. Paris: Cerf, 2021. 232p. €20.00.

Boulouque, Sylvain. *Julien Le Pen: Un lutteur syndicaliste et libertaire*. Lyon: Atelier de Création Libertaire, 2020. 372p. €18.00.

Buller, Robin Margaret. "Ottoman Jews in Paris: Sephardi Immigrant Community, Culture, and Identity, 1918–1939." PhD diss., University of North Carolina at Chapel Hill, 2021.

Cattanéo, Bernard. *Mésentente cordiale: Les Anglais vus par les Français au tournant du XXe siècle*. Paris: Harmattan, 2020. 174p. €18.50.

Cole, Jenn. *Hysteria in Performance*. Montreal: McGill-Queen's University Press, 2021. 264p. CAD$37.95.

Collectif de Sociétés d'Histoire et d'Archéologie de l'Oise. *1918, finir la guerre dans l'Oise: Actes du colloque, Compiègne, 2–3 novembre 2018*. Berteaucourt-les-Thennes: Sociétés d'Histoire Moderne et Contemporaine de Compiègne, 2020. 306p. €30.00.

Dasi, Pierre. *Penser et représenter la nature à l'école sous la Troisième République*. Paris: Harmattan, 2021. 330p. €34.00.

Ducange, Jean-Numa. *Jules Guesde: The Birth of Socialism and Marxism in France*, translated by David Broder. Cham: Palgrave Macmillan, 2020. 213p. $74.99.

Fein, Julius. *Hitler's Refugees and the French Response, 1933–1938*. Lanham, MD: Lexington, 2021. 297p. $120.00.

Girault, Jacques, and Jean-Louis Robert. *1920, le Congrès de Tours: Présentation, extraits, résolutions*. Montreuil: Temps des Cerises, 2020. 203p. €15.00.

Grieu, Eric. *Amère victoire: Des soldats méridionaux de juin 1919 à juin 1940; Une collection pour servir leur histoire*. Brignon: Editions de la Fenestrelle, 2020. 127p. €25.00.

Grousselas, Camille. *Jean Jaurès: Oser l'idéal*. Nancy: Arbre Bleu, 2020. 225p. €20.00.

Guelton, Frédéric. *1919, de la paix aux reconstructions dans la Marne: Journées d'étude, 5 et 6 décembre 2019, Tinqueux-Suippes*. Châlons-en-Champagne: Département de la Marne, 2020. 267p. €25.00.

Henning, Jérôme. *Le radicalisme d'Edouard Herriot et la crise des institutions (1905–1954)*. Paris: Dalloz, 2019. 671p. €70.00.

Herpin, Vincent. *Les exécutions sommaires: Un non-dit historique*. Louvier: Ysec, 2021. 150p. €20.00.

Holekamp, Abigail A. "Citizens and Comrades: Entangled Revolutions and the Production of Knowledge between Russia and France, 1905–1936." PhD diss., Georgetown University, 2021.

Jacquet, Benjamin. *Les malades de la Grande Guerre: Les poilus et leurs médecins face à la maladie*. Paris: Ellipses, 2021. 263p. €24.00.

Jamin, Jean. *Tableaux d'une exposition: Chronique d'une famille ouvrière ardennaise sous la IIIe République*. Paris: Nouvelles Editions Place, 2021. 213p. €22.00.

Kalifa, Dominique. *The Belle Epoque: A Cultural History, Paris and Beyond*, edited and translated by Susan Emanuel and Venita Datta. New York: Columbia University Press, 2021. 252p. $120.00.

Karila-Cohen, Pierre. *Monsieur le préfet: Incarner l'Etat dans la France du XIXe siècle*. Ceyzérieu: Champ Vallon, 2021. 368p. €24.00.

Kessler, Marni Reva. *Discomfort Food: The Culinary Imagination in Late Nineteenth-Century French Art*. Minneapolis: University of Minnesota Press, 2021. 320p. $120.00 cloth, $30.00 paper.

Lalouette, Marie, and Daniel Jennepin. *Femme courage: Histoire de l'épouse d'un poilu qui vécut la Première Guerre mondiale à Signy-le-Petit alors que son époux se battait sur le front*. La Neuville-aux-Joutes: Flament, 2021. 183p. €19.00.

Lehman, Eric. *Alliées et rivales: L'Italie et la France dans la Grande Guerre*. Grenoble: Université Grenoble Alpes, 2021. 246p. €24.00.

Marsaud de Labouygue, Richard Alain. *Il portait l'ancre d'or: Colonel Christian Marsaud de Labouygue, de l'infanterie coloniale (1880–1952); Attaché à la personne du président de la République (1930–1940)*. Versailles: VA, 2021. 88p. €20.00.

Morlat, Patrice. *"Orients" extrêmes: Les loges coloniales du Grand Orient de France (1870–1940)*. Paris: Indes Savantes, 2021. 433p. €30.00.

Paulhan, Claire. *Port-Cros en 1886, île de quarantaine*. Hyères: Association des Amis de Port-Cros, 2021. 88p. €10.00.

Peyvel, Pierre. *De la guerre à la paix: Le département de la Loire en 1919; Actes du colloque tenu à Montbrison le 22 novembre 2019*. Montbrison: Diana, 2020. 198p. €24.00.

Plantié, Léon, Madeleine Plantié, and Cécile Plantié. *Que de baisers perdus . . . : La correspondance intime de Léon et Madeleine Plantié (1914–1917)*. Pessac: Presses Universitaires de Bordeaux, 2020. 517p. €33.00.

Rexer, Raisa. *The Fallen Veil: A Literary and Cultural History of the Photographic Nude in Nineteenth-Century France*. Philadelphia: University of Pennsylvania Press, 2021. 328p. $59.95.

Richefort, Isabelle, ed. *Aux sources de la paix: Les archives du service français de la SDN*. Aubervilliers: Comité des Travaux Historiques et Scientifiques, 2020. 523p. €19.00.

Rizzo, Jean-Louis. *Albert Sarraut: Au coeur de la République parlementaire et coloniale*. Paris: Harmattan, 2021. 256p. €26.00.

Rollet, Catherine, and Virginie De Luca Barrusse. *Dans l'ombre de la réforme sociale: Paul Strauss, 1852–1942*. Paris: Institut National d'Etudes Démographiques, 2020. 287p. €25.00.

Schmauch, Joseph. *Réintégrer les départements annexés: Le gouvernement et les services d'Alsace-Lorraine, 1914–1919*. Metz: Paraiges Histoire, 2019. 548p. €25.00.

Société Française pour le Droit International. *Le traité de Versailles: Regards franco-allemands en droit international à l'occasion du centenaire; 11èmes journées franco-allemande*. Paris: Pedone, 2020. 318p. €48.00.

Thevenet, Charles. *Carnets de notes du général Thevenet (1914–1917): Suivi de Réflexions sur la nation armée*, edited by Yves de Mestier du Bourg. Paris: Harmattan, 2021. 189p. €20.00.

Verardi, Virginia. *Bâtir la paix: Léon Bourgeois, prix Nobel (1920–2020)*. Gand: Snoeck, 2021. 255p. €35.00.

Vidalenc, Gabriel. *De Rethondes, 11 novembre 1918, à Rethondes, 22 juin 1940: Une histoire de France et d'Allemagne*. Paris: Harmattan, 2020. 536p. €48.00.

Vildrac, Charles, and Georges Monnet. *Souvenirs militaires de la Grande Guerre*. Paris: Paulhan, 2021. 286p. €28.00.

Post-1940

Archives Départementales des Ardennes. *Andrée et Pierre Vienot, pensée et action: Actes du colloque; Bastion du Dauphin, rue Dauphine, Rocroy, samedi 8 octobre 2016*. Charleville-Mézières: Terres Ardennaises, 2020. 107p. €17.00.

Aubert, Antoine. "Devenir(s) révolutionnaire(s): Enquête sur les intellectuels 'marxistes' en France (années 1968–années 1990): Contribution à une histoire sociale des idées." PhD diss., Université de Paris 1, 2020.

Bat, Jean-Pierre. *Pierre Messmer (1916–2007)*. Paris: Cerf, 2021. 151p. €14.00.

Batardy, Christophe. *Le programme commun de la gauche (1972–1977): C'était le temps des programmes*. Pessac: Presses Universitaires de Bordeaux, 2021. 450p. €29.00.

Beltramo, Noémie. *Vivre sa polonité en territoire minier: L'évolution de trois générations à travers les milieux associatif et familial (1945–2015)*. Arras: Artois Presses Université, 2021. 338p. €25.00.

Benoist-Lucy, Odile, Michèle Agniel, and Sophie Carquain. *Nous étions Résistantes*. Paris: Alisio, Témoignages et Documents, 2020. 189p. €18.00.

Bonet, Gérard, and Jean-Yves Mollier. *L'agence Inter-France de Pétain à Hitler: Une entreprise de manipulation de la presse de province (1936–1950)*. Paris: Félin, 2021. 901p. €35.00.

Bourachot, André, and Henri Ortholan. *Les épurations de l'armée française, 1940–1966: Le conflit de devoir de l'officier*. Paris: Giovanangeli, 2021. 493p. €25.00.

Brun, Jean-Pierre. *De Gaulle et l'armée, la fatale équivoque*. Paris: Dualpha, 2021. 566p. €25.00.

Buton, Philippe. *Histoire du gauchisme: L'héritage de mai 68*. Paris: Perrin, 2021. 560p. €26.00.

Büttner, Christian, and Jacqueline Tabuteau. *Prisonniers de guerre allemands en Médoc*. Pauillac: Publication de la Société Archéologique et Historique du Médoc, 2020. 91p. €8.00.

Canuel, Hugues. *The Fall and Rise of French Sea Power: France's Quest for an Independent Naval Policy, 1940–1963*. Annapolis, MD: Naval Institute Press, 2021. 344p. $54.95.

Castaingts, Yves. *Basse-Navarre et Soule sous l'Occupation: Témoignages*. Ciboure: Arteaz, 2021. 360p. €20.85.

Charnow, Sally Debra. *Edmond Fleg and Jewish Minority Culture in Twentieth-Century France*. New York: Routledge, 2021. 238p. $160.00.

Charpentier, Pierre-Frédéric. *Imbéciles, c'est pour vous que je meurs! . . . : Valentin Feldman (1909–1942)*. Paris: Centre National de la Recherche Scientifique, 2021. 330p. €25.00.

Chion, Thierry. *France 1940—Massacrés: Le triste sort des soldats africains et indochinois en Picardie et Normandie*. Thônes: Choucas, 2021. 208p. €25.00.

Christophe, Francine. *L'enfant des camps*. Paris: Grasset, 2021. 120p. €12.90.

Collins, Jacob. *The Anthropological Turn: French Political Thought after 1968*. Philadelphia: University of Pennsylvania Press, 2020. 304p. $65.00.

Cordier, Daniel. *La victoire en pleurant: Alias Caracalla, 1943–1946*. Paris: Gallimard, 2021. 323p. €21.00.

Courtès-Bordes, Geneviève, and Georges Courtès. *Présences juives dans le Gers (1939–1945)*. Orthez: Gascogne, 2021. 322p. €23.00.

Delhomme, Patrice. *Eugène Deloncle, de la Cagoule au MSR (juin 1936–7 janvier 1944)*. Paris: Dualpha, 2021. 358p. €31.00.

Denis, Cécile. *La Résistance allemande et autrichienne en France: D'après sa presse clandestine; L'histoire de trois réseaux germanophones actifs en France pendant la Seconde Guerre mondiale au travers de leurs journaux et de leurs tracts*. Paris: Harmattan, 2021. 315p. €33.00.

Denis, Eric. *L'armée de Terre française du 10 mai 1940*. Paris: Economica, 2020. 200p. €39.00.

Di Maggio, Marco. *The Rise and Fall of Communist Parties in France and Italy: Entangled Historical Approaches*. Cham: Palgrave Macmillan, 2021. 288p. $108.99.

Domenach, Léa, and Hugo Domenach. *Les murs blancs*. Paris: Grasset, 2021. 320p. €20.00.

Drake, Laurie. "Feeding France's Outcasts: Rationing and Hunger in Vichy's Internment Camps, 1940–1944." PhD diss., University of Toronto, 2020.

Dreux, William B. *No Bridges Blown: With the OSS Jedburghs in Nazi-Occupied France*. Notre Dame, IN: University of Notre Dame Press, 2020. 346p. $125.00 cloth, $22.00 paper.

Dreyfus, Nicole, and Gilbert Haas. *Fuir pour vivre: Parcours d'une famille juive d'Alsace en Occitanie*. Albi: Autre Reg'art, 2021. 234p. €19.00.

Emler, David. *La politique, l'histoire, la mémoire: Les usages politiques du passé en France dans les années 1990 et 2000*. Paris: Harmattan, 2021. 248p. €25.00.

Fauroux, Camille. *Produire la guerre, produire le genre: Des Françaises au travail dans l'Allemagne nationale-socialiste (1940–1945)*. Paris: Ecole des Hautes Etudes en Sciences Sociales, 2020. 310p. €19.00.

Fontaine, Juliette. *Vichy face aux instituteurs: Réformer les politiques scolaires en contexte autoritaire*. Paris: Dalloz, 2021. 600p. €65.00.

Fortat, Richard. *Le pasteur Yves Crespin (1906–1944): Un chrétien dans la Résistance*. Carrières-sous-Poissy: Cause, 2020. 195p. €13.00.

Frager, Dominique. *Socialisme ou barbarie: L'aventure d'un groupe (1946–1969)*. Paris: Syllepse, 2021. 215p. €17.00.

Frioux, Stéphane, ed. *Une France en transition: Urbanisation, risques environnementaux et horizon écologique dans le second XXe siècle*. Ceyzérieu: Champ Vallon, 2020. 408p. €27.00.

Gay, Vincent. *Pour la dignité: Ouvriers immigrés et conflits sociaux dans les années 1980*. Lyon: Presses Universitaires de Lyon, 2021. 311p. €22.00.

Ginsburger, Nicolas. *Géographes français en Seconde Guerre mondiale*. Paris: Editions de la Sorbonne, 2021. 442p. €37.00.

Graf, Marie-Laure. *L'étoffe des héros? Actes du colloque "L'engagement étranger dans la Résistance française": Modalités, impacts et construction mémorielle, tenu à l'Université de Genève, 21–22 juin 2018*. Chêne-Bourg: Georg, 2021. 286p. €18.00.

Greminger, Marie-Françoise. *Une rafle: Bourganeuf, 21 juillet 1944*. Eguzon: Points d'Aencrage, 2020. 98p. €10.00.

Harté, Yves, and Jean-Pierre Tuquoi. *Latche: Mitterrand et la maison des secrets*. Paris: Seuil, 2021. 235p. €18.00.

Head, Piper. "Immovable Force: The Survival of Parisian Haute Couture, 1940–1944." PhD diss., Iowa State University, 2020.

Horowitz, Sara R., Amira Bojadzija-Dan, and Julia Creet, eds. *Shadows in the City of Light: Paris in Postwar French Jewish Writing*. Albany: State University of New York Press, 2021. 264p. $95.00.

Humbert, Laure. *Reinventing French Aid: The Politics of Humanitarian Relief in French-Occupied Germany, 1945–1952*. New York: Cambridge University Press, 2021. 357p. $120.00.

Jamme, Paul. *Histoire d'un instructeur saboteur, compagnon de la Libération*. Saint-Maur-des-Fossés: Jets d'Encre, 2020. 473p. €27.40.

Job, Mariette. *Se souvenir d'Hélène Berr: Une célébration collective*. Paris: Fayard, 2021. 287p. €22.00.

Jouan, Ophélie. *Rose Valland: Une vie à l'oeuvre; Exposition, Musée Dauphinois, Grenoble, 6 novembre 2019–27 avril 2020, Musée de la Résistance et de la Déportation de l'Isère, 23 novembre 2019–18 mai 2020*. Grenoble: Patrimoine en Isère, Musée de la Résistance et de la Déportation de l'Isère, Maison des Droits de l'Homme, 2019. 95p. €12.00.

Kervella, André. *Le réseau Jade: L'Intelligence Service britannique au coeur de la Résistance française (Paris, Bordeaux, Brest, Lyon . . .)*. Paris: Nouveau Monde, 2021. 511p. €24.00.

Klein, Richard. *High-Rise Buildings in France: A Modern Heritage, 1945–1975*. Paris: Hermann, 2021. 206p. €28.00.

Krop, Jérôme, and Corinne Vézirian. *Le massacre d'Ascq, 1er avril 1944: Enseigner un traumatisme de l'histoire*. Villeneuve-d'Ascq: Presses Universitaires du Septentrion, 2021. 114p. €15.00.

Kupecek Domankiewicz, Danielle. *Une constellation dans la nuit: L'Entraide temporaire; Un réseau de sauvetage d'enfants juifs sous l'Occupation*. Paris: Harmattan, 2021. 276p. €29.00.

Leblanc, Cécile, and Patrick Cabanel. *Marie Médard, une jeune résistante: Du Quartier latin à Ravensbrück*. Maisons-Laffitte: Ampelos, 2021. 141p. €12.00.

Ledoux, Sébastien. *La nation en récit: Des années 1970 à nos jours*. Paris: Belin, 2021. 345p. €23.00.

Lee, Adeline. *Les Français de Mauthausen: Par-delà la foule de leurs noms*. Paris: Tallandier, 2021. 731p. €32.00.

Lormier, Dominique. *Les vérités cachées de la France sous l'Occupation*. Monaco: Rocher, 2021. 460p. €19.90.

Lowenbach, Gérard. *Frédéric Lowenbach: Un Français, agent secret au MI6 de 1940 à 1945*. Paris: Impliqués, 2021. 253p. €25.50.

Magida, Arthur J. *Code Name Madeleine: A Sufi Spy in Nazi-Occupied Paris*. New York: Norton, 2020. 324p. $27.95.

Marandin, Jean-Pierre. *César-Stockbroker: Un réseau franco-britannique en Franche-Comté Bourgogne, 1942–1944*. Besançon: Sekoya, 2021. 288p. €25.00.

Marchand, Thierry. *La "drôle de guerre" des indésirables français: Le cas de la région parisienne (septembre 1939–juin 1940)*. Condé-sur-Noireau: Corlet, 2021. 258p. €25.90.

Martigny, Vincent, Laurent Martin, and Emmanuel Wallon, eds. *Les années Lang: Une histoire des politiques culturelles, 1981–1993*. Paris: Documentation Française, 2021. 600p. €27.00.

Masconi, Marie-José. *Et les femmes se sont levées: Portraits de résistantes alsaciennes et lorraines*. Strasbourg: Nuée Bleue, 2021. 256p. €22.00.

Mauger, Pierre, Jean Rousseau, and François Blanchet. *Pierre Mauger, 17 ans en 1940: Résistance, prison, déportation; Entretiens avec Jean Rousseau et François Blanchet*. La Roche-sur-Yon: Centre Vendéen de Recherches Historiques, 2021. 158p. €13.00.

Melchior, Jean-Philippe, and Philippe Tétart. *Mai 68, cinquante ans après: Mémoire[s], trace[s] et représentation[s]*. Etival-lès-Le Mans: Jamet, 2020. 203p. €14.00.

Merle Georgevail, Andrée. *4 rue Duphot: Mémoires de Maria Lhande*. Saint-Laurent-de-Mure: Pottok, 2021. 132p. €12.00.

Moore, Celeste Day. *Soundscapes of Liberation: African American Music in Postwar France*. Durham, NC: Duke University Press, 2021. 312p. $104.95 cloth, $27.95 paper.

Nattiez, Laura, Denis Peschanski, and Cécile Hochard. *13 novembre: Des témoignages, un récit*. Paris: Jacob, 2020. 304p. €19.00.

Odic, Robert. *Un autre regard sur de Gaulle: Front populaire, Vichy, Alger, Londres, Pentagone, 1936–1944*. Paris: Harmattan, 2021. 175p. €19.00.

Paul, Jean-Louis Mohand. *Mais que peut-on savoir du 17 octobre 1961? Un essai récapitulatif*. Coeuvres: Ressouvenances, 2021. 130p. €14.99.

Peaucelle-Delelis, Véronique. *Mont-Valérien: Un lieu d'exécution dans la Seconde Guerre mondiale; Mémoires intimes, mémoire nationale*. Rennes: Ouest-France, 2021. 231p. €26.50.

Pike, Robert. *Silent Village: Life and Death in Occupied France*. Cheltenham: History Press, 2021. 384p. $34.95.

Poirier, Sylviane, and Julie Ranslant. *1940, retours dans l'Alsace annexée: Témoignages; Schiltigheim*. Strasbourg: Bout de Chemin, 2020. 302p. €24.00.

Poirriez, Jean. *L'épopée des marins de la France libre: Dunkerque-Flandre maritime, 1940–1945*. Dunkerque: Société Dunkerquoise d'Histoire et d'Archéologie, 2020. 296p. €30.00.

Poulhès, Louis. *L'Etat contre les communistes, 1938–1944*. Neuilly-sur-Seine: Atlande, 2021. 821p. €19.00.

Riche, Rémi. *Des jours sombres à l'espoir: L'Ain, 1939–1945; L'histoire au regard des archives*. Bourg-en-Bresse: Chroniques de Bresse, 2020. 142p. €18.50.

Rizzo, Jean-Louis. *De Gaulle, le gaullisme et la République*. Paris: Glyphe, 2021. 218p. €18.00.

Robcis, Camille. *Disalienation: Politics, Philosophy, and Radical Psychiatry in Postwar France*. Chicago: University of Chicago Press, 2021. 240p. $105.00 cloth, $35.00 paper.

Rose, Raymonde, and David Fuks. *Journal d'une juive française à Paris durant l'Occupation (1939–1943)*. Paris: Editions de Paris, 2021. 214p. €18.00.

Rozier, Jacques, and François Rozier. *Journal de guerre de Jacques Rozier, 1940–1941*. Avon-les-Roches: Lamarque, 2021. 92p. €42.00.

Sicard-Bouvatier, Karine. *Déportés, leur ultime transmission*. Paris: Martinière, 2021. 190p. €25.00.

Sirinelli, Jean-François. *Ce monde que nous avons perdu: Une histoire du vivre-ensemble*. Paris: Tallandier, 2021. 393p. €21.90.

Smith, Andy. *Made in France: Societal Structures and Political Work*. Manchester: Manchester University Press, 2021. 240p. £80.00.

Sommier, Isabelle, ed. *Violences politiques en France: De 1986 à nos jours*. Paris: Presses de la Fondation Nationale des Sciences Politiques, 2021. 411p. €24.00.

Staedtler, René. "The Price of Reconciliation: West Germany, France, and the Arc of Postwar Justice for the Crimes of Nazi Germany, 1944–1963." PhD diss., University of Maryland, College Park, 2020.

Stiver, Jean-Luc. *Avaient-ils le choix? Réquisition de la main-d'œuvre dans le département de l'Indre, 1942–1945*. Eguzon: Points d'Aencrage, 2020. 372p. €23.00.

Taïeb, Karen. *Je vous ecris d'Auschwitz: Les lettres retrouvées*. Paris: Tallandier, 2021. 267p. €19.90.

Teyssier, Arnaud. *L'énigme Pompidou–de Gaulle*. Paris: Perrin, 2021. 361p. €23.00.

Thiery, Laurent. *Le livre des 9000 déportés de France à Mittelbau-Dora*. Paris: Cherche Midi, 2020. 2,414p. €49.00.

Tillon, Fabien. *Charles Tillon: Le chef des FTP trahi par les siens*. Paris: Seuil, 2021. 299p. €22.00.

Trocmé, Magda. *Souvenirs d'une vie d'engagements*, edited by Nicolas Bourguinat, Frédéric Rognon, and Patrick Cabanel. Strasbourg: Presses Universitaires de Strasbourg, 2021. 343p. €26.00.

Union Nationale des Associations de Déportés, Internés et Familles de Disparus (Deux-Sèvres). *Résistants en Deux-Sèvres: Elie Cousseau, Louis Michaud*. La Crèche: Geste, 2020. 186p. €20.00.

Vargo, Marc E. *The French Terror Wave, 2015–2016: Al-Qaeda and ISIS Attacks from Charlie Hebdo to the Bataclan Theatre*. Jefferson, NC: McFarland, 2021. 256p. $39.95.

Veillon, Dominique. *Paris allemand: Entre refus et soumission, 1939–1945*. Paris: Tallandier, 2021. 367p. €22.00.

Woodruff, Lily. *Disordering the Establishment: Participatory Art and Institutional Critique in France, 1958–1981*. Durham, NC: Duke University Press, 2020. 336p. $104.95 cloth, $28.95 paper.

Zinsou, Cameron. "Occupied: The Civilian Experience in Montélimar, 1939–1945." PhD diss., Mississippi State University, 2021.

France and the World

Agag-Boudjahlat, Fatiha. *Nostalgériades: Nostalgie, Algérie, jérémiades*. Paris: Cerf, 2021. 138p. €16.00.

Arnaud, Lionel, and Jean Terrine. *La politique des tambours: Cultures populaires et contestations postcoloniales en Martinique*. Paris: Karthala, 2021. 320p. €25.00.

Balazuc, Jean. *Les troupes indigènes: Ils sont morts pour la France*. Paris: Harmattan, 2021. 513p. €45.00.

Baraton, Edouard. *Les Français perdus: Essai historique sur la nationalité française en Amérique du Nord du XVIIIe siècle à aujourd'hui*. Lyon: Baudelaire, 2019. 276p. €20.00.

Becker, Bert. *France and Germany in the South China Sea, c. 1840–1930: Maritime Competition and Imperial Power*. Basingstoke: Palgrave Macmillan, 2021. 484p. $139.99.

Carotenuto, Audrey. *Esclaves et résistances à l'île Bourbon (1750–1848): De la désobéissance ordinaire à la révolte*. Paris: Indes Savantes, 2021. 511p. €35.00.

Carr, Thomas M., Jr. *A Touch of Fire: Marie-André Duplessis, the Hôtel-Dieu of Quebec, and the Writing of New France*. Montreal: McGill-Queen's University Press, 2020. 370p. $37.95.

Charlevoix, Pierre de, and Micah True. *The Jesuit Pierre-François-Xavier de Charlevoix's (1682–1761) "Journal of a Voyage in North America": An Annotated Translation*. Leiden: Brill, 2019. 549p. $224.00.

Cohen-Addad, Nicole, Aïssa Kadri, and Tramor Quemeneur, eds. *8 novembre 1942: Résistance et débarquement allié en Afrique du Nord; Dynamiques historiques, politiques et socioculturelles; Actes du colloque international, Paris, Musée de l'armée, 12–13 novembre 2017*. Vol. 1. Vulaines-sur-Seine: Croquant, 2021. 334p. €20.00.

Duclert, Vincent. *La France, le Rwanda et le génocide des Tutsi (1990–1994): Rapport remis au Président de la République le 26 mars 2021*. Malakoff: Colin, 2021. 380p. €49.00.

Duflot-Ciccotelli, Chloé. *La franc-maçonnerie en Guadeloupe, miroir d'une société coloniale en tensions (1770–1848)*. Pessac: Presses Universitaires de Bordeaux, 2021. 360p. €20.00.

Fageol, Pierre-Eric. *Identité coloniale et sentiment d'appartenance nationale sur les bancs de l'école à la Réunion (1870–1946)*. Saint-Denis (Réunion): Presses Universitaires Indianocéaniques, 2020. 279p. €11.00.

Fardella, Kattia. *De l'esclavage à 1910: La femme noire guadeloupéenne ou la reconstruction de soi*. Gourbeyre: Nestor, 2020. 130p. €18.00.

Figeac, Michel. *Echanges et métissage des cultures matérielles entre la Nouvelle-Aquitaine et les outre-mers (XVIIIe–XIXe siècles)*. Pessac: Maison des Sciences de l'Homme d'Aquitaine, 2021. 282p. €29.00.

Gaida, Peter. *Le travail forcé dans les colonies françaises (1900–1946): "L'empire de la contrainte."* Paris: Indes Savantes, 2021. 294p. €25.00.

Gay, Jean-Christophe. *La France d'outre-mer: Terres éparses, sociétés vivantes*. Malakoff: Colin, 2021. 288p. €27.00.

Gérard, Gilles, Jean Barbier, and Jérémy Boutier. *L'étrange histoire de Furcy Madeleine, 1786–1856: Livre de l'exposition*. Saint-Gilles-les-Hauts (Réunion): Musée Historique de Villèle, 2020. 296p. €12.00.

Grenet, Mathieu. *La maison consulaire: Espaces, fonctions et usagers, XVIe–XXIe siècle*. Aix-en-Provence: Presses Universitaires de Provence, 2021. 265p. €26.00.

Ha, Marie-Paule. *La femme française et l'empire: Textes choisis et commentés*. Paris: Harmattan, 2020. 221p. €22.00.

Harrigan, Michael. *Life and Death on the Plantations: Selected Jesuit Letters from the Caribbean*. Cambridge: Modern Humanities Research Association, 2021. 282p. £12.99.

Hazareesingh, Sudhir. *Black Spartacus: The Epic Life of Toussaint Louverture*. New York: Farrar, Straus and Giroux, 2020. 427p. $30.00.

Johnson, Jessica Marie. *Wicked Flesh: Black Women, Intimacy, and Freedom in the Atlantic World*. Philadelphia: University of Pennsylvania Press, 2020. 360p. $34.95.

Khudori, Darwis. *La France et Bandung: Batailles diplomatiques entre la France, l'Afrique du Nord et l'Indochine en Indonésie (1950–1955)*. Paris: Indes Savantes, 2021. 312p. €26.00.

Klein, Jean-François. *Pennequin, le "sorcier de la pacification": Madagascar-Indochine (1849–1916)*. Paris: Maisonneuve et Larose, 2021. 488p. €28.00.

Labadie, Jean-Christophe. *La guerre d'Algérie vécue des Basses-Alpes*. Digne-les-Bains: Archives Départementales des Alpes de Haute-Provence, 2020. 174p. €20.00.

Laborde, Jacques. *L'homme du choléra: Retour sur l'acquittement surprise des trois prévenus du procès du Mascareignes*. Saint-Denis: Orphie, 2021. 150p. €14.00.

Lalouette, Jacqueline. *Les statues de la discorde*. Paris: Passés Composés, 2021. 238p. €17.00.

Lambert, Léopold. *Etats d'urgence: Une histoire spatiale du continuum colonial français*. Toulouse: Premiers Matins de Novembre, 2021. 334p. €18.00.

Le Crom, Jean-Pierre, and Marc Boninchi, eds. *La chicotte et le pécule: Les travailleurs à l'épreuve du droit colonial français (XIXe–XXe siècles)*. Rennes: Presses Universitaires de Rennes, 2021. 336p. €25.00.

Lefebvre, Camille. *Des pays au crépuscule: Le moment de l'occupation coloniale (Sahara-Sahel)*. Paris: Fayard, 2021. 352p. €24.00.

Legg, Charlotte Ann. *The New White Race: Settler Colonialism and the Press in French Algeria, 1860–1914*. Lincoln: University of Nebraska Press, 2021. 304p. $55.00.

Le Glaunec, Jean-Pierre. *The Cry of Vertières: Liberation, Memory, and the Beginning of Haiti*, translated by Jonathan Kaplansky. Montreal: McGill-Queen's University Press, 2020. 216p. $29.95.

Leperre, Michel. *Journal de ma guerre d'Algérie: Classe 55-2B (Constantinois, 1956–1958)*. Le Quai: Maule, 2020. 244p. €25.00.

Lotem, Itay. *The Memory of Colonialism in Britain and France: The Sins of Silence*. Cham: Palgrave Macmillan, 2021. 428p. $109.99.

Luguern, Liêm-Khê. *Les "travailleurs indochinois": Etude socio-historique d'une immigration coloniale (1939–1954)*. Paris: Indes Savantes, 2021. 661p. €35.00.

Mahé, Alain, and Emile Masqueray. *Emile Masqueray et la crise allemande de la pensée française dans l'Algérie coloniale: Suivi de Formation des cités chez les populations sédentaires de l'Algérie; Kabyles du Djurdjura, Chaouïas de l'Aurès, Beni Mezab*. Saint-Denis: Bouchène, 2020. 460p. €30.00.

Maneuvrier-Hervieu, Paul. "La Normandie dans l'économie atlantique au dix-huitième siècle: Production, commerce et crises." PhD diss., Université de Normandie, 2020.

Martinez, Jean-Louis. *Algérie 1962—disparus et oubliés*. Sète: Plume-de-Soi, 2020. 257p. €17.00.

Mongey, Vanessa. *Rouge Revolutionaries: The Fight for Legitimacy in the Greater Caribbean*. Philadelphia: University of Pennsylvania Press, 2020. 288p. $45.00.

Mulich, Jeppe. *In a Sea of Empires: Networks and Crossings in the Revolutionary Caribbean*. Cambridge: Cambridge University Press, 2020. 300p. $99.99.

Namakkal, Jessica. *Unsettling Utopia: The Making and Unmaking of French India*. New York: Columbia University Press, 2021. 328p. $120.00 cloth, $30.00 paper.

Pan, Cong. "La guerre d'Algérie et les relations franco-chinoises." PhD diss., Université de Lyon, 2020.

Panon, Xavier. *Un Français de la coloniale: Les mille vies d'Hubert (Afrique, Chine, Mandchourie, Algérie)*. Carnac: Menhir, 2021. 500p. €25.90.

Peabody, Rebecca, Steven Nelson, and Dominic Thomas, eds. *Visualizing Empire: Africa, Europe, and the Politics of Representation*. Los Angeles: Getty Research Institute, 2021. 191p. $55.00.

Peiretti, Delphine. *Corps noirs et médecins blancs: La fabrique du préjugé racial, XIXe–XXe siècles*. Paris: Découverte, 2021. 350p. €22.00.

Rivet, Daniel. *Henry de Castries (1850–1927): Du faubourg Saint-Germain au Maroc, un aristocrate islamophile en République*. Paris: Karthala, 2021. 239p. €23.00.

Rocard, Michel. *Faire la paix: Ce que nous enseignent les accords de Matignon*. Joinville-le-Pont: Double Ponctuation, 2021. 112p. €13.00.

Safi, Omar. *The Intelligence State in Tunisia: Security and Mukhabarat, 1881–1965*. London: Tauris, 2020. 344p. $108.00.

Schnakenbourg, Christian. *L'économie de plantation aux Antilles françaises, XVIIIe siècle*. Paris: Harmattan, 2021. 362p. €37.00.

Tardieu, Jean-Pierre. *Biassou, Jean-François, Toussaint Louverture et les Noirs français de Saint-Domingue: L'apport des archives espagnoles (1792–1804)*. Paris: Harmattan, 2021. 224p. €24.00.

Todd, David. *A Velvet Empire: French Informal Imperialism in the Nineteenth Century*. Princeton, NJ: Princeton University Press, 2021. 368p. $39.95.

Trouillot, Michel-Rolph. *Stirring the Pot of Haitian History*, edited and translated by Mariana F. Past and Benjamin Hebblethwaite. Liverpool: Liverpool University Press, 2021. 240p. $130.00.

Vaïsse, Maurice. *Le putsch d'Alger*. Paris: Jacob, 2021. 336p. €25.90.

Villerbu, Soazig, ed. *La France et les Amériques entre révolutions et nations, 1776–1871*. Rennes: Presses Universitaires de Rennes, 2021. 196p. €20.00.

Vince, Natalya. *The Algerian War, the Algerian Revolution*. Cham: Palgrave Macmillan, 2020. 227p. $29.99.

Weber, Jacques. *La France et l'Inde des origines à nos jours* Vol. 3, *Regards croisés*. Paris: Indes Savantes, 2021. 673p. €36.00.

Wenzel, Eric. *La Grenade française et ses institutions coloniales aux XVIIe et XVIIIe siècles: Entre échanges et dépendance*. Paris: Harmattan, 2020. 270p. €27.00.

Williard, Ashley M. *Engendering Islands: Sexuality, Reproduction, and Violence in the Early French Caribbean*. Lincoln: University of Nebraska Press, 2021. 310p. $65.00.

Translated Abstracts

DOWNING A. THOMAS

Les sons du Siam : Environnements sonores de la diplomatie franco-siamois au XVIIe siècle

Une série de contacts diplomatiques entre la France et le Siam a commencé dans les années 1660, principalement à travers des activités missionnaires et l'expansion du réseau commercial de la France. Ces efforts diplomatiques et leur importance historique ont été l'objet d'études visant à comprendre les ambitions globales de Louis XIV et ses efforts à façonner une image royale. Un aspect de ces échanges qui a été moins étudié est l'attention donnée dans les commentaires et chroniques de l'époque à l'espace sonore siamois : comment les sons—musicaux ou autres—que les voyageurs ont rencontrés auraient empêché ou bien avancé leurs efforts diplomatiques. Dans le contexte de l'influence mondiale croissante de la France sous Louis XIV, les sons et les silences décrits par les voyageurs français offrent d'importants aperçus concernant les initiatives diplomatiques et les tentatives de comprendre le Siam et sa culture.

JENNA HARMON

« Il n'est plus guère de mode : tant pis » : Repenser l'obsolescence du vaudeville au XVIIIe siècle

Au XVIIIe siècle, Charles Collé a déclaré que « le vaudeville est aujourd'hui totalement tombé », « tué » par le genre musical actuellement à la mode à Paris, l'ariette. Pourtant, cette affirmation est démentie par la présence des vaudevilles dans la culture de l'imprimé pendant la deuxième moitié du XVIIIe, et même les premières années du XIXe siècle. Les sources imprimées nous proposent donc une histoire différente de celle qui décrit un vaudeville moribond au milieu du XVIIIe siècle. Cet article affirme que l'histoire de la mort prématurée du vaudeville est l'effet d'une confusion simple mais cruciale entre deux pratiques chansonnières distinctes, mais également appelées « vaudeville ». Les origines de cette confusion remontent aux dictionnaires musicaux du XVIIIe siècle. Finalement, cet article examine le rôle des vaudevilles extra-théâtraux dans les romans, les journaux, et les chansonniers politiques pour démontrer que le vaudeville a conservé son intérêt malgré les rumeurs de sa mort.

ANNELIES ANDRIES
Mobiliser l'historicité et la couleur locale dans *Fernand Cortez* (1809) :
Raconter l'Empire à l'Opéra

Pourquoi les créateurs d'opéras napoléoniens étaient-ils si zélés de souligner que leur méthode de représenter l'histoire s'appuyait sur des sources de référence ? L'analyse de *Fernand Cortez* de Gaspare Spontini (1809) montre que ce désir s'est développé dans le cadre d'une épistémologie du « réalisme historique » qui promet une véritable connaissance du passé. Cette confiance épistémologique a poussé les historiens et les artistes à mobiliser l' « historicité » et la « couleur locale » pour propager des récits d'empire fondés sur le processus de civilisation. Dans *Cortez*, ces techniques visaient à transformer le scepticisme des philosophes vis-à-vis le colonialisme du XVIe siècle en un récit de succès, en vue de susciter l'enthousiasme pour la guerre napoléonienne contre l'Espagne. Bien que ces détails historisants aient brouillé le message propagandiste de *Cortez*, cet opéra a réussi à fournir un modèle qui sert à vulgariser et diffuser des idéologies d'empire et de civilisation au-delà du monde savant.

DIANA R. HALLMAN
La commémoration napoléonienne sur la scène lyrique :
Le retour des cendres et *La reine de Chypre* d'Halévy

Le retour des cendres, le rapatriement commémoratif de la dépouille de Napoléon en 1840, faisait partie d'un ensemble de gestes de restauration napoléonienne pendant la monarchie de Juillet : monuments, peintures, œuvres d'histoire, pièces de théâtre et panégyriques à l'empereur vaincu. La commémoration du règne impérial par la monarchie atteint la scène de l'Opéra de Paris en 1841, avec le début de *La reine de Chypre*, le grand opéra en cinq actes de Fromental Halévy et Henri de Saint-Georges. L'opéra fait résonner des allusions sonores, visuelles, littéraires et politiques à la légende napoléonienne et des références manifestes au retour des cendres, y compris l'utilisation des grandes trompettes du cortège de Napoléon et de la cérémonie d'inhumation aux Invalides. Dans son remodelage historique de la montée au pouvoir en Chypre de Catarina Cornaro au début du XVe siècle et de son mépris de la tyrannie vénitienne, le portrait nostalgique des chevaliers français exilés, en particulier le roi mourant Lusignan, évoque le héros déchu de la France tout en renouvelant la mémoire impériale.

PAUL COHEN
« Le zouk est le seul médicament dont nous avons besoin » :
Kassav et la politique culturelle de la musique dans la Caraïbe française

Cet article analyse comment l'histoire de Kassav, le groupe musical antillais fondé en 1979, permet de mieux comprendre la politique culturelle de la musique des Antilles françaises ainsi que l'histoire « mondiale » de la France. La musique de Kassav représente une réponse culturelle et commerciale inventive à des structures d'exclusion néocoloniales et capitalistes dans les Antilles françaises, une réponse qui puisait dans les ressources culturelles propres aux îles, afin de façonner un nouveau genre de musique (le zouk) qui a exercé une influence importante. Kassav doit son succès commercial en partie à une industrie musicale mondialisée à l'affût de musiques issues des périphéries postcoloniales et au rôle de Paris comme capitale de la « musique du monde ». Que la musique de Kassav ait été perçue en France métropolitaine comme « antillaise » ou « du monde », plutôt que « française », témoigne des lignes de faille historiques et raciales qui occultent l'appartenance française des Antilles aux yeux de nombreux habitants de l'Hexagone.

Eugen Weber Book Prize

The UCLA Department of History is pleased to announce that

Judith G. Coffin,

Professor of History at the University of Texas at Austin, has been awarded the **2022 Weber Book Award**. A prize for the best book in modern French history (post 1815) over the previous two years, this award is named for the eminent UCLA French historian Eugen Weber (1925-2007) and brings a cash award of $15,000. Judith G. Coffin's beautifully written book, *Sex, Love, and Letters: Writing Simone de Beauvoir*, explores the neglected archive of letters written to Simone de Beauvoir by ordinary women and men. This innovative cultural history examines the twentieth century as an embodied experience, showing the intimate connections between the geopolitical and the personal.

Honorable Mention

Camille Fauroux, Associate Professor of History, Université Toulouse II Jean Jaurès
Produire la guerre, produire le genre: Des Françaises au travail dans l'Allemagne nationale-socialiste (1940-1945)

Annette K. Joseph-Gabriel, Assistant Professor of French, University of Michigan Romance Languages and Literature
Reimagining Liberation: How Black Women Transformed Citizenship in the French Empire

John Warne Monroe, Associate Professor of History, Iowa State University
Metropolitan Fetish: African Sculpture and the Imperial French Invention of Primitive Art

Andrew Israel Ross, Assistant Professor of History, Loyola University Maryland
Public City/Public Sex: Homosexuality, Prostitution, and Urban Culture in Nineteenth-Century Paris

Claire Zalc, Professor of History, École des hautes études en sciences sociales
Denaturalized: How Thousands Lost Their Citizenship and Lives in Vichy France

---

For more information, visit http://history.ucla.edu.

UCLA College | Social Sciences
History

Keep up to date on new scholarship

Issue alerts are a great way to stay current on all the cutting-edge scholarship from your favorite Duke University Press journals. This free service delivers tables of contents directly to your inbox, informing you of the latest groundbreaking work as soon as it is published.

To sign up for issue alerts:

1. Visit **dukeu.press/register** and register for an account. You do not need to provide a customer number.

2. After registering, visit **dukeu.press/alerts**.

3. Go to "Latest Issue Alerts" and click on "Add Alerts."

4. Select as many publications as you would like from the pop-up window and click "Add Alerts."

Printed and bound by CPI Group (UK) Ltd, Croydon, CR0 4YY

10/10/2023

08128424-0001